Joan Orme
David Shemmings

Developing Research
Based Social Work Practice

palgrave
macmillan

First published 2010 by
PALGRAVE MACMILLAN

Palgrave Macmillan in the UK is an imprint of Macmillan Publishers Limited, registered in England, company number 785998, of Houndmills, Basingstoke, Hampshire RG21 6XS.

Palgrave Macmillan in the US is a division of St Martin's Press LLC, 175 Fifth Avenue, New York, NY 10010.

Palgrave Macmillan is the global academic imprint of the above companies and has companies and representatives throughout the world.

Palgrave® and Macmillan® are registered trademarks in the United States, the United Kingdom, Europe and other countries

ISBN 978–0–230–20045–6

This book is printed on paper suitable for recycling and made from fully managed and sustained forest sources. Logging, pulping and manufacturing processes are expected to conform to the environmental regulations of the country of origin.

A catalogue record for this book is available from the British Library.

A catalog record for this book is available from the Library of Congress.

10 9 8 7 6 5 4 3 2 1
19 18 17 16 15 14 13 12 11 10

Printed in China

This text is dedicated to the memory of Jo Campling who provided the original inspiration and to Professor Martin Davies who has supported the careers of both authors.

Contents

Tables and figures

Tables

Figures

Acknowledgements

We would like to acknowledge the variety of opportunities we have had in research teaching and research development that have informed the writing of this text.

Joan Orme has taught on research training programmes at both the University of Southampton and the University of Glasgow. The enthusiasm and critical feedback from students over more than two decades of such teaching have taught her much. She has also benefited as a member of the ESRC Training Board from the many visits to research training courses in the social sciences at numerous universities. The willingness of colleagues to share their enthusiasm and to be critically reflective has enabled her to put social work in the wider context. This generosity was also apparent in the social work colleagues and postgraduate research students with whom she worked on the first Researcher Development Initiative for social work. Finally, as ever, she is indebted to Geoff for his unfailing support and endless sustenance.

David Shemmings has taught social work research to social workers at the Universities of East Anglia, Middlesex and Kent during the past twenty years. He has recently been the director of the second Researcher Development Initiative across the UK, aimed at increasing the confidence and ability of a large number of social work academics in obtaining research grants from public funding bodies. He has presented innovative sessions on research methodology in Athens, Naples and more recently to the ESRC's Methods festival at Oxford University. David is very grateful to his partner Yvonne for her love and encouragement.

In addition we would like to acknowledge our indebtedness to Esher Coren (Canterbury Christchurch University), whose presentation to the UK's Researcher Development Initiative for social work (RDI 2) in February 2009 and her expert knowledge provided the basis for Chapter 4. We are also grateful to SCIE for permission to quote at length from Bates and Coren, *The Extent and Impact of Parental Mental Health Problems on Families* (SCIE, 2003) in Chapter 4. Finally, we thank Denise Parris for preparing the Index.

Introduction

The aim of this text is to consider how to develop a research base for social work practice. This introduction sets the context by telling the story so far, while the body of the text highlights what building a research base for professional practice actually involves. It is intended to encourage academics, students and practitioners to consider what is meant by research, how they can use it in their practice and why they should do so. It is also hoped that it will encourage academics, practitioners, students, service users and carers to reflect on their own involvement in research by generating topics and issues to be researched and undertaking research themselves.

In doing this, as the title indicates, we are focusing on social work practice. That is the practice undertaken by those who have a professional qualification in social work. The terminology used in agencies delivering social work services includes both social work and social care. Some definitions identify social work as one activity within the provision of social (and at times health) care. Marsh and Fisher (2005), describing the infrastructure for 'social work and social care', reason: 'the term "social care" describes the welfare sector ... we argue that "social work" is the core research discipline underpinning the knowledge base for policy and practice (there is no academic subject of social care)' (Marsh and Fisher, 2005, p. 1).

We support this position and suggest that the need to develop a research base for social work practice permeates both academia and practice. By using the term social work we are addressing both the core research discipline and professional practice. The practice on which we focus and the initiatives on which we draw are predominantly those aimed at people with a social work qualification and are designed to develop research-minded practitioners, or as we have also termed it, reflective practitioner researchers. This should not limit the usefulness of this text to others working in the social care and health care fields. The underpinning theories, the implications and challenges of developing a

1

research base for professional practice and the strategies used are all transferable.

Why do we need research based social work practice?

Social work practice involves a mixture of skills and knowledge. The knowledge required includes theoretical knowledge (about subjects such as human growth and development), legal knowledge and knowledge about the impact of interventions. Underpinning all knowledge is research. Social work interventions should be based on reflections on research that inform the skills and decision-making of the practitioner.

However, it is difficult to achieve this when social work has been identified as having a deficit in research capacity. This deficit is in both the research produced and its utilization by practitioners. A demographic review of the social sciences identified that only a small number of social work academics were undertaking research (Mills *et al.*, 2006). The impact of this has been compounded in assessments of academic research over time, including the measures employed by an exercise that assesses the research of all subjects in UK universities (the Research Assessment Exercise or RAE). Social work has been repeatedly assessed as not performing well (Lyons and Orme, 1998; Fisher, 1999; Fisher and Marsh, 2001). While this is only one measure of effectiveness in research, it is an important one because the funding that flows from the assessment is intended to stimulate further high quality research and it is difficult to improve the research base without funding. Further, the status of a subject, or discipline, was seen to be reflected in its performance in the RAE. The implications for social work are illustrated by the fact that in the 2008 RAE, despite much lobbying, social work research was assessed jointly with criminology and social policy research. The effect of this was to make the performance of social work research invisible in the results of that assessment. This reflects social work's ongoing struggle for status in UK universities (Lyons, 1999; Orme, 2000a, b), which has implications for the future of education and training of the workforce.

At the same time debates about practice have drawn attention to a lack of a research base, or more accurately to the lack of utilization of research by those in practice. This has had major implications for social work. The 'what works' debate in criminal justice social work in the 1990s (Furniss, 1998) is one example of how criticisms of the effectiveness of services and an assumed unwillingness on the part of practitioners to evaluate effectiveness led to the demise of the Probation Service in England. More positive attempts to develop a research base include the availability of government funding for 'messages from research' for practitioners (Aldgate, 2001). However, making research results available is not always enough. The research undertaken has to be meaningful to practitioners in terms of both its focus and the way it is undertaken. Its results have to be in readily available formats that are understood, and transferable to practice. Moreover, practitioners have to have the time, the means and the motivation to access, understand and utilize the findings from research. Despite attempts over time by organizations such as Research in Practice (RiP) and Making Research Count (MRC), the use of research by practitioners is still patchy (Walter *et al.*, 2004). The reasons for this are complex and relate to the lack of attention to research in the education and training of social workers and the culture of organizations (Orme and Powell, 2008).

What is to be done to develop a research base for practice?

A number of initiatives have been designed to rectify this. In 2001 the Social Care Institute for Excellence (SCIE) was established with the mission to identify and spread knowledge about good practice to the social care workforce, including social workers. While not focusing purely on research, SCIE provides a research register and has commissioned studies that have underpinned the work of developing research-based social work practice. In addition to the study by Walter *et al.* (2004) on utilization there has been work on different kinds of knowledge (Pawson *et al.*, 2003) and the development of overviews or systematic reviews of existing research (Coren and Fisher, 2006).

In 1999 the Joint University Council Social Work Education Committee (JUC SWEC), an organization that represents courses that provide university-based social work and social care education and training, undertook a seminar series funded by the Economic and Social Research Council (ESRC), the major independent research funding body in the UK, on 'Theorising Social Work Research' (papers available at http://www.scie.org.uk/publications/misc/tswr/index.asp). This was the beginning of a concerted effort to achieve recognition of social work research, and to gain resources for an infrastructure for a research base for social work. The seminars led to further work by JUC SWEC on a strategy to increase the capacity and capability of social work research (JUC SWEC, 2006; Bywaters, 2008). Work funded by SCIE on the relationship between social work and the ESRC (Shaw *et al.*, 2004) and jointly funded work on the kinds and quality of social work research (Shaw and Norton, 2007, 2008) highlighted what had been achieved, but pointed out that more was needed.

Such initiatives have had an impact and the ESRC is working with social work academics to develop a research infrastructure. In Scotland the *Changing Lives* report (Scottish Executive, 2006) gave a strong commitment to practitioner research and in May 2008 the UK government announced funding for a National School for Social Care Research in England. In launching the initiative the then minister identified the need to improve the evidence for social care practice so that people are provided with better and more effective services in the future.

Alongside these initiatives the introduction in 2003 of a degree level qualification for entry to the social work profession was perhaps the most significant opportunity to produce research-minded practitioners, a necessary prerequisite for research based social work practice. While qualifying students are not the most powerful in the organization and cannot be expected to change the culture single handed, it is vital that they begin professional practice with a clear understanding of, and commitment to, the importance of research for social work policy and practice.

The degree took different formats in the four countries of the UK but all drew on a benchmark statement for undergraduate education in social work (HEFCE, 2000) and National Occupational Standards (NOS) for social work (TOPSS, 2002). While the latter made scant reference to research, the benchmark statement was clear that knowledge and understanding for social work includes the ability to use research and enquiry techniques with reflective awareness to collect, analyse and interpret relevant information (HEFCE, 2000, 5.1.1), and that such understanding should take place in practice learning as well as university-based learning. It asserts that beginning social workers should be taught research-based concepts and critical explanations and that they should be able to undertake critical appraisal of relevant social research and evaluation methodologies (HEFCE, 2000, 3.1.4). These very clear expectations are reiterated and strengthened in the revised benchmark statement (QAA, 2008).

It was therefore anticipated that research methods would have a much higher profile in qualifying education and training but this is not necessarily the case. An audit of learning and teaching about research on the degree funded by the ESRC (Orme *et al.*, 2008) indicated that although they were prepared to draw on research findings in teaching on, for example, child care or adult services, there was some hesitancy on the part of social work educators about undertaking direct teaching on research methods. This was because of their lack of training in the area. There was an even greater resistance to addressing research in practice because of a similar lack of confidence among practitioners.

This suggests that more needs to be done in qualifying education and training for social workers and across the professional life course to introduce practitioners to research and to explain and demystify the research process. Further, service users and carers, practitioners and managers require a change of culture in agencies to create an environment where research is not only utilized, but also undertaken.

The aim of this book is to introduce social work students, practitioners, managers and those who utilize services to the complexities of developing a social work specific research base but also to encourage them to share our enthusiasm and excitement that doing so will enhance the quality of services. We also hope that it will stimulate students, practitioners, service users and carers to become involved in the research process in different ways. This will ensure that they will contribute to the knowledge base necessary for developing research based social work.

The organization of the text

This text therefore introduces social work students, practitioners, managers, service users and carers at different levels to the context of social work research in the wider social sciences; to explore the rationale for undertaking and utilizing research in social work; and to explain the processes and practices of undertaking research. In doing this it illustrates not only how social work research draws on other social sciences, but also how some distinctive elements of social work research can contribute to other disciplines in the social sciences. It is not a 'how to do it' text, although there is discussion and description of particular approaches and methods.

There are a large number of texts on research in the social sciences but few address the distinctiveness and complexity of social work research. There are also texts that have focused on social work specific research (for example Everitt *et al.*, 1992; Shaw and Gould, 2001; D'Cruz and Jones, 2004; Corby, 2006; McLaughlin, 2007). Each of these has made an important contribution to the definition and exploration of social work specific research. However, there are few texts that situate social work research in the wider social sciences and explore the implications of this for the research base for social work

To achieve this broad remit the text is divided into three parts. While links with the wider social sciences are drawn throughout the book, Part 1, on the *context of social work research*, focuses specifically on the debates within the wider social sciences about the meaning and purpose of research and, in Chapter 2, specifically social research. These debates are examined in terms of the implications for social work research.

In Part 2, on the *process of social work research*, the chapters move through the different stages of undertaking research. In doing this each chapter discusses the practical implications in a theoretical context. The part overall also moves from theoretical discussion to practical examples. Hence Chapter 3 explores the specific ethical issues of researching the interpersonal and private dimensions of people's lives that are the focus of social work research and practice. This links with Chapter 4, which discusses methods for exploring the available resources and existing research before commencing a project. Chapter 5 provides a backdrop to the next three chapters. Before deciding on how to undertake research it is necessary to understand the implications of different approaches and the distinctions in terminology. These are discussed in Chapter 5. Chapters 6, 7 and 8 present different methods in more detail, explaining what they involve and the implications of using them. These chapters provide examples of research methods developed from and for practice research.

Part 3, *implications of social work research*, returns to the underpinning theme of the book, developing research based social work practice. Chapter 9 explores the implications of research for social work practice in terms of who commissions it and who undertakes it, while Chapter 10 explores how it can be disseminated. For social work to be research based the research has to be useful – that is, it has to make a difference to practice.

Part 1 | Context of Social Work Research

1 | What is research for?

Introduction

The Introduction explained why social work needs a research base, and some of the initiatives, policies and processes that have been developed to improve the quality and quantity of research for social work. This chapter and the next take a slight step back to help us understand social work research in context. In the first instance this context is the broader field of social science and the role of research in society in general. Hence it addresses questions such as what is research? What is research for?

The second part of the chapter concentrates on research in social work. In considering what social work research is for, two major issues emerge. The first is the concept of evidence based policy and practice. This is not unique to social work but it has played an important role in developing social work research and has been the focus of much discussion. It is therefore important to set out the arguments at a very early stage because they raise questions about the role of research in enhancing social work practice.

The other major theme concerns what is known as participatory and/or emancipatory research. This has gained prominence in social work research and is sometimes identified as *the* defining feature of social work research. In responding to the question 'what is research for?' this approach challenges some of the accepted norms of social sciences research. Considering this distinctive focus of social work research helps to focus attention on the relationship of social work to the wider social sciences and the implications for developing a research base for practice.

Social work and social sciences

Social work as a subject and as an area of study and research is complex. In universities social work can be found in a number of different departments depending upon the organization of the university and how social work is understood. In some it can be found in health or even science departments because it is seen to be part of 'health-related' professions. In others it is associated with education, or in departments or faculties known as professional studies. Less often is has associations with law and criminal justice. Finally it can be associated with other social sciences, usually with sociology and social policy, but sometimes with psychology.

These different arrangements for social work in universities, and the way social work is perceived, are a result of its research tradition and in particular the links between practice, education and research. It has been suggested that social work is *only* the appliance of social science, inferring that social work has no theory or research of its own (Orme, 2000a). This is an unfair description. No one suggests that medicine is *only* the appliance of science. Both medicine and social work share characteristics of drawing on other subjects for their theory base and applying this theory to practice (Orme, 2000b). Doing this enables social work to build up a theory base of its own, the theory of interventions (Howe, 1987; Payne, 1997).

Context

At the end of the nineteenth century the early beginnings of social work in universities involved collaboration between a practice-based organization, the Charity Organisation Society (COS), and educational institutions in London and Liverpool (Lyons, 1999). The emphasis was on general training for social work. In 1912 the London-based course became part of the Department of Social Science and Administration in the London School of Economics. This and other courses set up at the time offered a range of 'academic' and 'professional' subjects. This split was, according to Lyons (1999), the origin of the status difference between social science 'academics' and social work 'educators'.

The history of the development of social work education and the tensions between practice and education are well documented by, among others, Jones (1979) and Lyons (1999). The implications for developing research have been explored by Orme and Powell (2008). However, what is evident is that over time the curriculum for training for social work has clearly drawn on social science subjects to inform the knowledge base for social work practice (CCETSW, 1989; DoH, 2002). The analysis of how and why we need to develop a research base for social work will demonstrate that social work also draws on theories and methods of research from the social sciences.

Social sciences

Subjects grouped as social sciences also differ between universities but whatever their configurations the emphasis is on subjects that study people: on the social. Different subjects focus on different aspects of social behaviour: the way people behave (psychology), the way they live their lives (anthropology, sociology), the way they organize themselves and/or are organized (politics). This is an extremely simplistic analysis and one that constantly changes as different disciplines (or areas of study) develop either in their own right or as part of larger disciplines. The place of social work, for example, has already been described as complex, and we shall see below how that complexity becomes significant in understandings of research.

It is difficult to get absolute clarity about either the commencement of what we now call the social sciences, or what actually constitutes them (Delanty, 1997). However, a useful overview is provided by the Economic and Social Research Council (ESRC), the main UK research council for the social sciences, which describes social science as, in its broadest sense, '*the study of society and the manner in which people behave and impact on the world around us*' (ESRC website). For our purposes this description would support the inclusion of social work in the social sciences. Moreover, social work brings an added dimension to the social sciences in that it emphasizes study of the way that society impacts on individuals.

The ESRC claims that social scientists shape people's lives. It argues that research findings provide invaluable insights into all aspects of the lives of individuals, families, groups, communities and nations. This suggests that the purpose of research is to have an effect, and that this effect is in some ways an improvement and therefore 'good'. However, as is discussed later, this is contentious. The assumption that one purpose of research is to change social life raises questions about who makes decisions about what is 'improvement' and what is 'good' (Hammersley, 1995). It also raises questions about whether research can provide unambiguous insights into social life. Both of these questions are connected to discussions about what research is for, but before answering this we need to clarify what constitutes research.

What is research?

The term research is ubiquitous. Its use can usually be divided into three main categories. The first is the very general and loose application that we all use. For example, when buying a product such as a car people often talk about 'doing their research' before committing to the expense of the product. On the other hand there is the formal use of the term 'research', which often conjures up pictures of people in white coats in laboratories mixing chemicals or peering through microscopes. Somewhere in between are groups such as journalists who refer to doing research for their news stories. This can involve reading documents, gathering data, conducting interviews to get different opinions or using various methods to observe people in different situations. In this middle category we might include students of all ages and stages who are often encouraged to 'research' topics as part of their study. This usually involves either reading widely around a subject or undertaking 'projects' as part of their studies.

These different uses might seem to confuse any definition of research but in fact what they do is illustrate that the term can mean different things in different situations, and over time its use has both grown and become more diffuse. However, what has to be avoided is the suggestion that 'anything goes' in research.

At a very simple level research is carried out in order to discover something about the world (Hughes, 1990) by collecting information and thinking about it (D'Cruz and Jones, 2004). This involves looking again, trying to understand or find out about something for a purpose: gaining more information and/or producing knowledge about it. The distinction between gaining information and producing knowledge is a crucial one and is at the core of many debates about the meaning and purpose of research. Many of the uses described in the preceding paragraph are about gaining information – the price of the car, what happens when chemicals are mixed, what a cell looks like under a microscope. This is predominantly descriptive. What distinguishes research from mere inquiry or inquisitiveness is that it is systematic investigation, the process of searching, investigating and or discovering facts 'through scientific enquiry' (Holosko, 2001, p. 204).

In the area of social work and social care the framework for research governance defines research as: the attempt to derive generalizable new knowledge by addressing clearly defined questions with systematic and rigorous methods. This includes studies that aim to generate hypotheses as well as studies that aim to test them (DoH, 2005).

Research is therefore systematic and rigorous enquiry that involves, or leads to, understandings of how things are as they are, or how they work. This involves gathering information and producing knowledge. The production of knowledge requires something more than description. It requires explanation, which involves reflection on what is found out, observed or discovered. It also involves consideration of how things are known, or are found out. This can help to lead to explanatory theories. This search for information, understanding and knowledge is a consequence of changes that have been brought about by Enlightenment thinking.

Enlightenment thinking

There is no one theory of the Enlightenment or agreement about when it commenced. Enlightenment thinking evolved over time and involved questioning accepted norms of the organization of the world. These norms had been governed by and grounded in religion, theology and philosophy. The questioning of the acceptance that all rules and phenomena were god-given and challenging reliance on religion, revelation and tradition (Hammersley, 1995) led to the creation of a new framework of ideas about man [*sic*], society and nature (May, 1996, p. 8). However, the emergent framework of ideas led to different and sometimes contradictory philosophical positions.

According to May (1996) three core principles underpin Enlightenment thinking and emphasize the move away from a universal acceptance of knowledge being god-given. They are:

- an autonomous human who is capable of acting in a conscious manner;
- the pursuit of universal 'truth';
- a belief in the natural sciences as the model for thinking about the social and natural world.

A number of texts outline the various philosophical traditions that have contributed to discussions about what can be known, how things are known and the relevance of these for research (for example, Bulmer, 1982; Hammersley, 1995; May, 1996).

May (1996), for example, suggests that underpinning much of the discussions about research are the writings of Kant, which incorporated notions of *rationalism* and *empiricism*. *Rationalism* is reflected in the thinking of the seventeenth-century philosopher Descartes, who tried to discern how people 'know' that the knowledge they possess is true. The famous statement 'I think therefore I am' as the only certainty reflects the rationalist position that the only basis for knowledge is reason (May, 1996).

The school of thought known as *empiricism* suggested that knowledge of the social and physical world can only be known as it is experienced, as it appears to us. Data (or information) constitutes an end in itself and does not provide a theory or explanation to guide the collection of data or to interpret it. It is summed up in the belief that 'the facts speak for themselves' (Bulmer, 1982, p. 31). An alternative explanation is that there is a world out there that can be recorded and analysed, independently of people's interpretation of it (May, 1997). This is often associated with the 'science' of social science.

Scientific method

Discussions have ranged about the meaning of research, and the distinctions that are drawn between 'scientific' research and research in the social sciences. It is the consideration of how we know things and how we know that what we know is 'true' that distinguishes rigorous research from a mere search on the Internet. In chemistry this might involve knowing about the number of different chemicals involved in an experiment, and knowing that nothing else was involved in the mixture. In social work, or the situations that social sciences research, this is more complicated. How can we demonstrate that if we put someone in a particular circumstance such as a 'sink' housing estate they will commit a crime? How do we know how much crime is committed? Are the crime statistics gathered by the police on arrests and convictions the 'truth'? Are the different figures drawn from victim studies, where people tell researchers of their experience of crime, even if they have not reported it, more accurate? Or is the definitive truth the self-report studies where individuals report their involvement in crime? They all give different versions of the truth, and, in that they may be referring to different definitions of information about crime (or even understandings of what constitutes a crime), they may all be correct. This is the complexity of research in the social world.

The previous example highlights a major debate in research, which is how research undertakes the search for truth. Sometimes this is framed as being able to demonstrate the *validity* of the information collected: that the explanation of the information is the only one available, and therefore the most likely one. One way of demonstrating validity is to demonstrate how ideas or facts are arrived at. Hence a very basic definition of research is: '*systematic investigation into and study of material sources etc. in order to establish the facts and reach new conclusions*' (*Concise Oxford Dictionary*, 1990). However, even simple definitions have alternatives. Research is not only about discovering new facts. The notion of 'looking again' can also involve testing and critiquing conclusions that have been previously arrived at by others. Hence an alternative dictionary definition of research is: '*an endeavour to discover or collate old facts etc. by the scientific study of a subject or by a course of critical investigation' (Concise Oxford Dictionary, 1990).*

However, both of these definitions tend to reflect a scientific approach to research, which can be controversial. Barber (1996) suggests that scientific method is breathtakingly simple:

> Measure or gather information about an event that interests you, look for a pattern, generate an idea or hypothesis that would explain the pattern, make a prediction on the basis of your hypothesis, and test to see if you are right or wrong. (Barber, 1996, p. 380)

If you are right you have the answer, the truth, and you will be able to replicate your results again and again. If you are wrong you start again or, as Barber says, build another model. This definition introduces another important concept related to validity, and that is *falsification*. The process Barber describes raises questions about whether you can ever prove that something is true, or whether you can only ever falsify – that is, prove that it is not true. The philosopher Popper (1965) gives as an example the claim that 'all swans are white'. This can only be true as long as no black swan is observed. Observing one black swan falsifies the claim that all swans are white. You can then say with certainty 'not all swans are white', but until you observe all swans you can only claim that 'as far as I have observed, all swans are white'.

Science usually refers to studying the physical world. The term 'scientific approaches' and the methods described by Barber are most often used in, for example, gathering and logging information and facts such as the colour of swans or how many crimes are committed. However, the dual aims of knowing about the social and physical world and the *ways* of knowing about it are core to all research. Put very simply, the distinction between science and social science is that medics want to understand illness and disease, biologists want to understand life and engineers want to understand how machines and/or or structures work, while social scientists want to understand how people operate in and are influenced by the world, which is both social and physical. The purpose of research, the way that research is undertaken and the implications of the results or findings are also the subject of much debate in the social sciences generally and social work in particular.

The distinction between finding absolute truth and finding out how the world works raises again the question: what is research for? This includes questions about the purpose of the knowledge gleaned or created.

Purposes of research

The distinction between describing the world and understanding it is sometimes presented as the distinction between basic and applied research. An alternative description of basic research as 'pure' research indicates that there is a sense in which one approach might be better than another! It also reflects a tension between scholars about the purpose of research

At a very simple level basic (pure) research is concerned with producing theory, while applied research is devoted to the application of theoretical knowledge in order to solve practical problems (Hammersley, 1995). The question is whether it is appropriate for social scientists to only produce theories about the world, or should social sciences use those theories to solve problems? This is an important distinction for social work because, as has been said, the need to develop research-based practice has meant greater emphasis has been placed on applied research. It is this emphasis that has at times led to social work being described as 'practice-based' and having no theory of its own. The epithet of social work as the 'appliance' of social science relegates its importance in contributing to knowledge generation – suggesting that social work research is about how to do social work, rather than contributing to knowledge about social problems and theoretical understandings of these.

The distinctions between basic and applied research are sometimes linked to the distance or objectivity from the subject of the research. Applied research is at times criticized for lacking distance and objectivity. Other, more fundamental critiques of the notion of applied research (sometimes known as the 'engineering' model: Janowitz, 1972) are directed at the assumption that research can provide knowledge about the 'right' ways to intervene in social situations in order to bring about change for the good. For example, the ESRC definition given earlier suggests that there is a growing body of opinion that the knowledge produced by social sciences should be able to contribute to the improvement of society.

For Hammersley (1995) the suggestion that social sciences can improve society involves acceptance that social life can be improved in the interest of all through deliberative interventions and that the most effective basis for intervention is scientific (rational, theoretical) knowledge. The assumption is that such knowledge is achievable through research, and that the purpose of research is therefore to identify practices that bring about change for the good. However, Hammersley questions the notion of research 'doing good' because this assumes that someone is in a position to make judgements about the intended outcomes of research, and that those outcomes can be predicted (Hammersley, 1995, 2003). This, he argues, compromises rigour in research. His position challenges some important developments in social work research, so it is necessary to look more specifically at social work research and what it can tell us about the purposes of research.

Social work research

The emphasis of this text is on developing research based social work practice. So far in this chapter social work has been discussed in the context of social sciences research. The focus now is on social work research, but this begs a number of definitions: social work research can be *for* social work, *on* social work or *from* social work that is *by* social workers.

Research *for* social work can be generated by many social sciences disciplines, and by subjects such as medicine and other health-based subjects. Such research helps social workers understand physical and social development.

Social work and the situations in which social workers intervene are also the focus of researchers in these other subjects. Social policy in particular researches interventions by social workers, as can be seen in the developments of community care and the introduction of care management (Challis and Davies, 1986). This constitutes research *on* social work: practitioners and service users become the focus of research by others.

However, developing research based practice requires generating knowledge about social work *from* practice. The situations experienced by those receiving services and the interventions by social work in these situations generate important research questions. Those involved are also significant sources of knowledge and can contribute to the research process in a variety of ways. One implication of developing research-based practice is that research might be undertaken *by* those involved in the situation.

Research for social work

In the very first volume of the *British Journal of Social Work* Robinson (1970) hints at tensions in social work research. Social service departments need to show 'results' but there has existed over time a school of thought that contended that the content of social work was incapable of 'scientific' evaluation. Parton and Kirk (2009) highlight another tension when they suggest that while social work has regarded itself as a carrier of the human tradition of compassion, it has drawn on science both as a model of practice and as a knowledge base, suggesting that the two might be incompatible. This relationship of science and social work is also discussed in greater detail by Kirk and Reid (2002).

Social work has come a long way since the language of social work practice, particularly in the USA, borrowed the terminology of medicine (cases, diagnosis, treatment, symptoms, pathology, recovery and reha-bilitation) but in its relationship with social sciences there remain tensions about social work's production of knowledge through research and the use of that knowledge in practice.

In an overview of social work research Trinder (1996) identifies three dominant research traditions in social work. Reminiscent of Robinson, these include the scientific agenda of rigorous measurement, pragmatist perspective and participatory/critical research. Locating social work in the wider social sciences, and the profound changes in the social politi-cal and intellectual context within which it operates, she argues, however, that certain methodologies matter to social work because they support and sustain particular approaches to social work practice (Trinder, 1996, p. 233). Hence the iteration between research and prac-tice becomes a recurring and significant theme.

Other attempts at defining social work research include describing it as 'professional supervised activities which produce and/or analyse information relevant to practice delivery systems and management in social work' (Broad, 1999). This highlights the need for relevance, to practice and management. A wider view is taken by Lyons (1999, 2000), who suggests that a defining aspect of social work research is that it should involve knowledge production: it should contribute to knowledge transmission (teaching and learning) and to knowledge application (practice). Such reviews are not exclusive to the UK and in North America work is being undertaken to analyse and identify agendas for practice research in social work (Fortune *et al.*, forthcoming).

Powell's analysis of the changing conditions of social work research in the UK concludes that there is a widely held view that the primary purpose of any research is to 'promote the development and improve-ment of social work practice' (Powell, 2002, p. 21). Supporting Trinder's (1996) 'pragmatic approach', she agrees that what is needed is not any one particular method of doing research, but the best method that fits the purpose.

The examples so far would therefore suggest that as long as research is contributing to the improvement of social work practice then particu-lar approaches to research are not important. However, the commentary on the IFSW/IASSW definition of social work makes a specific reference to 'evidence based' and raises an issue that is core to developing research based social work practice, but is nevertheless contentious: 'Social work bases its methodology on a systematic body of evidence based knowledge derived from research and practice evaluation' (IASSW/IFSW 2000).

Evidence based policy and practice

Much of the discussion about research in twenty-first-century social work reflects on or responds to the concept of evidence based policy and practice (EBP). Debates about EBP are at the heart of the relationship between research and practice and their impact on social work has been global, as demonstrated by the 'world' definition given above and the contentiousness of debates in North America (see Gambrill, 2003, 2007 as an example).

However, discussions of EBP are not confined to, nor did they originate in, social work. The origins of EBP were in medicine. In a well cited article Sackett and colleagues (1996) argue that the philosophical origins of evidence based medicine are the conscientious, explicit and judicious use of current best evidence in making decisions about the care of individual patients. They answer critics by denying that this leads to 'cookbook' medicine. They also assert that it does not privilege evidence from any particular methodological approach. Their conclusion, that it involves tracking down the best external evidence with which to answer clinical questions, is in many ways uncontentious. However, the introduction of EBP into social work and social care has caused dynamic, and sometimes bitter, disputes.

Definitions of EBP more relevant to social work describe it as an approach 'that helps people make well-informed decisions about policies, programmes and projects by putting the best available evidence from research at the heart of policy developments and implementation' (Davies, 2004, quoted in Nutley et al., 2007, p. 13). Social work cannot argue with the need to have the best possible evidence for practice. However, it has been suggested that on the one hand social workers have been reluctant to hear negative messages about traditional ways of intervening in social situations (Sheldon and Chilvers, 2002). On the other hand, it is argued that the quality of evidence in social work and social care research is such that there is little 'evidence' that anything works, or put another way: nothing works.

Perhaps the clearest account of the positive and negative effects of the EBP agenda in social work involves developments in the probation service in the UK. In the mid-1970s academic and government thinking concluded that interventions of the probation service had little impact on offending behaviour: nothing worked (Chapman and Hough, 1998). Paradoxically this nihilistic approach was followed by one that argued that if any intervention had marginal impact, and was less expensive than prison, then it should be supported on the basis of cost rationing. This period of 'anything works' was quickly curtailed by economic factors. These required value for money to be demonstrated in all interventions. Significantly this was accompanied by some research evidence that suggested that probation practice could do *some* things to change the behaviour of *some* offenders.

The case for EBP in the probation service, according to Chapman and Hough (1998), is therefore about *improving effectiveness* and *demonstrating effectiveness*, and achieving this involved two core elements. Probation services had to:

1. Ensure that the existing knowledge base about effective practice is comprehensively applied.
2. Extend the knowledge base.

Put another away, research had to be undertaken that tested and evaluated work with offenders, and the results of this research, and all other relevant research, were to be made available to, and used by, practitioners.

These principles are core to developing a research base for any social work practice. They reinforce the case that research has to be about and for practice. What then caused resistance in social work to EBP?

First, it is important to note that resistance to EBP was not just in social work. Nutley and colleagues (2007), discussing EBP in public services generally, identified opposition because EBP was associated with a particular kind of methodological approach in research, or was seen to promote particular interventions. In social work the critiques are not just knee jerk resistance to EBP, as suggested by Sheldon and Chilvers (2002).

Second, while there is some evidence that social work practitioners do not utilize research evidence effectively (McDonald *et al.*, 1992; Sheldon and Chilvers, 2001; Walter *et al.*, 2004), as a research finding this is open to different interpretations and there are many complicating factors (Orme, 2000a). Webb (2001), for example, argues that an EBP approach relies on particular theories of how people (social workers) process information. He questions the underlying assumption that the existence of evidence will necessarily lead to certain actions, and sees the process of decision-making in social work as more complex than this. This is supported to some extent by Fisher (1999), who suggests that conclusions that social workers do not use evidence may be drawn because they do not articulate the research evidence they are drawing on when they are discussing their practice.

However, there is some resistance to EBP in social work and the reasons for this can be analysed in the following ways:

1. It prescribes practice. There is concern that an EBP approach will lead to the privileging of certain kinds of intervention and in doing so will deny practitioners' professional skills and decision-making. These fears are not unfounded. Sheldon's argument for the use of cognitive behaviour therapy (Sheldon, 2000) is seen to be 'evidence' of this. In the probation service reliance on evidence led to a 'programmatic' approach where 'off the shelf' groupwork programmes were devised for certain kinds of offending behaviour: anger management; driving with excess alcohol; working with perpetrators of domestic violence. Such programmes also draw on the principles of cognitive behaviour therapy, which are deemed to be the most effective, based on the evidence (McDonald, 1994).

This approach, sometimes referred to as 'manualization', has also emerged in the United States, where in some states manuals for practice, again usually employing cognitive behavioural therapy, have been developed for use by practitioners in mental health services. The fact that the state is determining how practitioners should intervene is seen to reflect a managerialist approach.

2. It represents a managerialist approach. This relates to concerns that using an evidence base to support particular interventions would be associated with more prescription by management and less professional autonomy. The ultimate in prescription occurs in the USA, as described above, when particular approaches or 'programs' become legislated for. See, for example, discussion of the case for multi-systemic therapy (Littell, 2006). The potential clash between professional autonomy and the freedom of social workers to choose how to intervene, with the use of schedules and pro formas, based on the outcomes of research, to systematize practice is problematic. Every death of a child known to social services leads to enquiries that produce guidelines for future practice. These enquiries often draw on academic research, but also gather their own evidence for explanations of what led to particular 'failures' in particular situations (Laming, 2003). Lessons learnt from such enquiries should be incorporated into best practice. The question is: what is the most effective way to achieve this?

Another influence on practice is the distillation of research evidence into documents that can be used to inform practice. One approach is that of Aldgate (2001), who provides an excellent reference source of studies undertaken, but also provide guidelines for practice based on the evidence collated and assessed. More 'extreme' versions of the use of research to inform practice, however, are seen to be more managerial, and to encroach upon professional practice. Work on the development needs of children has been incorporated into assessment frameworks (Ward, 2000) that have to be completed by all involved in assessing children. The impact of such an approach is demonstrated by the fact that the Australian Research Council supported a study testing the use of such frameworks in Australian child care practices (Fernandez and Romeo, 2003).

The principle of assessment frameworks may be a very positive one, but the practice is problematic. Reducing assessment to the routine completion of forms can diminish the assessment process as social workers become reliant on the forms, rather than using their professional judgement when they are collecting the necessary information (see the chapter on assessment in Coulshed and Orme, 2004). Put another way, it ignores the processes of deliberation and choice operating when social workers make judgements (Webb, 2001).

Some of these concerns have been addressed in the work of the Social Care Institute for Excellence (SCIE). The mission of SCIE is to identify and disseminate the knowledge base for good practice in all aspects of social care throughout the United Kingdom. It argues that only by understanding what works in practice – and what does not – can services be improved, and the status of the workforce be raised (http://www.scie.org.uk/about/index.asp).

The guidance produced by SCIE takes the position that empirical evidence, whether qualitative or quantitative in design, provides the best evidence of effectiveness of particular interventions (Coren and Fisher, 2006, p. 2). It also argues that user and carer testimony should be a core of systematic review of evidence (see Braye and Preston-Shoot, 2007, for discussion how this is achieved in particular systematic reviews). This position therefore acknowledges both a rigorous methodological approach and what might be deemed an emancipatory approach, recognizing the need for user and carer participation in the process.

3. It determines what counts as evidence. In his critique of EBP Webb (2001) expresses concern at what is deemed to be 'evidence'. Early proponents of EBP tended to draw on the results of studies that were empirical, and used a particular methodological approach such as

random control trials and experimental designs, which Webb (2001) calls scientific. The different methodological approaches and their significance are discussed in the next chapter, but it is important to say that 'scientific' methods were thought to exclude professional and service user knowledge and did not meet the 'emancipatory' criteria that some social work writers and the SCIE reviews required.

That these approaches predominated may have been because this was the most rigorous evidence available at the time. McDonald (1999) has acknowledged the need for a 'rapprochement' between qualitative and quantitative methods. In doing so she argues that researchers should: be explicit about underpinning values and assumptions; use methods that are robust and do not oppress either the researcher or the researched; and produce knowledge that can be used by service users themselves (McDonald, 1999, p. 98).

The most contentious of these suggestions is the notion of robustness. McDonald argues that this has to address questions of validity. However, as discussed earlier the notion of what is 'valid' knowledge is the subject of much discussion. Coren and Fisher (2006) suggest that knowledge is valid only if it has been subject to user and carer testimony. This is not a test of validity in the wider social sciences.

The notion of 'usefulness' is also contentious. Pawson and colleagues (2003) in another SCIE study identify different kinds of knowledge for social work. They propose a set of generic principles known as TAPUPA: Transparency; Accuracy; Purposivity; Utility; Propriety; Accessibility. The emergence of evidence based practice, they argue, means that for research knowledge there is more emphasis on 'relevance' and 'utility'. However, knowledge that is to be useful also has to have been arrived at using rigorous methods, whether these are qualitative or quantitative methods. It also has to have some degree of accuracy, although this too is a contentious term.

Finally, Shaw and Norton (2007) give a useful 'illuminative' overview of frameworks for considering the quality of social work research (see Chapter 2 of the report). Defining the quality of research is extremely complex and they conclude that the notion of 'fit for purpose' in social work research should include developing guidance on how different stakeholder communities should apply quality judgement 'selectively but not self-servingly' (Shaw and Norton, 2007, p. 23).

Emancipatory and participatory research

A second distinctive approach to research in social work alluded to above involves a commitment to participatory and/or emancipatory approaches to research. There are some links between these approaches and approaches in social sciences known as critical approaches. In critical approaches research is directed to progressive social change in emancipatory terms and a particular theory (e.g. Marxism, feminism) plays a crucial role in guiding the process of change. Feminist scholars drawing on Marxist traditions emphasize this interdependence. Arguing for a notion of *praxis*, Stanley (1990) suggests that the point of (feminist) approaches to research is to change the world, not just to study it (Stanley, 1990, p. 15). Such a stance challenges the more traditional positions on what research is for, but is relevant to social work where research is integrally linked to improving practice (Orme, 1997).

Participatory and emancipatory approaches have many similar characteristics, but the distinctions between them are to do with the processes of research, how it is conducted, and the outcomes.

Participatory approaches acknowledge particular philosophical and practical approaches to knowledge production. In terms of what research is for they have the fairly conservative aim of including research participants. This can take a number of forms, from asking groups of service users what troubles them and making this the focus of research, to including service users and carers as full partners in the research process. This partnership might involve them in steering groups or being investigators, carrying out data collection and writing analyses of the finding. Powell (2002) argues that participatory approaches that seek ways of taking account of diversity are consistent with the aims of social work practice, which might be seen as a form of emancipatory practice

Emancipatory research can be participatory but does not have to be. The aim of such research is that by the process of the research, and/or by the findings, the outcome will be significantly changed and improved conditions. This can involve, for example, evaluating pilots for schemes such as the use of direct payments that ultimately give people requiring care the freedom to purchase their own care. Or it might involve an action research project for an advocacy service where the researcher works with service users to set up, evaluate and produce the necessary analyses to establish such a service on a long-term basis. However, an equally valid emancipatory approach to research is to provide statistics for government departments to influence policy in ways that might be emancipatory. For example, data on levels of poverty especially among single parents have led to a raft of benefit initiatives to try to 'release' people from poverty.

Some people question whether a 'pure' statistical analysis can be truly emancipatory. The debates flag up interesting distinctions between purposes of research. Here the immediate purpose is to influence policy, the consequences of which are to improve the situation. In other contexts the purpose of the approach and methods used is to bring immediate relief and improvement, by empowering individuals who are part of the process.

The involvement of service users in research has been an important and distinctive theme in social work research over decades (Beresford and Croft, 1986; Beresford, 1999, 2000; Fisher, 2002). It is one of the characteristics identified by Dominelli (2005), who, in outlining the defining features of social work research, suggests that *all* social work research should involve change, egalitarian relationships, accountability to service users and holistic engagement (Dominelli, 2005, p. 230). Reflecting a stance taken in one of the early texts on social work research (Everitt *et al.*, 1992), both McLaughlin (2007) and D'Cruz and Jones (2004) suggest that social work research is value driven. Corby (2006), while agreeing that social work research is driven by social work's distinctive values, acknowledges that other researchers may share those values. What Corby sees as distinctive is that social work's research emphasis on these values means that social work research places as much importance on process as it does on outcomes.

These discussions of social work research resonate with Shaw and Gould (2001), who identify a fourfold purpose for social work research, which is more far reaching than other definitions. For them the process and outcomes of social work research should:

- contribute to the development and evaluation of social work practice and services;
- enhance social work's moral purpose;
- strengthen social work's disciplinary character and location;
- promote social work inquiry marked by rigour, range, variety, depth and progression (Shaw and Gould, 2001, p. 3).

Emancipatory positions have been criticized for following the ideologically driven pendulum swings of policy fashion (Sheldon and McDonald, 1999). It is suggested that those who ascribe to approaches to social work research aligned to a value base have supported social work approaches based on personal preference rather than a careful analysis of the available evidence. This, it is argued, does detriment to service users and to social work in general. It also raises questions about what is research, or what is rigorous research.

Emancipatory approaches are usually associated with small-scale qualitative studies. However, some have suggested that such approaches do not necessarily provide a rigorous evidence base for social work research. McDonald (1999), for example, recognises the need to research aspects of individual experience and the structures that impact on individuals, but argues that social work research should embrace a wide variety of methods to ensure improved services for social work clients and service users (McDonald, 1999, p. 89). This should make social work open to different methodological approaches that not only bring about change, but also explore causal factors that have contributed to the problems.

These tensions between research that is value driven and research that is scientifically driven are at the heart of debates about what constitutes research and whether different kinds of research, such as social research, can incorporate both positions.

Conclusion

In thinking about developing research based social work it is necessary to think through questions about what constitutes research and what research can achieve.

This chapter has introduced some important and basic concepts. It has explained how the influence of the Enlightenment on understanding and knowing about the world has had important implications for the ways that we undertake research and the relationship of research to the world. The researcher, the epistemological approach and the methodological considerations are all informed by understanding, or more accurately questions, about how it is possible to know about both the physical and the social world.

Having started with a wide view of the social sciences the chapter explored the relationship between research and practice and, particularly, research designed to bring about change. This led to a specific focus on social work in the context of social sciences research. The chapter has demonstrated that social work research has been influenced by wider movements in research such as evidence based policy and practice. However, drawing on its value base social work has also contributed to significant developments in understanding the impact of research and the research process. These include ways of knowledge generation that involve those who are affected by policy and practice: practitioners and service users.

One recurring question is whether social work is unique or distinctive in its approach to research, or part of a wider set of activities within research known as social research. This is explored in the next chapter.

putting it into practice

To help reflect on the contents of this chapter it is useful to spend some time reflecting on what research means to you.

- Have you ever undertaken a piece of research?
- What was the purpose of the research?
- What were you trying to find out?
- What methods did you use?

If you have not undertaken a piece of research, think of a piece of research that you have become aware of and use in some way in your social work practice:

- Why do you think the research was undertaken?
- Why is this research important to you?
- In what ways do you 'use' it in your practice?

Would you describe the piece of research as social work research?

- Why?
- What is distinctive about it?

Recommended reading

Hammersley, M. (1995) *The Politics of Social Research*. London, Sage. Chapters 6 and 7 raise interesting questions about the role and purpose of research.

May, T. (1997) *Social Research: Issues, Methods and Process*. Buckingham, Open University Press. Chapters 1 and 2 give a very readable introduction to the issues and theories underpinning social research.

2 | Understanding social research

Introduction

In Chapter 1 we looked at the place of social work research in the wider social sciences and identified some elements of its distinctiveness. In this chapter social work research is contextualized in debates about what is called social research.

To understand social research the chapter explores both the definitions and the development of social research. In doing this it continues to explore the implications for developing research based social work, the contribution social work research makes to the wider context and what, if anything, makes social work research distinctive from social research.

The chapter ends with a synthesis of the implications of understandings of social research for the processes and methodological approaches involved in undertaking social work research.

Social research

The term social research is widely used to distinguish certain approaches to research from those that are deemed to be scientific. The implications and limitations of 'scientific' approaches have been alluded to in Chapter 1 but need some further clarification. In suggesting that social research is a balancing act between empirical data and theory, Shipman (1988) recognizes that there are limitations in all research. These relate to distinctions between the certainties of data collection and the tentative nature of theory building. Shipman argues that a 'scientistic' approach leads researchers to make bold claims rather than acknowledge limitations. The implications for social research are that the limitations of trying to emulate 'scientist' approaches in social sciences provide an opportunity to explore what he calls the 'middle ground' of social research, where theory and data can be related. This middle ground is creative, exciting and important: 'The focus on the gap between ideal and real, intended and unintended in the middle range is the exciting part of social research' (Shipman, 1988, p. 176).

However, other than identifying it as 'the middle range' it is hard to find more detailed definitions of 'social research'. This may be because of the way that the use of the term emerged. Stacey (1969) in a very early text suggests that because of the way that it developed (which we explore later) social research was often confused with social surveys. To counteract this she offers five different types of social research. However, there is very little synthesis to give a definition, other than a statement that the purpose of social research is to increase knowledge of 'the facts of social life' or to further our research into social matters (Stacey, 1969, p. 1). This suggests that social research is about social relations.

Texts on the philosophy of social research (Hughes, 1990; Hammersley, 1993) do not give much more help with understanding social research as a phenomenon, or a category. Hughes (1990, p. 10) suggests that social researchers claim their methods and procedures are superior to others and that they have moral authority, but his discussion is primarily about the methodology of social research. Babbie's definition – that social research is the 'systematic observation of social life for the purpose of finding and understanding patterns among what is observed' (Babbie, 1998, p. 1) – goes a little further in associating method with purpose. He uses the metaphor of the 'hologram' to describe social research as the search for patterns. He goes on to offer 'layers' to the definition: social researchers study people but also the variables/variabilities; and they study the relationships among the variables (Babbie, 1998). Social research is therefore about discovering patterns that imply rules governing the ways people interact with one another in society.

Walliman (2006), in a text designed to help students of research methods, suggests the difference is in the approach of the researcher. He argues that the way questions are formulated in social research and the way it is carried out are based on the ontological viewpoint of the researcher, the way they see the world. This will influence what is researched and how it is researched, and therefore the information/knowledge that is revealed. Therefore, as well as the distinctions between theory and data identified by Shipman, there now emerge distinctions in the use of language, which involves terms such as 'information' and 'knowledge' rather than 'facts'.

However, these distinctions might lead to assumptions that social research should only be associated with qualitative methods and constructivist accounts For example, Holosko (2001) discusses social research in a chapter on qualitative methods. This suggests that social research only uses qualitative methods, which is not necessarily the case. His explanation of the process of social research is that it includes, to varying degrees, four elements: observation; questioning, collecting information and analysis. But does not all research include these stages? Moreover, the four components identified could equally involve the use of quantitative methods, or a mixture of both qualitative and quantitative.

The suggestion that social research is dependent upon qualtitative methods is counteracted by Babbie's position, no doubt influenced by his own background in survey methods, that social research is organized around measurement and interpretation (Babbie, 1998). Henn and colleagues (2006) are more inclusive in their suggestion that social research makes no assumptions about what they call research 'styles'. They suggest that those involved in social research have a common aim, which is 'the pursuit of information gathering to answer questions about some aspect of social life' (Henn *et al.*, 2006, p. 8).

This return to the use of the term 'social life' raises another conundrum in that in Chapter 1 we identified that all social sciences was about studying social life. The notion of the 'social' used by Henn and colleagues (2006), which involves examining human behaviour and relationships with other human beings, groups, (sub)cultures and organizations, does little to clarify any distinctions.

The tendency to confuse social science research and social research, or more accurately not make the distinction between them, is acknowledged by Bryman (2008), who suggests that social research is not separate from social science research, but that methods of social research are closely tied to different visions of how social reality should be studied. He identifies a number of ways in which researchers should question how research methods connect with the wider social sciences. The most significant is in theories of knowledge creation and how research is undertaken. Echoing Shipman's (1988) definition, Bryman (2008) argues that theory is important to social research as a backdrop to, and rationale for, research. Any particular approach has to be acknowledged and theoretically justified. For Bryman theory also provides a framework within which social phenomena are understood (Bryman, 2008, p. 6). This assertion of the importance of theory becomes a significant theme in claims about the distinctiveness of social research. However, it also leads to the need to defend its rigour in comparison to other approaches. Shipman (1988), for example, suggests that designing research through the adoption of theoretical models is the pathway to bias and 'if theory is to be grounded in the data as they are collected, the scope for bias is further increased' (1988, p. 164). However, as Guba and

Lincoln (1989) point out, *all* research involves bias. One of the strengths of social research and one of its main characteristics is that it is open and transparent about the 'biases' it holds. Hence social research demands not only an evaluation of outcomes but also a reflexive analysis of the research process and the place of the researcher in it. This involves a critical scrutiny of the epistemological commitments of any research (Usher, 1997).

These discussions seem to be polarizing social research as being associated with theorists while those involved in technical empirical data gathering have been called researchers. This carries implications that those committed to theory and theorizing are not proper researchers. Hence Bulmer's (1982) reflection that the challenge for social research is the need to manage the balance between empirical evidence and theoretical interpretation is very relevant: 'Theory needs to be confronted with empirical evidence in basic research. Evidence needs to be informed by theory and interpreted in the light of it in policy research' (Bulmer, 1982, p. 15). May (1997) also argues that the split between theory and evidence is a false one. He suggests that there is a constant relationship between social theory and social research. Social researchers do not seek one overarching monolithic theory for the social world. Through a combination of reflective experience and practice, which for him is the hallmark of social research, more becomes known about the social world (May, 1997, p. 28).

> Instead of descending upon the social world armed with a body of theoretical propositions about how social relations exist and work as they do, we should first observe those relations, collect data on them, and then proceed to generate theoretical propositions. (May, 1997, p. 29)

From this review of writing on social research it is possible to make tentative conclusions that social research is not necessarily defined by the methods used, but by the interrelationship between empirical evidence or 'facts' and the development of theory in the research process and in the interpretation of the outcomes. The focus of social research is on social relations, which include relations between individuals and relations of individuals and groups with their environment. This broad definition helps to situate social work research within social research.

Developments in social research

Another way of identifying how social work research relates to social research is by considering the developments of social research over time.

In doing this we can observe not only how social work research has developed from other traditions, but also how developing a research base for social work can contribute to even better understandings of the social world.

Bulmer (1982) suggests that the beginnings of social research were associated with the collection of data to describe the population. The first UK census in 1801 involved the collection of data and was initially associated with the science of statistics. However, the emphasis very soon changed from the mere collection of data to the collection of population data for specific purposes, which in turn led to theory building.

The notion of social inquiry, which involved what was called objective scientific study into social conditions, led to reports such as the *Royal Commission on the Poor Law* (1832–4). While such reports were concerned with empirical measurement of social conditions they also revealed injustices (e.g. differential living conditions between groups of people). The collection and analysis of data enabled associations to be made between, for example, poverty, poor housing and other social phenomena such as illness and crime. While collecting census data and scientific inquiry continued the information that became available was used by social reformers, who began to conduct social investigations. This involved more targeted and specific data collection than global statistical descriptions of conditions. Social investigation also involved different kinds of data or knowledge. For example, Mayhew's *London Labour and the London Poor* (1861) included what is now known as qualitative evidence: accounts of social conditions from those who were experiencing those conditions. Rowntree's study in York, *Poverty: A Study of Town Life* (1901), involved interviewing people in their homes. This was also significant as, building on Booth's study of London (*Life and Labour of London's Poor*, 1886–1903), it began to classify degrees of poverty and to establish measures and definitions of poverty. The development of the notion of a 'poverty cycle' is an early example of how information collected and the way it is collected gives insight into social conditions and how these are experienced.

It was the development of these processes, the coming together of empirical data with social commentary and social movements, that marked a shift in the development of social research. The work of social reformers such as Beatrice and Sidney Webb began to combine 'scientific' enquiry with participation in social movements. Data was collected for political purposes rather than just description. The Webbs undertook historical and institutional analysis combining social sciences and political action: they aimed to know not just how things were but what caused them (Webb and Webb, 1968). This, according to Shipman, involves 'probing into the gap between intention and practice' (Shipman 1988, p. 176) and involves methods of enquiry that reveal how the evidence supporting injustices is itself constructed. Social research therefore involves a critical (political) edge that highlights how existing structures have to be challenged rather than assumed to be legitimate.

By the beginning of the twentieth century social research had become institutionalized and inhabited what was defined as the 'middle ground' (Hammersley, 1995). This is slightly different from the middle ground between data and theory and involved two expectations: that it was scientific (that is, it functioned in the way that the natural sciences functioned by providing statistical data); and that it delivered practical solutions, in the way that science had done.

By the 1950s social research was further influenced by developments in the social sciences, which included a growing influence of political philosophy, a revival of what are known as 'grand theories' in social sciences and a growing popularity of qualitative methods (Hammersley, 1993). However, the notion of social surveys continued in social science and involved factual inquiries.

These traditions can be seen in the development of subjects within the social sciences. Subjects such as demography and social statistics discussed the collection of data and philosophy, politics and some branches of sociology looked at the emerging data in the light of theories. There are also examples of subjects emerging where the study of phenomena such as illness and interventions often brought together statistics and data. In health the study of epidemiology brought together the incidence of illness and disease with theories about the causes, which could lead to the discovery of cures. This is significant for social work research because such approaches influenced early developments when researchers were attempting to identify causes of and cures for social problems (Davies, 1969; Robinson, 1970).

As has been indicated in Chapter 1 differences emerged between those social researchers who continued to try to emulate a scientific approach claiming that the only credible knowledge came from quantitative data and those who argued that the 'social' nature of what was being researched was different from phenomena in the natural world. The fact that people exercise free will, can interpret their surroundings and will act on the basis of their interpretation (Hammersley, 1993, p. viii) has implications for research in terms of the kinds of research questions asked of the social world, the process of gathering knowledge to answer the questions and the way that the knowledge is interpreted (Hammersley, 1995; Delanty, 1997).

The differences and distinctions between different subject approaches to research in the social sciences continued. In social policy and related subjects the principles of social research became more inductive – that is, they tried to understand and ascertain knowledge about social situations rather than impose theories on them. This involved making connections between surveys and action, knowledge and policy. Although they drew on technical approaches such as sampling, they began to include speculation about causal theories and potential political activity that at times touched on moralism: 'Research has a directly political function, to describe and so expose the unacceptable with the aim of shifting policy and practice' (Hood et al., 1999, p. 5).

There are some features of social order where description is both necessary and sufficient because the unacceptable aspects of a situation will be obvious. Examples of this are evident in the early studies on poverty. However, the need for a political perspective that included social research acknowledging the involvement of those being researched marked distinctive developments (Hood et al., 1999). This shift is seen as a swing in social sciences from the search for laws of observed behaviour to the search for meanings that individuals give to events (Shipman, 1988, p. 161). Shipman sees social researchers becoming engaged in a social and political process as a rejection of the role of neutral observer. This was also the ultimate rejection of 'scientism' (Shipman, 1988, p. 165).

Limitations

While developments in social research meant that there were closer links between research and social work practice, there were limitations. For example, the involvement of those who were frequently the focus of social researcher, the users of social services, was circumscribed. Further, the way that research questions were framed often problematized the experiences of those being researched.

As part of becoming more political there were developments in social research that recognized that it was necessary to enable the voice to be heard of individuals and groups who might be described collectively as disadvantaged. However, no assumptions were made about the methods to be used to make such voices audible. Hood et al. (1999) point out that large-scale data has provided 'evidence' of inequalities in access to health services and the complex inequalities of black and minority ethnic groups. For them, therefore, there is no assumption about the *right* method, what is important is to use the method appropriate for the question (Hood et al., 1999, p. 3).

Others acknowledged the need to hear the voices of those within the social situations being investigated. However, while they sought to identify the structural determinants of people's problems and include the views of those within social situations there remained the sense that the researcher was the expert, in both collecting the data and interpreting it. The politics of the research process involved power differentials within that process. No matter how 'egalitarian' social researchers try to be they can be constrained by the requirements of funding bodies and/or policy agendas that require them to interpret and impute meaning to the accounts that have been collected. It took the participatory approaches of social work research to develop methods that not only gave voice to those in research, but began to challenge the very process of researching (Mayer and Timms, 1970; Sainsbury, 1975, 1987).

Other limitations in social research were the constraints of organizing factors such as who becomes the focus of research and how experiences are categorized. In the 1980s in social research those who were the focus of research were known as 'subjects' and were organized into hierarchies usually focusing on the poor, the deprived and the powerless (Shipman, 1988). The subject matter defined who and what is researched: 'It is top down, rarely concerned with those with power and rarely challenges their right to hold it (Shipman, 1988, p. 165).

A final set of limitations involve social research attempting to find a comfortable modus operandi. Attempts to become more egalitarian led to criticism that developments in social research brought social scientists closer to media reports and to literature (Shipman, 1988, p. 162). This was a direct result of methodological development that involved attempts to be distanced from associations with 'science'. Initially social researchers stressed the scientific character of social research as being separate from journalism and literature. However, as they developed, methods involving discourse and narrative research were seen more as a form of writing that has something in common with prose and poetry. For some (Hood et al., 1999) the fact that research can be akin to journalism is a strength of social research. It is associated with the political function of research to make social conditions known: to describe and so expose the unacceptable with the aim of shifting policy and practice (Hood et al., 1999, p. 5).

Towards a definition?

It has been suggested that the field of social research might be thought of as a war zone in which competing assumptions about the purposes and possibilities fight it out (Hammersley, 1993, p. xii). While the scope of discussions about methodology in social research is great it is possible to synthesize some core principles.

Social research focuses on the social world, but uses critical perspectives to observe that world and to identify, understand and explain what is revealed, and how it is revealed. It places emphasis on the way theory influences both the research questions and the research processes. Social research therefore focuses not just on the knowledge created, but on how the research process contributes to knowledge creation. Those involved in social research argue that while it is important to undertake empirical research to describe the way that the world is, it is also important to try to understand and explain the world from the perspective of those experiencing it and to explore the processes of knowledge creation that contribute to the different explanation. This tends to favour qualitative research methods, but is not exclusive to these approaches.

Social research and social work

The emerging definition of social research has two implications for developing a research base for social work. Social research deals with the *social* world and focuses on people and their interactions with agencies, organizations, policies and structures. It is therefore studying the world in which social work practitioners intervene. Social work practice therefore becomes the focus of research. However, social research can be enhanced by social work – in particular the ways in which social work researchers have gained insights from researching practice. So, for example, it is possible to research school phobia by focusing on the education system and gathering data on those who do not attend school. But the idea of 'school' and attitudes towards school attendance differ depending on parenting experiences, family dynamics, preparation for school, educational attainment and many other factors. To fully understand patterns of school attendance research has to be conducted in ways that allow these different perspectives to emerge.

Social work research therefore, by being both the subject of research and a contributor of research insights, enhances the ways in which social life can be understood. Social research is a social process. The results of social research feed into social life and by doing so influence practices and understandings, both of those participating in the research and of society more generally.

Research based social work practice is an example of this process. Social workers require research to understand the social world in which they intervene, but also need to understand that those very interventions are part of the social world. Social work cannot merely undertake empirical research and 'use' the results in formulating assessments or deciding in what ways to intervene. Decisions about whether to use a particular method of intervention (for example, task-centred case work, crisis intervention or cognitive behavioural therapy) require ways of understanding the particular situation, not just textbook knowledge about what each approach involves. As each abuse or neglect enquiry highlights, decisions about whether to take a child into the care of the local authority or to provide residential care for an older person involve a delicate balance of understanding the research evidence on the consequences of acting, or not acting, and the implications for this person or family at this particular point in their lives.

Early debates about the relationship between social work practice and research began in the USA. They followed a 'scientific' line (Thyer, 1989) and argued that to prove social work effectiveness design studies were needed to inform conclusions about whether or not a given programme had been of benefit or not. Such studies include Fischer (1973), who looked at the efficacy of case work in North America, and Reid and Shyne's (1969) work, which was used to bring about changes in the way social workers went about their practice. Work in the UK included Robinson (1970) in the area of casework, Folkard (1974), who evaluated the effect of intensive supervision in the probation service, and Sainsbury's (1975) analysis of the effectiveness of work with families. These illustrate some of Thyer's (1989) suggestions for what was required in social work research. These include:

● design studies that allow the researcher to conclude whether interventions are of benefit;
● a rigorous methodology in defence of the professional activity (social work, health, education etc.);
● the use of research principles (methodology and methods) that are appropriate for the investigation;
● possibly less emphasis on *outcome* studies that can render the process of interventions immune from analysis (Thyer, 1989).

Although not necessarily supporting all Thyer's recommendations, White (1997) certainly supports the last one. She questions the wisdom of putting all social work's research eggs in the 'outcomes' basket. This is often associated with what has been called the 'magic bullet' approach to social work – the assumption that there is a particular social work method of intervention that will 'cure' social ills.

White's questioning comes about because of the 'dynamic' nature of the situations in which social work intervenes. This dynamism is not only relevant to practitioners, it is relevant to the way that research is carried out, and used. Those with whom social workers work have the capacity to be free agents, to understand their own world, interpret it and change their behaviour – making it more complicated for social work research to understand it, and making it more difficult for practitioners to intervene. This is often referred to in social work textbooks as focusing on 'the person in their situation' and is associated with individualization as one of the fundamental values in social work (Plant, 1973). Understanding the 'person', the individual in the situation, requires complex understandings of human behaviour and motivation at the micro-level from biology, physiology and physical and social psychology. The 'situation' or the macro-level requires understanding of political, economic and sociological analysis of the functioning of social systems from families to governments, recognizing differences and diversity. White (1997) suggests that the concentration in research on outcomes can render the intricacies of social work practice immune from analysis. Understanding in social work and therefore social work research has to go beyond what she calls 'retroduction', arguing that the process of understanding is more important than outcomes.

This distinction is not unique to social work research. Others researching the 'social' recognize the interaction between individuals and systems. Williams and colleagues' (1999) analysis of welfare reform over time led them to identify changing paradigms in social research. Some of the major changes included:

- people are no longer seen as 'beneficiaries' of welfare;
- people are no longer seen as one-dimensional fixed categories, and therefore there is recognition of diversity;
- people are active agents with the capacity for reflexivity.

This leads them to conclude that:

> The challenge [for welfare research] is to explore the nature of subjectivity and agency, and the complexity of social divisions, but also find middle range concepts which can tie these concerns to the structural contexts of widespread poverty, equality, globalisation and the international structuring of welfare. (Williams *et al.*, 1999, p. 7)

In developing research based social work this has implications for the kind of research needed to help develop good practice. One important area that has developed is the evaluation of practice (Shaw and Lishman, 1999). However, social work research also needs to draw upon and develop methodologies that enhance knowledge for practice. This has to include knowledge from those involved in the social and interpersonal situations in which social work intervenes.

This knowledge has to be both global and local, about populations and individuals. Jones (2001), for example, drawing on both empirical research and journalism, outlines the level of poverty that social workers encounter among service users' groups and reveals social workers' sense of demoralization. Part of their frustration was caused by the lack of attention paid to the impact of this poverty by either politicians or social work managers.

Practitioners, managers and policy-makers contribute and have access to many and diverse databases that give broad brush pictures of social conditions. In both practice and research there is a tendency to avoid analysis of these databases. This may be because they are seen to be too impersonal, or it may be because of the lack of attention paid to teaching statistics and quantitative methods on social work training courses (Orme *et al.*, 2008). However, social workers need to have a sense that the issues they are dealing with are part of wider social trends, and need to be alert to the fact that those issues may also be part of phenomena that have wider implications.

For example, in the early days of working with survivors of domestic violence, social work tended to see the problem as being relevant to that particular family at that particular time (Maynard, 1985). As feminist writers and practitioners began to share their experiences of working with these situations it became apparent that the problem was widespread and required a policy response (Mullender, 1996; Orme and Briar Lawson, 2009). Social work that addresses the person in their environment has to be alert to the conditions of that environment.

Social work researchers therefore have a responsibility to provide data on the conditions that service users and carers are experiencing and in which social work is operating. This can be done by drawing on data collected for other purposes, but also building up data sets, statistical information that will provide arguments for particular research and evaluation.

The counterpoint to this approach to research is that social work also deals with the intimate, private, personal and interpersonal aspects of people's lives and with what is at times anti-social and unacceptable behaviour. To ensure best practice in these areas it is necessary to undertake research into both the issues and the methods of intervention or practice. As has been said, the process and practice of evaluation is a growing area in social work research. However, such situations require more than evaluation of outcomes and processes. They require attention to research methods that are sensitive to the situations that are being 'investigated' and deal with the complexities of understanding them. Often emancipatory approaches are effective in such circumstances, but sometimes social work and therefore social research has to deal with contradictory claims and competing needs. To return to the example of domestic violence, it required new methodologies and very careful work to enable women who had experienced abuse to reveal the extent and different manifestations of the phenomena (Mullender, 1996). It requires equally complex work to develop methods that will enable research to explore what factors contribute to and precipitate such abuse and to inform practice with those who perpetrate the abuse (Orme, 2004).

Conclusion

This chapter has explored social research as a particular aspect of social sciences research. It has identified that social research occupies what is called the middle ground. That is, it focuses on the interrelationships between individuals and groups and the relationships of individuals and groups with their wider environment. It also occupies the middle ground, or more accurately a mediating role between different methodological approaches. As such it has much that is relevant to developing a research base for social work: to inform practice with 'the person in their situation'.

In saying this, no assumptions are made about the methodological approach or methods used in social research. The contribution of social research can help to make sense of situations by gathering 'hard' data about the extent and nature of social problems or issues. However, it is fundamental to social research and social work research that methods are developed to access knowledge about social situations from those within them.

Finally, recognizing another 'middle ground' held by social research, researchers have to reflect on all information gathered and the processes of gathering that information to look for patterns and give it meaning – to develop theory.

putting it into practice

Think about a case in which you might have to intervene as a social worker. Write down what you think you need to know about this situation before you intervene.

It is likely that you thought first of the information you need to know to undertake a social work assessment, based on the nature of the case and the agency policy. You probably identified that you needed to talk to those involved in the situation to help your understanding of the situation. You probably also thought that you would need to check out legislation and agency policy to establish what you should do and what you could do.

Now reflect on what you have written:

- Did you identify that you need to know about how many people are in this situation: nationally; in your area; on your case load?
- Did you identify that you need to know about what happens to different people in different circumstances, how they are affected by them — for example, on the basis of their gender, ethnicity, age etc.?
- Did you identify that you need to know what other practitioners have done in similar situations?
- Did you identify a need to know what service users (and carers) in similar situations have said about their experiences?
- If you identified any (or all) of the above, would you know where to go for the information that you require?

Research can provide this kind of information to assist the process of making an assessment. It is necessary to think through such questions not only at the outset of an assessment, but also at different stages, because as you gather more information it leads to more questions.

So, think about the situation again and identify what research based information would help your understanding.

Recommended reading

Bulmer, M. (1982) *The Uses of Social Research.* London, Allen & Unwin. Provides an illuminative account of the origins of social research.

Orme, J. and Briar-Lawson, K. (2009) 'Knowledge and Theories of Social Problems and Policies', in I. Shaw, K. Briar-Lawson, J. Orme and R. Ruckdeschel (eds) *The Handbook of Social Work Research*. London, Sage. Explores the development of social work research.

Part 2 | Process of Social Work Research

3 | Ethics and ethical approval

Introduction

This chapter is the first of this part, which addresses the implications of developing research based practice for the processes involved in undertaking research. The previous chapters have set out how research is not just a matter of collecting data or information and 'telling it how it is'. It is a complicated process of thinking about what information is required and how different ways of thinking about the world, and therefore different ways of collecting and interpreting information, have implications for the research that is undertaken and its usefulness. This is particularly so in social work, where research is about people, their situations and the way that those situations are perceived and interpreted by those who are in them and those outside them, such as policy-makers.

All research is subject to ethical rules. Because social science research is about people and their situations these rules are more overt. Social work research has further ethical implications because increasingly social work is about the very personal and intimate aspects of people's behaviour and relationships. To be meaningful and useful at times it also investigates aspects of people's behaviour that are unacceptable and/or they are reluctant to reveal, such as violent behaviour or inappropriate or illegal sexual behaviour. Having said that, social work research is undertaken in a practice culture that includes a value base that seeks to respect individuals, no matter how abhorrent their behaviour.

Over the past decade there has been active consideration of ethics for research, not least because rapid developments in health and medical research have raised crucial dilemmas. Moreover, research is becoming more transparent. Results are becoming more available through resources such as Internet sites and media interest, which brings added ethical dimensions. Finally, legislation in the areas of human rights, freedom of information and data protection must underpin legal and ethical considerations. There are rightly ever more constraints on what research can be undertaken, by whom and with whom, and there is more public scrutiny of research and researchers. Social work research is informed by such developments. It also contributes to ethical debates both through the influence of the value base of practice and because of its commitment to widening the range of individuals and groups who undertake research.

The response to these developments within the social and health care field has been to introduce aspects of governance that attempt to regulate research for the protection of all and to try to codify ethical questions to provide guidance for researchers. This surveillance role is important but for social work the fact that much of the guidance to which it is subject emanates from health and medical research means that either it creates inappropriate demands or it does not address the nuances of subject and method that are distinctive in social work research.

In the past decade these issues of control and 'governance' in research have had implications for developing a social work research base. They have acted as both a hindrance and a catalyst.

Therefore to understand the development of research practice that can contribute to a strong research base for social work it is necessary to understand the thinking behind the developments. This chapter starts with the broader context of research governance. Discussion of the social work response, which includes the development of a code of ethics for social work research, then leads to a consideration of some of the complexities of undertaking ethical research in social work both in the broad context and for individual researchers.

Research governance

Research governance is intended to ensure that research is conducted to high scientific and ethical standards. It includes the broad range of guidance to help achieve, and continuously improve, research quality. To this end it seeks to determine best practice and rules governing how to ensure that the process of allocating funding is free and fair and leads to the most appropriate ways of undertaking research for each project. Hugman (2009) analyses arrangements for research governance in the USA, Australia and the UK and finds that there are similarities between them. Notably, the rules for governance are invariably established by government or para-government organizations whereas ethical codes for social work research evolve from professional organizations.

In the UK, because different governments and assemblies have responsibility for commissioning research and each has responsibilities and rules about financial probity and laws governing the use of public funds, each of the four countries has its own research governance framework.

The purpose of the Research Governance Framework in England (Department of Health, first published in 2001 and revised in 2005) is to respond to the rights of the public in a variety of ways: 'The public has a right to expect high scientific, ethical and financial standards, transparent decision making processes, clear allocation of responsibilities and robust monitoring arrangements' (DoH, 2005, p. 2). In that the Department of Health in England is responsible for both medical and social care research, the Research Governance Framework, which covers all activity in that area, has to cover many aspects of legislation that are controversial, such as research involving human tissue and stem cell research.

This was seen to be problematic by social work researchers, who argued that some of the organization and principles of research in social work and social care were different from those in medical and health research. Social work researchers felt disadvantaged by the forms and procedures, which were not tailored to the nuances of social work research.

While the Research Governance Framework argues that the same principles apply across health and social care research, it does acknowledge that the way in which the relevant standards are achieved will differ according to the research type, context and method. In particular it recognizes differences in the mix of stakeholders, the organizational context and the range of academic disciplines involved in social work and social care research.

The Framework addresses issues of respect for persons, the underpinning social work value, by asserting that the dignity, rights, safety and well-being of participants must be the primary consideration in any research study and that informed consent is at the heart of ethical research. However, it also recognizes that social work and social care has a commitment to the involvement of service users and the need for research and those pursuing it to reflect the diversity of society, and in particular the multicultural nature of society.

This difference in interpretation begins to illustrate the complexities of having a catch-all set of guidance. Another example is the issue of risk. Issues of risk are more often associated with medical research: with the administration of drugs or medical interventions that can do obvious harm. Social work research is unlikely to involve the administration of harmful drugs or the withholding of potentially helpful ones but risks in research manifest themselves in different ways. The risks associated with social work research are more subtle, in that engagement with those who are experiencing disadvantage and poor social conditions can lead to raising the hopes of those with whom the researcher is in touch. Social work research also often involves making contact with those who for a variety of reasons are isolated and excluded. This can lead to unrealistic expectations of the research relationship. The impact is not always foreseen, especially when not the central focus of the research.

For example, research into the workload of probation officers (Orme, 1995) involved contacting offenders on whom reports had been written, asking them to complete a questionnaire. Some of those contacted were in prison. One person who responded while in prison answered the questions but also filled every blank space on the form writing about his situation, offering further help in the research and asking for continued contact. On the one hand it could be argued that this person had been given some status by being thought important enough to have his views sought. On the other hand he had his expectations raised of ongoing contact, which could only lead to disappointment. While this does not constitute 'harm' in the same way as administering drugs might cause harm, it does highlight the unintended consequences of research practice.

Such examples illustrate the need for governance and guidance. Other aspects of governance might seem to be good practice, including:

- undertaking a review of existing evidence;
- subjecting research proposals to peer review;
- guidance on the protection and storage of data collected on individuals;
- availability of information on the research being conducted and the findings;
- openness to critical review.

However, the critique of a generic framework is that it was not always responsive or relevant to the particular aspects of social work research. These criticisms were also made of the arrangements for research ethics committees set up to operationalize the guidance.

Research ethics committees

The mechanisms by which research governance operates include research ethics committees. These committees have become gatekeepers of the research agenda. Once a research proposal has been developed consideration has to be given to whether it is necessary to take it to a research ethics committee, and if so which one.

Research ethics committees have an important tradition. In 1964 the Helsinki Declaration (WMA, 1964) was developed to try to prevent the abuses that had been revealed as having been perpetrated by the Nazis at Nuremburg. It led to the proliferation of committees that had oversight of research that involved human subjects. These committees were therefore established to provide an independent opinion on the extent to which proposals for a study comply with recognized ethical standards. They were required to be independent when formulating advice on the ethics of the proposed research. To ensure the composition and regulation of research ethics committees their establishment was subject to legislation and governance.

The purpose of ethics committees is beyond dispute: 'The dignity, rights, safety and well-being of participants must be the primary consideration in any research study' (Governance Arrangements for Research Ethics Committees (GAfREC), 2001). However, with the development of a more discrete and distinctive research base in social sciences the focus of the committees and the criteria with which they operated were seen to be dominated by science-based concerns (Dominelli and Holloway, 2008).

The Research Governance Framework for Health and Social Care in the UK (2005) indicated that the arrangements for ethics review in social care research were less well developed than in the NHS. There was no system comparable to the NHS Research Ethics Committees, although those involved in social work and social care research were obviously using their best endeavours to ensure it is conducted to high ethical standards. Wherever possible they drew on existing arrangements for independent ethics review. In addition to using existing arrangements in health and/or in universities there were also systems developed in social work agencies. For example, the (as was) Association of Directors of Social Services (ADSS) research group advised the ADSS and individual directors and social services on the ethics, quality and relevance of proposals. This was because while research ethics committees provide an independent opinion each director or head of a care organization has a duty of care to those receiving services and is responsible for giving permission for research in that organization, acknowledging not only ethical principles but also local and personal factors that might make individuals and groups vulnerable.

For example, in the early 1990s in the UK when there were dramatic changes in the organization of services brought about by community care legislation a great deal of research was undertaken to evaluate the effects of the changes. Directors of social services and research ethics committees had to be mindful that certain groups, particularly older people, were at risk of being over-researched. The balance of ensuring effective evaluation of service development alongside the need to protect service users raises many issues that are both ethical and political.

Developing social work systems

Despite, or because of, the plethora of ethics review committees, social work researchers felt disadvantaged by the forms and procedures that, they argued, were not tailored to the nuances of social work research. In the UK a social work specific code of ethics (Butler, 2002) was developed and the principles of this are discussed below. This was thought necessary because the code of ethics for practice developed by the British Association of Social Work did not cover research. In the USA, Australia and New Zealand codes for practice did include research.

Arguments for the development of social work research specific systems, reflected in that code, emerged from the 'Theorising Social Work Research' seminars and were part of the case for the distinctiveness of social work research and the need for different rules of governance.

Discussions about governance involved a working party, which included representatives from government, social work academics, practitioners and service users and carers, and undertook a review of arrangements for ethical oversight in social care (which in their remit included social work) research in England (Pahl, 2007). The working party acknowledged the complexity of arrangements for researchers in social care (and therefore social work). They also recognized that the systems in place were based on assumptions that research would be undertaken by academics, government or contract researchers. There was no proportionate and transparent single system for the review of ethics in social care research proposals where the investigator was not attached to a university. This could be a problem for many stakeholders, but particularly excluded people who use services and their carers and their organizations. That this was a major consideration in the ethical infrastructure is one illustration of the distinctiveness of social work and social care research. Service users and carers now play a variety of key roles in social work and social care research and robust procedures for ethical review are required to enable a more diverse body of researchers.

The recommendations of the working party led to proposals to set up in England a national Social Care Research Ethics Committee (SCREC) to provide a resource for researchers to enable and promote ethically sound research. In the light of the observations above it was essential to ensure that all perspectives are represented. Therefore the proposed committee will include service commissioners, service providers and those who use services and members who represent the general public. The involvement of services users and carers is distinctive of approaches in both government and the social work and social care professions in the UK to work towards social inclusion, and is not necessarily reflected in the arrangements of other countries.

In order to undertake their work efficiently and to ensure some standardization of practice, ethics committees ask two important questions. The first is 'what are the ethical dimensions to this project?' The answer to this question is obviously important as it gives an indication of the nature of the research, and whether the person applying understands the implications of what they are intending to do. The second is about codes of ethics. The existence of numerous codes of ethics is an indication of how researchers and professional bodies are taking the impact of research very seriously. However, the fact that there are numerous codes of ethics can also be confusing. It is therefore important to understand the thinking behind codes of ethics, and in particular the implications of codes of ethics for social work research.

Principles of codes of ethics

One implication of developing a research base for practice is that research in social work should be guided by social work values. This raises two issues. The first is an implicit suggestion that other social science research does not have a value base, or if it does it is significantly different from that of social work. The diversity of methodological approaches contributes to this perception because there is the suggestion in some that facts can be collected without implying value judgement. In fact the involvement of values or value judgement is considered to be problematic: researchers should be 'disinterested' and 'value free'. However, others have argued that all researchers are influenced by values and this permeates the whole research process. The very identification of something as a 'problem' or a puzzle involves a value judgement on behalf of the researcher (Guba and Lincoln, 1998). Moreover, to undertake any analysis of the data involves interpretation, which will be influenced by the researcher.

Developments in social research associated with critical theory (May, 1997) have advocated being overt about the value base from which research is being undertaken. The most obvious example of this is research that is feminist in orientation. While there may be different approaches to research that can be called feminist (Harding, 1987;

Stanley, 1990), all are conducted from the perspective of identifying and/or overcoming women's oppression.

The discussion of values therefore highlights that it is necessary to have certain standards to guide how a community of researchers conducts itself when undertaking research. The machinery of research governance provides oversight of these, but more detailed sets of guidance emerge in codes of ethics for research. Ethical practice involves decisions about what is right and just in the interests of all who are involved in the research. It also has to be contextualized in the community in which it is being undertaken because it often involves discussion of the micro-decisions that each individual researcher has to make in each research interaction. Hence different organizations, professions and institutions have developed their own codes. It is this level of detail that makes codes of ethics both necessary and problematic.

Social work research code of ethics

Social work practice has a very clear value base although there have been debates over time about which values are pre-eminent (see Biestek, 1961; Plant, 1973; Horne, 1987; Hugman and Smith, 1995; Clark, 2000; Banks, 2006). These have been codified at both a national level (see, for example, the British Association of Social Workers code of ethics) and a global level (see the statement of ethics by the International Federation of Social Work (IFSW) and the International Association of Schools of Social Work (IASSW); IFSW/IASSW, 2004).

Few of these texts address the issue of ethics and values in research. This is partly because of the lack of acknowledgement of a distinctive approach to social work research. In the UK social work researchers have drawn on codes devised by other disciplines and developed over time such as those of the Social Policy Association (SPA, 2008) or the Social Research Association (SRA, 2003). Researchers seeking funding from the ESRC now have to be mindful of its codes (ESRC, 2007).

Such codes are sufficient for broad decisions to be made to ensure the ethical conduct of research, but as with the principles of research governance they do not sufficiently address the complexities and distinctiveness of social work research.

Underpinning most approaches to ethics and social research are two principles:

● *The ethics of inherent duty* (deontology): ethical judgements should guide the conduct of research, are universal and should be followed irrespective of the position in which the researcher finds himself or herself. As Hugman (2009) puts it, 'something is right because it accords with the duties that follow from the moral nature of humanity'.

- *The ethics of consequence* (consequentialsim or teleology): ethical judgements in research are not based on absolute rules but are influenced by the possible consequences of undertaking the research: 'something is right because it leads to "good" outcomes' (Hugman, 2009).

Hugman (2009) also suggests that at times research ethics may draw on 'virtue ethics' or the ethics of character, in which what is right is encountered in the qualities of the person acting. It is virtue ethics that at times has been uppermost in discussions of social work research, where such research is defined as that undertaken by those with an understanding of the profession and the commitment to the value base. However, as will be seen, one of the problems of developing a code of ethics for social work is defining what is meant by social work research.

In developing a specific code of ethics for social work and social care Butler (2000) drew on the work of two Americans, Beauchamp and Childress (1989), who developed the 'four principles plus scope' approach. By this it is argued that there are four basic principles underpinning ethical research: respect for autonomy, beneficence (doing good), non-maleficence (not doing harm) and justice. While this does not make explicit reference to deontology and teleology, the definition of scope, which refers to the process of deciding about to whom and in what circumstances the particular moral obligation applies (Butler, 2002), indicates leaning towards consequentialism rather than an absolute set of rules to be applied in every circumstance. The scope can therefore be influenced by the professional context in which the research is being conducted – be that the background of the researcher or the subject being researched.

Hugman (2009) points out that the practical ethics of a profession often combine the different approaches. The underpinning principles that Butler developed for a social work specific code in the UK seem to be such an amalgam and include:

1. Every human being has a unique value, which justifies moral consideration for that person.
2. Each individual has the right to self-fulfillment to the extent that it does not encroach upon the same right of others, and has an obligation to contribute to the well-being of society.

3. Each society, regardless of its form, should function to provide the maximum benefits for all its members.
4. Social workers have a commitment to social justice.
5. Social workers have the responsibility to devote objective and disciplined knowledge and skill to aid individuals, groups, communities and societies in their development and resolution of personal–societal conflicts and their consequences.
6. Social workers are expected to provide the best possible assistance to anybody seeking their help or advice, without unfair discrimination on the basis of gender, age, disability, colour, social class, race, religion, language, political beliefs or sexual orientation (Scie website http://www.scie.org.uk/publications/misc/tswr/seminar6/butler.asp).

The resultant fifteen-point code of ethics for social work research (Butler, 2002, p. 214) also sought to challenge the hierarchical relationships that are frequently constructed in the research process. This was particularly important because social work as a discipline was seeking to democratize the research process by involving service users in ways other than being the 'subject' (or object) of research. Challenging power bases in the construction of knowledge is addressed to some extent through methodological approaches discussed in other parts of this text, but in constructing the code of ethics for social work research it was thought necessary to foreground principles, not just of non-maleficence but of empowerment.

Social work research is not the only area which has sought to address power imbalances in research processes. Feminist approaches to research, which permeate all social science disciplines, have challenged hierarchies of knowledge and knowledge production (Stanley and Wise, 1983). Whether this is possible or appropriate is questioned by Hammersley (1995), who argues that 'the proper relationship' between researcher and researched cannot be legislated by methodology, and dilemmas and inequalities that exist throughout the social world cannot be avoided in research (Hammersley, 1995, p. 61).

Such discussions alert us to the fact that while it might seem appropriate to develop codes of ethics to ensure the protection of individuals and groups, doing so is not unproblematic. The assumption that there are certain ways to proceed when undertaking research, and certain practices to avoid, might seem obvious, but researchers, like practitioners, are constantly faced with situations that challenge accepted norms and present dilemmas.

Limitations of codes of ethics

Constructing codes of ethics is not without criticism in the social sciences generally (Bauman, 1993), in social work practice (Banks, 2006; Orme and Rennie, 2006) and in social work research (Shaw 2008; Hugman, 2009). In describing the process of constructing such a code in the UK Butler (2002) acknowledges that having a social work specific code of ethics for research raises many questions: whether it applies only to social work researchers, or to other researchers when undertaking social work research; and what is 'social work research'? He suggests that the benefit of attempting to codify ethics for research is not in the provision of absolute rules but in the criticism that it evokes and the dialogue that follows.

A similar but different point is made by those who argue for a dialogic approach to research (Powell, 2002) and ethics (Rossiter et al., 2000). They suggest that it is not helpful to have rules or codes that have to be slavishly followed, not least because every situation is different and involves different nuances, different dilemmas and different challenges. The process of reflection is core to good social work practice and leads to what Husband (1995) calls the 'morally active practitioner'. Such principles should be equally embedded in social work research practice, whatever methodological approach is being utilized. The aim is to ensure morally *active* researchers.

Morally active researchers

That each research project presents different dilemmas that cannot be resolved by unquestioning following of rules means that there needs to be active consideration of all aspects of the research throughout the process. An example of one problematic of ethical codes is provided in the area of domestic violence, where what might be seen as competing values are in operation. Much research in the area of domestic violence has rightly been with women, attempting to glean information about the nature and extent of the phenomenon to inform understanding. However, in that, to our knowledge, most domestic violence is perpetrated by men on women, it is necessary to involve men in the research process to try to identify motivation, triggers and other potential causes of domestic violence (Gilgun, 2008).

In this situation respecting men who have been violent to women, giving them a voice in the research process and giving validity to what might be seen as justifications or excuses for their behaviour would be an anathema to some feminist researchers. However, the research is needed to ensure that there is full understanding of domestic violence in order to protect women. Researchers have to be mindful of the conflicts and develop research methods that enable information to be gathered about male violence in ways that constructively add to the understanding of the phenomenon, but do not necessarily 'privilege' the male perspective (Orme, 2004). Many other social work research projects present similar dilemmas. Often the principles and values of practice have to be considered alongside the ethics of research. In child abuse, for example, the principle of the paramouncy of the rights of the child – to protection and care – might be met by attention to the conditions of parents who abuse them. Only if we can discern what precipitates violence can we work towards its elimination.

Shaw (2008) asserts that research ethics permeate the whole research project, right through to the dissemination of results. His concern is that ethics become bound up with governance and process and are only addressed at the beginning of the process. In looking specifically at qualitative methods he illustrates that there are aspects of the research process that cannot be anticipated at the beginning. This means that, for example, it is not really possible to gain informed consent if the researcher does not know what might emerge during the research. Moreover, there are some methodological approaches that require the researcher to be constantly vigilant and reflective. Those agreeing to participate in the research might not be aware of this and might not realize that note is being taken of, for example, their demeanour or their home circumstances and not just the answers to the research questions.

This is particularly significant in social work research into sensitive subjects. There is always the possibility that information about other abuses, or unacceptable or illegal behaviour, might emerge. Researchers with a practice background might be particularly alert to indications. This can present dilemmas for researchers who, on the basis of good ethical practice, have guaranteed confidentiality at the outset. Dominelli (2005) has suggested that a more helpful principle would be 'contingent confidentiality', where social workers when engaging people in research set out at the beginning the conditions under which confidentiality could not be maintained – for example, if criminal acts are disclosed.

However, it is not only overt conflicts or dilemmas that are presented to social work and social care researchers. Some are created by what might be described as role conflict. In that many researchers in social work research have a practice background they are sometimes presented with situations that test their adherence to their role as researcher.

For example, a social worker with a mental health nursing background was undertaking research with users of mental health services into their persceptions of workers from black and ethnic minority backgrounds. The research involved undertaking interviews in the homes of service users. On one visit the researcher was certain that the service user was experiencing a psychotic episode and was at risk to themselves, but not necessarily to the public. The dilemma in such a situation is whether to step out of the role of the researcher and take action as a social worker. This is not just the dilemma of compromising the research but more the ethics of intervening in a case or situation where you do not have full information.

Moreover, the morally active researcher is faced with challenges when not all ethical principles can be optimized, or there is a conflict of ethical principles. Healy (in Banks *et al.*, 2008) discusses this in relation to practice in the USA, but her points are equally relevant to research globally. She highlights the tension between universalism and relativism, arguing that there may be differences in perception between practitioner and service user. She suggests that ways of resolving this include discussion of the reasons for action and the possible consequences with the service user. While it might not always be practical to discuss with those who have been recruited to a research project the detailed implications of competing ethical concepts, Healy does alert us to the need to perceive the impact of the research from a variety of perspectives.

Her arguments also relate to an even more contentious set of challenges presented by research with marginalized groups such as refugees and indigenous people (Briskman, 2009). Briskman, based on her work with indigenous and marginalized groups in Australia, suggests that the normative 'gate-keeping' role that codes of ethics and ethics bodies perform is challenged by the need to adopt unorthodox measures to secure access and to give voice to such groups. There is a need to extend research hegemony for the greater good of communities, states and the international domain. A similar point is made by Mertens (2008), who argues that if social work is committed to social justice then being constrained by ethical codes and governance that have been formed by governments, professional associations and ethics boards is fraught with tension.

Implications for developing social work research

This leaves an interesting set of challenges. It is obviously necessary to have some checks and balances on who does research and how it is undertaken. It is not possible to accept everyone as bona fide researchers. It is also important to recognize that although service users and carers are citizens in their own right who can in the main make choices, it is not appropriate to subject them to a barrage of requests to participate in research just because they are in receipt of services. This is particularly important because social work in developing a research base will require more research to be undertaken.

Setting the research agenda

At a simple level there have to be rules about the accessibility of, for example, contact data. Mechanisms that require practitioners and managers to seek consent for this information to be passed to potential researchers can be time consuming. However, to ensure that there is a robust and useful research base for social work practice ways have to be found and systems devised to ensure that research does take place and that service users and carers are involved. At national and local level these systems must ensure that the research agendas are discussed and agreed, involving service users and carers as well as politicians, managers and practitioners.

Reflecting on ethical implications

As has been said, when applying for research funding or submitting a research proposal to an institution it is necessary to think through the ethical implications of the project. The discussions so far highlighted that it is important to think beyond the basic questions that are the main concern of ethical committees, such as:

- Will this project do any harm?
- How will I obtain consent?
- How will I ensure confidentiality?
- How will I store the data?

As has been indicated, it is sometimes impossible to anticipate all of the impact of the research process. Two examples illustrate the unanticipated impact of research:

1. Someone with a family history of heart disease is asked to participate in a research project about diet and heart disease. When questioned, the researcher explains that GPs have been asked to supply names at random. The person receiving the invitation to participate finds it hard to accept that she has not been 'marked' as a potential heart disease sufferer.

2. At the opposite end of the process is the impact of research findings. It is apparent in health research that when results about the impact of diet or lifestyle are published some people will have concerns. However, there are more subtle impacts of research results. Every year statistics on abortion are published with media debate about the implications of the statistics. Although these have been appropriately anonymized in line with ethical guidelines, it is important to remember that they relate to the very intense personal experiences of particular women who may have had to make difficult decisions. In this context Guba and Lincoln's (1998, p. 199) reference to the 'value ladeness of facts is appropriate. The publication of the statistics and the ensuing debate might revive memories for some women, even if they are not one of those anonymized numbers.

These two examples illustrate that in undertaking social work research it is sometimes useful to draw on social work concepts and skills. The concept of empathy, of trying to understand the situation of another person from their perspective, is vital in undertaking research. This means that: no assumptions are made about what might, or might not, be a problem; thought is given to the experience of participating in research and the likely impact of the results. These are only some of the areas that require careful thought before research is undertaken and are generally not the areas considered by research ethics committees.

Who is the research for?

In Chapter 9 we discuss who owns social research, which has further implications for the ethics of research. However, in considering here the principles underpinning ethical implications of undertaking research it is important to flag up that when embarking on research, and indeed throughout the process, it is necessary to be clear who the research is for. This will help to ensure that no false promises are made and that due attention is paid to communicating with those who participate. This is particularly important in a climate where there are many different imperatives for academics, practitioners and students to undertake social research. The pressures for academic and other researchers to be successful in a grant application or for students and practitioners to have a proposal for a project related to a qualification accepted can be great. We have seen in earlier chapters that the position that all research has to 'do good' is contested. However, it is unethical to intrude into and investigate people's lives purely for one's own gain. Increasingly service users and carers are questioning requests to be involved in research and rightly ask what is in it for them.

The need for transparency and dialogue is paramount here as part of informed consent. Service users and carers might well be extremely happy to support a social work student in undertaking a project to help them achieve a qualification. But they also have a right to not participate.

Developing theory ethically

Finally, it is important to remember that while ethical permission has to be sought for research that involves direct contact with human subjects, a morally active researcher will consider the ethics of all research undertaken. Not all research involves empirical methods – there is an important role for what is sometimes called scholarship. There is a fine line to be drawn between censorship or restriction of academic freedom and ethical scholarship. However, the latter requires that those undertaking 'desk research' or developing theoretical positions are as rigorous in their approaches as those undertaking empirical research not least because, according to Guba and Lincoln (1998, p. 199), 'theories are value laden statements'.

At a practical level this requires that a comprehensive search of the relevant literature is undertaken, representing the spread of views and ensuring that due care is taken of the authenticity and rigour of the positions considered. It also means that the implications of explanations of research findings are presented in a balanced way. In social work research the risk is always that findings will be used by the media to negatively stereotype service users, or to condemn the actions of social work practitioners.

Conclusion

This chapter has not given a 'how to do it' account of applying for ethical approval and dealing with research governance. These can be found elsewhere (Pahl, 2004; McLaughlin, 2007). Instead the chapter has sought to complexify the subject by describing how developing a research base for social work has challenged existing arrangements for governance and gatekeeping and has led to social work specific codes of practice and research ethics committees. It has documented the development of procedures for the oversight of social care and social work research and the place of a code of ethics within this. However, in explaining the reasons for the specific social work approaches the chapter has also explored the contentious nature of such codes. It has emphasized that the existence of mechanisms and guidelines for ethical research does not absolve the researcher from being constantly alert to the impact of the research process on those who are involved in the research and those who might in any way be affected by the process and the outcomes of the research.

putting it into practice

You have been asked to submit a proposal to an older people's forum to undertake a research project to evaluate how older people can be consulted about the kinds of services they might require.

The forum consists of health and social work professionals and it wants the research to help to develop a model of consultation that will meet future needs and therefore inform their commissioning services. The area in which the forum operates includes many different ethnic and religious groups, some of whom have only recently arrived in the UK as refugees and/or economic migrants.

Devise a research project that might help you to meet the requirements of the project. In doing so consider the ethical questions that the research raises. Think not just about what you would do but also what the ethical implications of the request are. Who is asking for the research? What are purposes for which the results will be used?

When you have identified the ethical questions that you think arise in the way that you will address this project, analyse which aspects of ethical theory apply to each of the items that you have identified.

Finally, consult the code of ethics for social work research (this can be found at http://www.juc.ac.uk/swec-res-code.aspx or in Butler, 2002). How helpful do you find the code? In what ways does it address your ethical issues or help you to think more deeply about your research project?

Recommended reading

Hugman, R. (2005) *New Approaches in Ethics in the Caring Professions*. Basingstoke, Palgrave. An excellent overview of ethical principles underpinning social work practice – and research.

Seedhouse, D. (1998) *Ethics: The Heart of Health Care*. Chichester, John Wiley & Sons. Although not specifically about research it gives a good account, with exercises, of the relationship between ethics and providing care.

4 | Reviewing the literature

Introduction

In terms of the process of undertaking research the next stage, after considering the ethical dimensions of the project, is to consider it in its context. For social work that context is its relevance to practice, but also knowledge of what other research and scholarship has been undertaken that might inform the current work. In thinking about developing research based practice this is a vital part of the process because it helps to create an awareness of the scope of research that has already been undertaken. For social work this can be a particularly complex exercise because, as was discussed in Part 1, practice can draw on research findings from a number of different academic disciplines. However, it is important because doing such an exercise raises questions of the relevance and rigour of existing research and helps to identify the specific research needs of social work in this particular area.

This chapter therefore looks at how to find and summarize information about a topic of interest. The processes for doing this have traditionally used the techniques of literature review. However, as part of the development of a research base for social work practice there has been growing attention to the technique called systematic review. Both of these approaches are discussed and assessed.

In any literature review, it is useful to take a 'helicopter' viewpoint on a subject area: a wide-angle lens, rather than a microscope. We might want an in-depth, detailed look later, but at the beginning it is helpful to establish what is 'going on', who the key writers are and what are the key studies along with the main findings. But we should also seek to find out something else: in surveying a topic it is important to know the main points of conflict; in other words, what 'experts' disagree over and argue about, because it is usually in that space that lies relevant practice knowledge. This is particularly relevant to developing a research base for social work, where disagreements are often found within and between managers, practitioners, policy-makers and service users (the regularly contested field of what should be done when an allegation of child abuse arises is a prime example), but it is also evident in differences between researchers in their research questions, and in the interpretation of research outcomes.

Traditional literature reviews

An excellent example of what we consider to be an exemplar of a traditional literature review is Andy Alaszewski and Jill Manthorpe's 1993 review in the *British Journal of Social Work* of the research findings and other literature around the, new at the time, concept of 'quality' in welfare services. They point out that there is a wealth of difference between the concepts of quality as 'fit for purpose', on the one hand, and 'gold standard', on the other. The former definition would encompass the idea that a quality product (or service) 'does what it says on the tin'. It might not mean, however, that customers (or service users) will like it. The notion of quality as the 'gold standard' would suggest the idea of the Rolls-Royce car, which relies on a customer belief that there is a 'top-of-the-range' model to which many people aspire. These are remarkably different notions of quality and the fascinating conclusion in Alaszewski and Manthorpe's review is their demonstration of how most authors did not distinguish between these different concepts when they began to apply models of quality from the business world to the social care sphere (a not uncommon oversight, many would argue). Indeed, most authors switched between the different conceptualizations without acknowledging it.

Where to begin

A basic approach might well be to start a search by 'Googling' the topic. Where the terrain is relatively unknown, 'Google Scholar' will often prove useful as a filtering mechanism. However, both these sources will provide so many references that it is difficult to be discerning. One way of managing this material is to begin to read some of the sources and to list or map the references that are regularly cited. However, it is important to bear in mind that citation does not necessarily mean that this is an accurate or high quality source. Some material attracts citation because it is contentious – or just bad research. The obvious next step is to read the material and make a judgement, but it is this aspect of the process of the literature review that is problematic – the quality judgement. To develop a useful research base for practice it is vital that researchers, practitioners, managers and service users and carers are able to discern the quality of research.

Those already operating as reflective practitioner-researchers will be aware of the key journals relating to their area of practice interest, and this is often the best place to start, partly because they are relatively short (typically between 5,000 and 7,000 words) and usually relevant. The clear advantage of journals is that there are some quality control mechanisms. Articles are peer-reviewed by at least two other experts in the field, and they and the author(s) may have edited and re-written the paper many times before it is published. Different topics are found in different outlets. For example, the top-rated journals in the field of childhood attachment in social work include *Attachment and Human Development*, *Child Development*, the *Journal of Child and Family Social Work* and the *Journal of Social Work Practice*. On the other hand, in *adult* attachment relationships, the key journals are *Personal Relationships*, the *Journal of Social and Personal Relationships*, and the *Journal of Personality and Social Psychology*. Even within one specific topic area, the main sources will change depending on the precise nature of the review required.

A typical article provides a very brief synopsis of the main arguments and findings in the first 1,000 words and this assists practitioner researchers to stay above the ground, able to see the 'wood for the trees': to discern the focus and findings of the piece. It will also set out in the references other key authors, writers and researchers in the topic field. In the USA and in the health care field, where empirical studies predominate, some journals also require the authors to provide a section reflecting on the limitations of the study. This provides useful examples of critical reflection on research methods, and how to interpret results.

Other sources

Journal articles are not the only source for a literature review, and, according to the respondents in the survey undertaken by Shaw and Norton (2007), they are not always the source of the highest quality research. Most of us, for example, will have learned about social work by reading books, and while electronic versions are increasing replacing the notion of book as 'something to hold', they remain important. Authored books can give a coherent overview of a particular subject area, while edited books bring together experts around particular themes. The main contemporary alternatives to books include:

- Regulatory, inspection and policy documents – official, often government-initiated and owned, reports, legislation and statutory instruments.
- Practice-oriented guidance, briefings and digests – e.g. JRF Findings.
- User experience/autobiographical literature – e.g. INVOLVE (established to promote public involvement in research, in order to improve the way that research is prioritized, commissioned, undertaken, communicated and used).
- Research listings – e.g. Cochrane and Campbell Collaborations (see below).
- Portals – e.g. the SCIE website.
- Relevant service-based organisations – e.g. Age Concern, NSPPC, MIND.
- Media – e.g. *Guardian* newspaper reports on specific news items.
- e-Alerts – e.g. Research in Practice (http://www.rip.org.uk), which is the largest children and families implementation project in England and Wales and offers an automatic e-mail information alert service.

This range of resources illustrates the wealth of material available and highlights two main problems for the beginning researcher. The first is, as ever, time. There is no real short cut to a traditional literature review: it is very time consuming. The second concern is how researchers can judge the rigour and quality of the research reported. This is a particular challenge when the profession and discipline of social work is only just beginning to build its competence and confidence in the field of research.

Systematic review

It was because of both these concerns that SCIE committed resources to undertaking systematic reviews of research and, just as importantly for the process of developing a research base for social work, developed guidelines on how to undertake such reviews (Coren and Fisher, 2006; Sharland and Taylor, 2006). While systematic reviews are not unique to social work the resources developed by SCIE and the guidelines for producing them are innovative in the social work and social care field and have become a global resource for social work. The Evidence for Policy and Practice Information and Co-ordinating Centre (the EPPI-Centre), which is part of the Social Science Research Unit at the Institute of Education, University of London, has also pioneered many of the methods presented in this chapter. (The contribution of Josephine Kavanagh and Kelly Dickson has been especially important in the development of 'systematic mapping'.)

What is a systematic review?

The concept of a *systematic review* (SR) means far more than 'doing a traditional literature review very thoroughly': the key is in the word 'systematic'. The aim of a systematic review is to pool the findings of primary research by asking a very specific question in order to clarify what is known about it. It is this 'intentional specificity' behind an SR that is its hallmark.

In the early days, debates about SRs were linked to the argument that more 'evidence based' approaches needed to inform the choice or maintenance of social care interventions. SR proponents were often closely allied to the evidence based practice or 'what works?' movement. The net result was an overemphasis on the nature of 'evidence', with SR advocates such as Sheldon arguing forcefully for the random controlled trial (RCT) form of experimental design to be the 'gold standard' default when reviewing 'best evidence' (Sheldon, 2001). The resulting battles turned into familiar and, as we discuss in the next chapter, often rather fruitless epistemological 'paradigm wars', between the positivists and anti-positivists. Fortunately there is now a discernable rapprochement between the two 'sides'. This has been achieved by viewing research methodologies not as hierarchical, but as merely 'different'. Significantly, in the USA systematic reviews are now being used to question the evidence base of earlier studies that have been the basis for legislation about interventions (Little, 2005, 2006). This highlights the need to be rigorous and comprehensive in the review, and to be cautious in the conclusions that are drawn.

Questions such as 'What method or design should used?' depend on the *focus* of the enquiry, not on a predetermined *technique* for the enquiry: an RCT is *not* the gold standard if the research question is 'What are the views of parents about parenting classes?', but it might well be if the question were 'Do parenting classes based on cognitive behaviour therapy (CBT) work better than motivational interviewing methods with parents experiencing depression?'

As a result of this rapprochement there has been a noticeable increase in the inclusion of qualitative methods in SRs, which were omitted in the early days of SR. Popay (2006) identifies four specific ways in which qualitative research can contribute to Cochrane Intervention reviews for health policy and practice and these are relevant to social work and social care:

1. *Informing* reviews by using evidence from qualitative research to help to define and refine the question.

2. *Enhancing* reviews by synthesizing evidence from qualitative research identified while looking for evidence of effectiveness.
3. *Extending* reviews by undertaking a search and synthesis specifically of evidence from qualitative studies to address questions directly related to the effectiveness review.
4. *Supplementing* reviews by synthesizing qualitative evidence to address questions on aspects other than effectiveness.

In an SR a great deal of attention is paid to the formulation of an answerable (in the sense of 'capable of being explored') review question. One of the attractive aspects of SR for an inclusive approach to evidence-informed research and evaluation is that it is ideally placed to involve service users and other 'experts by experience' in the derivation and clarification of the question, as well as each of the other SR stages. Braye and Preston-Shoot (2007) provide a useful critical description of the involvement of service users in SR (as do Moriarty *et al.*, 2007).

Good SR studies are noted for being open and transparent because it is a requirement that 'search methods' as well as the 'inclusion and exclusion criteria' (see below) must be made explicit; this also means that an SR is easy to update or replicate. The conscious and deliberate reduction of 'bias' and 'error' is also a key element in an SR.

We now focus on these processes in a little more detail. Because this chapter is of necessity brief and provides only an overview of the process of SR we suggest you have a look at an SR. This can be done on a number of different websites for organizations developed to help health social work and social care practitioners worldwide to make well informed decisions. These include:

● the Cochrane Collaboration (http://www.cochrane.org/);
● the Campbell Collaboration (http://www.campbellcollaboration. org/);
● the Social Care Institute for Excellence (http://www.scie.org.uk/);
● the Evidence for Policy and Practice Information (EPPI) Centre (http://www.eppi.ioe.ac.uk/cms/).

You will find on each of the websites informative details about the purpose, conduct, uses and limitations of SRs and you will see that both qualitative and quantitative research is included in the reviews.

As an example of this inclusive approach, the EPPI-Centre conducted an SR into *Children and Healthy Eating: A Systematic Review of Barriers and Facilitators* (2003); specifically, the *review question* was 'What is known about the barriers to, and facilitators of, fruit and vegetable intake amongst children aged 4 to 10 years?' A total of 33 'trials' and eight 'opinion' studies were reviewed. With the trials, meta-analytic techniques – which combine samples in a large number of studies to compare 'effect sizes' (see Chapter 6) – were used; the opinion studies deployed thematic synthesis – a similar method to meta-analysis but for use with qualitative studies (and without the statistics!). This 'mixed methods' SR produced some fascinating results:

1. Children do not see it as their 'role' to be interested in health.
2. Children do not see future health consequences as personally relevant or credible.
3. Fruit, vegetables and confectionery have very different meanings for children.
4. Children actively seek ways to exercise their own choices with regard to foods.
5. Children value eating as a social occasion.
6. Children recognize contradiction between what is promoted and what is provided (Thomas *et al.*, 2009).

This example illustrates the different perspectives and kinds of information that can be drawn on and how this can be of assistance to practitioners, in this case in the health field.

The review question

Central to the SR is the derivation of the review question (RQ). It is the engine that powers all review process. More than a rephrasing of the topic of interest, the RQ is couched in terms that specify exactly what the investigation will focus upon. So, for example, in a traditional literature review RQs are usually wide-ranging and, in the area of child care, might look into 'What is written about disorganized attachment?' An SR, on the other hand, would begin with a question such as 'How are infant disorganized attachment and caregiver frightening behaviour related to subsequent psychosocial outcomes for the child?' Using a different example, on the subject of parenting interventions, a less specific SR question might be: 'Do parenting classes "work"?' but it would not include 'What is known about parenting classes?' or 'How can different approaches to parenting classes be distinguished?'

However, this is only the beginning because in an SR a number of factors – called *inclusion and exclusion criteria* – must be clarified before database searching begins. The acronym PICOS (Participants, Intervention, Comparison, Outcome and Study design) is often used to select the criteria. If we take parenting classes as our example, consideration needs to given to which *participants* are be included in the search. Are all children to be included or only a specified age-range (e.g. those under five)? Should mothers or fathers (or both) be included? We will then need to specify the type of *intervention* – for example, we could focus solely on (say) Webster–Stratton interventions, attachment-based interventions, CBT-based interventions etc. We might also consider the 'setting' in the criteria (e.g. UK-only, USA-only or community-based?). We might also wish to look at *comparisons* between interventions, e.g. are some interventions more effective than others? We also need to include *outcome* (or output) measures, such as scores on the Goodman's (modified) Strengths and Difficulties Scale (this and other psychometric measures are discussed in more detail in Chapter 7). Lastly, an SR needs to specify the *study design*: will we include case studies, experiments, service user opinion surveys etc.?

Below is a more detailed example of a systematic map (SM), often a precursor to a SR, in that it presents current literature in a way that can be explored further later, either in more depth or by 'skimming the surface', depending on the review questions and how much time is available for subsequent analysis. The resulting overview 'is a tool that offers policy makers, practitioners and researchers an explicit and transparent means to identify narrower policy and practice-relevant review questions. It also enables contextualisation of in-depth reviews within the broader literature, and helps identify the evidence base' (Bates *et al*., 2007). An investigation into *parental mental health* (PMH) was undertaken by Bates and Coren (SCIE, 2006). The full title is 'The extent and impact of parental mental health problems on families and the acceptability, accessibility and effectiveness of interventions' and it can be accessed by visiting http://www.scie.org.uk/publications/map/map01.pdf.

However, for the purpose of the SR the question needs more precision. The precise question therefore was 'What do we know about the extent and impact of parental mental health problems? What service interventions are available and what do we know about their acceptability, accessibility and effectiveness?' This study is considered here in greater detail to explain and illustrate the process of undertaking an SR.

Nowadays, a rigorous SR will always outline the scope of the review by providing full details of the systematic decision-making about what was and was not included in the many sub-questions. We reproduce below the details of the scope of the PMH Study to indicate the extent and level of specificity.

1. Scope of the parental mental health (PMH) study

To be included a study must examine parental mental health problems (PMHP), plus one of the following:

1. The extent of PMHP.
2. The impact of PMHP.
3. A service intervention.

This does not include studies of pharmacological interventions, unless they are evaluated in the context of service provision. Papers describing diagnostic/screening techniques are not included. Studies that assess the reliability or validity of population screening and/or diagnostic tools and explicitly relate findings to measuring the extent of PMHP are included. A study is examining mental health problems if:

1. The author or research subject says so.
2. The health problem has been diagnosed and conforms to those listed in DSM IV1 or ICD-10.
3. Relevant symptoms are described but are not yet subject to formal, or established, diagnosis.
4. It involves dual diagnosis of a mental health problem with substance misuse – i.e. alcohol and drugs and solvents.

A study is examining the extent of PMHP where it provides information on the prevalence or type of problem locally, regionally, nationally or internationally (where national data are presented). A study is examining the impact of PMHP where it describes biological, psychological and social (including economic) effects on any family member.

A study is examining an existing service intervention where it provides information on a service which is intended to benefit those affected by a PMHP (e.g. parents, children, wider family, family as a whole). We are interested in all levels and types of service provision, whether they are provided at a local, regional or national basis. We are interested in all types of service and intervention providers and developers (e.g. adult mental health services, child and adolescent mental health services, primary and secondary health care, antenatal or postnatal services, social workers, schools, family therapists, parenting coordinators, unregistered trainers and counsellors, police, forensic services, youth offending teams, probation, substance misuse workers, residential services, BME groups, researchers, etc.).

We also take service intervention to include those interventions that have been developed, and evaluated, but not yet in common practice. For the purposes of this systematic map, parents are taken to be anyone who has dependent children. This can include biological and nonbiological parents, legal guardians, and other primary care givers, whether resident or non-resident.

Studies are eligible if they:

- evaluate the EXTENT of PMHP, e.g. any study with prevalence data;
- evaluate the IMPACT of PMHP on any family member;
- evaluate the EFFECTIVENESS of any PMHP intervention on any outcome;
- evaluate the ACCESSIBILITY of any PMHP intervention, e.g. physical and/or social exclusion;
- evaluate the ACCEPTABLITY to people either receiving or providing a PMHP intervention.

We accept that a range of study designs including primary and secondary research may provide relevant data. This does not include individual case studies, briefings or opinion pieces.

We define 'parent' as anyone who has dependent children.
We also consider POPULATION to be regardless of residency and there is no exclusion on age, gender or ethnicity.

We include the extent or use for international impact and extent studies to decide impact uncertain exclusion criteria on sample size.

Studies will be also be included if carried out in the UK or inter-nationally if outcome evaluations, or internationally if providing data at a national level.

Studies must have been published between 1985 and 2005.

(Bates and Coren, 2006, p. 8)

In the spirit of openness, accountability and transparency, the authors of an SR will list the different databases consulted. The list from the PMH map included:

- *Health databases*: PsycInfo, Medline, EMBASE, CINAHL, HMIC, Cochrane Library, National Research Register.
- *Social science databases*: Social Services Abstracts (CSA Illumina), ASSIA, National Criminal Justice Reference Service Abstracts, ERIC, Campbell Collaboration.
- *Care databases*: Social Work Abstracts, CareData (now replaced by Social Care Online), ChildData, Communitywise.
- *General databases*: SIGLE, Journal searching.

The authors also add that:

> In addition to searching databases, journal table of contents were searched for the following journals: *Child Abuse and Neglect, Child Abuse Review, Children and Society, Psychiatric Bulletin, Families in Society, British Journal of Social Work, Health and Social Care in the Community, Journal of Substance Misuse*, and *Child and Family Social Work*. Key texts on the topic of PMH and interventions were used to identify search terms for the map. In addition, references were harvested from the citation lists of the key texts retrieved. (Bates and Coren, 2006, p. 9)

Based upon sophisticated electronic search techniques, SR methods are designed to interrogate knowledge databases. In a systematic map or review authors should be transparent about the precise search filtering strategy used, and this means being specific about the keywords used, as well as how they are linked using the logical connectors AND/OR. Here is part of the *keyword search strategy* used in the PMH map (but these conventions can vary between studies). The use of the dollar sign ($) in, for example, 'child$' means that the search$ will include any word, without spaces, beginning with 'child' (e.g. child/ren, child/care etc.) An asterisk (*) means 'AND' and, although it doesn't appear in the following example, the forward slash (/) means 'OR'.

---

2. An example of keyword search filters used in part of the SCIE PMH map

(The number in brackets indicates the number of results using the search filter.)

1. Parental mental health. (32)
2. Mentally ill parents. (31)
3. Parental psychopathology. (130)

> 4. ((Parent\$ or maternal or paternal or mother\$ or father\$) adj2 (psychiat\$ or depression or mental\$)).mp [mp = title, original title, abstract, name of substance word, subject heading word]. (2674)
> 5. ((Parent\$ or maternal or paternal or mother\$ or father\$) adj2 (psychiat\$ or depression or mental\$)). (769)
> 6. Postnatal depression. or *Depression, Postpartum. (1077)

What surprises most people when looking at the results from an SR or SM is the sheer size of the enterprise. With the most inclusive keyword searches – such as 'mental health' – the number of results will be in the region of tens, even hundreds, of thousands. If a logical modifiers such as 'AND child\$ protect\$ AND outcome\$ AND child\$ under 5' is added, the number of results will be reduced considerably (maybe into double figures). Adding 'AND England and Wales' will reduce it even further. Here is an extract to illustrate this from the PMH study.

3. Scoping results

The searches identified a total of 13,733 records. . . . A total of 2,790 duplicates were found and removed in EndNote prior to export to EPPI-Reviewer. A total of 10,943 records were exported to EPPI-Reviewer for screening. On the basis of titles and abstracts 754 records were judged to have met the inclusion criteria. These 754 papers were then obtained and the keywording strategy was applied. . . . A total of 754 studies were included in the final systematic map. . . . The largest number of records were excluded because they did not meet the scope of the map (10,189). A total of 1,482 records were excluded due to location criteria. This was because many non-UK studies were carried out at a local rather than a national level – one of the pre-set exclusion criteria. . . . A total of 1,071 records were excluded as they did not meet the study design criteria. For example, case studies made up a large proportion of the results and these were not included in the map. Some records were not mutually exclusive so were excluded on more than one criterion (for example, scope and location). In addition, 901 records were retrieved on the topic of post-natal depression and 94 records were found on

Munchausen's Syndrome by Proxy. These were also excluded but retained within the database in a separate list for use in possible future reviews.

(Bates and Coren, 2006, p. 11)

Critical appraisal

As with social work assessments in practice, gathering the information in a literature review is one thing; making sense of it, evaluating it and judging its worth are quite different questions (and, for the most part, are more important). As we have said it is not just the quantity of social work research that is vital to developing the research base that is to be developed for social work, it is also the quality, although what counts as social work research, and the quality measures to be used, are subject to much debate (Shaw and Norton, 2008). However, it is important that in addition to the processes of literature review and systematic review outlined so far in this chapter there are also numerous websites devoted to outlining ways of judging the quality of both qualitative and quantitative research. For qualitative studies see, for example, http://www.gsr.gov.uk/evaluating_policy/quality_framework/framework_table.asp and for quantitative studies, see http://www.ncddr.org/kt/products/focus/focus9/index.html.

In general, however, it is possible to summarize the key messages involved in *critical appraisal* as:

- How relevant is the study to the review question?
- How much information does it contribute?
- How trustworthy are its findings?
- How generalizable are its findings?
- Was it conducted ethically?

Try the mnemonic TAPUPAS:

- Transparency – is it open to scrutiny?
- Accuracy – is it plausible?
- Purposivity – is it fit for purpose?
- Utility – is it fit for use?
- Propriety – is it legal and ethical?
- Accessibility – is it intelligible?
- Specificity – does it meet source specific standards? (Pawson *et al.*, 2003)

Finally, as part of its Critical Appraisal Skills Programme (CASP – see http://www.phru.nhs.uk/Pages/PHD/CASP.htm) the UK's National Health Service provides a series of checklists for a number of different research and evaluative strategies, as follows:

- Systematic reviews: http://www.phru.nhs.uk/Doc_Links/S.Reviews%20Appraisal%20Tool.pdf
- Randomised control trials: http://www.phru.nhs.uk/Doc_Links/rct%20appraisal%20tool.pdf
- Qualitative studies: http://www.phru.nhs.uk/Doc_Links/Qualitative%20Appraisal%20Tool.pdf
- Economic evaluations: http://www.phru.nhs.uk/Doc_Links/Economic%20Evaluations%2010%20Questions.pdf

Conclusion

This chapter has provided an introduction to the process of undertaking a review of literature. In offering practical examples and pointers to the wealth of resources available it has demonstrated how those preparing to commence a research project can become aware of the research relevant to the area that they wish to research. However, just as importantly for developing a research base for social work, these resources are available to assist practitioners. For a research base to be effective it has to be accessible to enable practitioners to become familiar with relevant research for different aspects of practice to help them make informed decisions about the situations with which they are dealing and the range of possible interventions.

putting it into practice

Have a look at an assignment you did on your degree (or other social work qualifying course) that involved undertaking a review of literature. Now re-read it and reflect upon the extent to which you approached the review from the perspective of undertaking a *systematic review* of the subject area.

- How clear was your review question?
- How 'systematic' was your review?

Now have a look at one of the SCIE SRs on the website http://www.scie.org.uk/publications/.

Next, skim read an SR from the Cochrane website,
http://www.cochrane.org/.

● How do they differ?
● What similarities are there between them?

Recommended reading

Petticrew, M. and Roberts, H. (2006) *Systematic Reviews in the Social Sciences: A Practical Guide*. Oxford, Blackwell. A good introductory text.

Torgerson, C. (2003) *Systematic Reviews and Meta-Analysis*. London, Continuum Research Methods. A general text on the subject that provides a well written, thorough analysis.

5 | Methodologies and methods

Introduction

In the first two chapters we explored the meaning and purpose of research, and identified characteristics of social research. In doing this attention was drawn to the implications for social work research, whether social work research is distinctive from other social research and if so in what ways.

Chapter 2 concluded that social work research has to be 'fit for purpose'. That purpose might be informing policy, evaluating existing practice, exploring emerging social problems or testing out the effectiveness of interventions. All of these are relevant to developing research-based social work practice but above all research has to be relevant to practice and meaningful to practitioners and service users and carers.

To be fit for purpose social work research also has to be rigorous and methodologically sound. This does not mean that there are particular methodological approaches that have to be adopted by, or are unique to, social work research. Nor are there specific ways of undertaking research – that is, particular methods that have to be used. Different methodological approaches to undertaking research provide different knowledges for different purposes

This chapter first explores the difference between methodology and methods. This will help to explain the relevance of different approaches to social work. One consequence of considering relevance is to explore ways of bridging the assumed differences between methodological approaches. The chapter concludes with a discussion of ways in which this has been done. It therefore provides an introduction to the chapters that follow, where particular methods are discussed and illustrated in greater detail.

Methodologies, methods and design

There are two common assumptions made by beginning researchers. The first is that methodology and methods are the same thing. They are not. As the first two chapters indicated, the development of research in the social sciences has led to a number of different traditions of research and each of these represents an exploration of epistemological understandings. As was discussed in Chapter 1, epistemology refers to ways of knowing and it is the assumptions and/or understanding of ways of knowing that influence how researchers undertake their research.

Once the difference between methodological approaches (or methodologies) and methods has been understood and the various approaches or traditions have been identified, the second common assumption is that different methodological approaches have implications for the way (or method) in which information (or data) is collected. There is also confusion in this area. For example, some students when preparing to do research make the assertion that it is social work and therefore it has to be qualitative; or it is small scale and therefore it has to be qualitative. This is then frequently followed by a description of methods that include a very quantitative questionnaire and attempts to analyse what information is collected by comparing numbers.

The fact that there is confusion means that it is important to understand the differences, but also explore the implications for social work research.

Methodology

Methodology is at the very basic the study of methods (Becker and Bryman, 2004). But what does this mean? The confusion about methodology is to some extent caused by the relationship between theory and methods – that is, the explanation of how we know what we know and how to find out. The relationship between theory and methods is said by May (1997) to raise such intractable problems for researchers that it is often given a back stage position. Researchers get on with the research using methods without giving too much thought to the theory behind the methods. However, in developing research based social work it is important that researchers address their own conceptions of how the social world can be studied and understood. It is also important for practitioners to understand the way that research results have been arrived at, and how the framework for the collection of information and data influences both the results and the analysis.

For example, let us compare early studies of social work. In the USA Fischer used 'scientific' methods to try to answer the question 'is casework effective?' (Fischer, 1973). In the UK researchers (Mayer and Timms, 1970) sought to test the effectiveness of casework by recording the views of clients (as they were then designated) about the services they received. Sainsbury (1975) went further and analysed both client views and social worker views and noted that there were high levels of client satisfaction, irrespective of the 'outcomes' of the case (for example, whether people had had their needs met). However, he identified some of the limitations of the approach used, suggesting that asking pre-determined questions might not necessarily identify client expectations or what were the important issues for those who were receiving services (Sainsbury, 1987).

These different approaches all provide valuable information about social work interventions. However, Sainsbury's critique has been at the heart of moves to involve service users in research. This involvement includes helping to identify research questions rather than merely being respondents to a questionnaire drawn up by a researcher who has not been a service user. The assumption is that the way the world is experienced might not always be evident to those who do not share the experiences. The challenge for rigorous research is to include ways of enabling those in situations to describe them.

However, that suggests that there is only one approach to social research. As we have said, it is necessary to undertake different kinds of research for different purposes. The purpose will influence the kind of knowledge required and will also determine the kind of information that is needed. For example, debates about the level of funding for social care have a major impact on the kinds of social work that can be practised. Funding is linked to identified need but is also related to cost–benefit analysis. In the USA, because of the emphasis on the latter, social work researchers are urged to engage in research with economists. While such joint research is important it is necessary to acknowledge that other factors, such as how need is identified, are important.

One of the major factors in how understanding of need influences funding levels in adult services is the distinction between formal and informal care. Formal care provided by organizations, voluntary, private or state funded, is expensive. Informal care is demanding and it is necessary to know the extent of the care, who does it and what they do, to get the true costs of social care. Early studies undertaken by government agencies therefore tried to calculate levels of care undertaken. This was done by, for example, questions in the census or in the General Household Survey (for example, Green, 1988). The data gathered was challenged by feminists who adopted their own methodological approach (Stanley and Wise, 1983) to demonstrate that informal care was undertaken mainly by women (Ungerson, 1987). This led to important debates about methods used and the statistics gathered. There were challenges from those who thought feminists were operating with unhelpful gendered assumptions (Arber and Gilbert, 1989; Fisher, 1994). Issues to do with race were also seen to be poorly addressed in the research undertaken by government agencies (Atkin and Rolling, 1996), and those who were in receipt of services because of disability or impairment challenged the conclusions that were being drawn about care being a 'burden' on woman (Morris, 1993).

This discussion illustrates how trying to provide a research base for funding decisions is more complex than a 'pure' economic perspective, not least because establishing need can involve many different perspectives, or standpoints. In some approaches the researcher can have a particular view of the world and can be open about the fact that her/his research is taken from that particular perspective. Although this is controversial it does constitute a methodological option. If this methodological approach is adopted the theoretical perspective of the researcher has to be transparent so that it can be challenged. It is the declaration of the position or standpoint, the challenge and the response that can lead to the development of rigorous approaches to research.

Methods

Methods are often described merely as procedures for collecting research data (Becker and Bryman, 2004) – that is, techniques or ways of doing research. May (1997) suggests that an approach that separates out methods from theory and ethics is merely technicist. He argues that knowing about the different ideas about ways of knowing underpinning methods will lead to a clearer understanding of the applicability of different methods and therefore to better research.

In the first instance methods are often thought of as decisions between, for example: a questionnaire or an interview; a guided interview or an open interview. However, as more attention has been paid to ways of knowing and understanding how people construct the social world then the range of methods has broadened. Attention to the use of language, for example, has led to methods focusing on discourse and narrative (Hall, 1999; Riessman and Quinney, 2005; White and Featherstone, 2005). These have informed significant developments in understanding the complexities of social work interventions.

The range of methods is therefore broad and different texts include different methods and arrange them differently. This text, for example, describes methods that are relevant to social work research and tries in the three chapters that follow to give an overview of the kinds of methods that can be used to undertake research that will be relevant to social work practice. Other texts on more general social research (Becker and Bryman, 2004; Gilbert, 2008) give a greater range of methods and outline the more practical aspects of using them.

Describing the methods used, the different stages and reflections on the limitations as well as the strengths is an important part of undertaking research, as it indicates to the reader exactly what can be learnt from the research. It is also important because it enables others to undertake similar research either by exploring the same topic, or using the same method to explore different topics.

Design

To add another level of complexity, De Vaus (2001) talks about research design. By this he means something more than a work plan. Design involves decisions about the organization of the research that will ensure rigour: 'that the evidence obtained enables us to answer the initial question as unambiguously as possible' (De Vaus, 2001, p. 9). This is a helpful definition as it makes no assumption about the nature of the questions asked or the ways that the question will be answered. The design takes the approach of, given the research topic, determining what type of evidence is needed to answer the research question, or test the theory, in a convincing way. For de Vaus the question of 'how' – that is, what methods are used – is subsidiary to the question of what evidence is needed. However, his suggestion that how the data is collected is irrelevant to the logic of the design is challenged by some, especially in social work research, who argue that the logic of the design, the nature of the research questions asked and the process of collecting information all have to reflect underpinning assumptions or world view of the researcher (D'Cruz and Jones, 2004).

The notion of design is important and acknowledges that research needs to be approached with caution. De Vaus (2001) suggests that too often researchers rush to decisions about, for example, using questionnaires without thinking through what they actually need to address and the particular issue they are researching. An example of this is where a researcher wants to find out if a particular social work intervention makes a difference, brings about change. It is of limited value if the research merely describes the intervention after the event. Careful thought has to be given to what indicators of change will be used. This will be influenced by what information is available or can be found out about the situation before the social worker intervened. Decisions can then be made about what information can be collected before and after the social work involvement that will demonstrate change over time.

Another design option is that if the information about the situation before the intervention is not available, then a longitudinal study can be planned in which data/information is collected before, during and after the intervention.

The way an issue is addressed in research, what is considered useful information, how you decide whether change has occurred and what has contributed to the change all impact on what you need to know and are related to ways of knowing. For example, a criminal justice social work service might want to evaluate the effectiveness of a programme run for those who have been convicted of offences of domestic violence. The fact that someone has been violent could be assumed to have been established by the conviction (although some continue to deny their violence after conviction). An effectiveness measure might therefore be to discern whether the violent behaviour has stopped. But how do you do this? Devising a questionnaire asking those who attended the programme if they had stopped being violent to their partner would have limited value. Different ways of establishing the level and kinds of violence prior to the programme and on completion of the programme have to be identified. Basing the measure on the partner's reports of the level of violence raises ethical problems. Even if ways to gather data are found the researchers have to be clear about what the 'measures' indicate. Results might show that the offender has temporarily stopped being violent, but has the programme actually changed attitudes towards domestic violence? This of course relates to the aims of the programme – which takes us back to the research question and the design of the research.

These complexities of designing research for a particular issue help to illustrate that research design is important, and that there are many ways in which research can be conducted. Different designs will give answers to different questions and different methods will draw on different ways of knowing about a particular topic, issue or research question.

Ways of knowing

Discussion so far has suggested that there are different assumptions about the social world and how it can be investigated. These are sometimes referred to as *ontological* and *epistemological* assumptions. Put simply, the difference between ontology and epistemology is the difference between ways of being and ways of knowing.

The ideas behind these terms are complex, but they are fundamental to the understanding of research. For example, Kant argued that the combination of what can be known and how it is known enables human beings to reflect on nature and science in a rational manner (May, 1996). The terms used, and what they stand for, are influential in the development of different approaches and methods in undertaking research.

- *Ontology* refers to the nature of the world and what we can know about it. The search for knowledge *about* the social and physical world, how things are, involves considering ways of being or categories of existence in the sense of what it means to be human, the nature of the world and, ultimately, what is reality.
- *Epistemology* is concerned with knowledge claims. The search for understanding of how we know and find out about that world involves the theory of knowing, or how we know what we know and how we know that it is true. It is therefore concerned with the criteria used to distinguish knowledge claims, or assess their rigour and validity. Epistemological assumptions in research methods are therefore linked to different philosophies of how the social world should be studied.

As we saw in Chapter 1, approaches to research, or approaches to understanding the world, or epistemological positions, are often split between those that are described as *empirical* – that is, assumptions that there is an objective external reality that can be known – and those that are *theory driven* – that is, hypotheses or ideas for explaining the world that can be tested out.

These simple distinctions illustrate how terminology often sets up ideas in opposition to each other. This suggests that researchers have to choose one or other approach to research. As differences have emerged researchers have often argued their position very strongly and these arguments have been described as a paradigm war. The suggestion here is that there is now less polarized thinking about the different stances and it is therefore better to think about a paradigm debate rather than a war.

The 'paradigm debate'

Different positions that have developed over time since the Enlightenment (see Chapter 1) are testimony to the way that researchers and research traditions evolve out of knowledge discoveries, and reflections on the way that these discoveries have been made. The changes or trends in thinking, known as paradigm shifts, are much debated the social sciences.

Paradigms

In the first instance it is necessary to understand what is meant by a paradigm. At its simplest it is a cluster or pattern of beliefs and practices associated with a particular world view about how scientific practice should take place (Becker and Bryman, 2004, p. 400). Debates focus on the work of Kuhn (1970), who describes a paradigm as: 'The entire constellation of beliefs, techniques and so on shared by members of a given [scientific] community' (Kuhn, 1970, p. 175). Hence paradigms are frameworks for understanding the world that are powerful, self-contained and radically distinctive (Gilbert, 2008). Kuhn's ideas emerged from his analysis of the development of science. He argued that changes in thinking are a series of episodes – or shifts. It is only 'scientific revolutions' based on a misalignment between practices and assumptions that bring about dramatic change in the way scientists think about the world – a new paradigm replaces the old.

Opinions differ on whether Kuhn's ideas are relevant to the social sciences. On the one hand May (1997) describes Kuhn's work as a seminal contribution because it gives us a different way of thinking about how ideas develop. On the other hand Hammersley (1995) is of the opinion that looking at social research methodology in terms of competing paradigms is unhelpful. He suggests that social scientists draw conclusions from Kuhn that 'all knowledge is founded on assumptions which are arbitrary from a rational point of view, and that ultimately it is a matter of taste or politics which paradigm one adopts' (Hammersley, 1995, p. 13). In other words it could be interpreted as anything goes!

A less cynical approach is that there are different ways of understanding how we acquire knowledge and how that knowledge is tested. This means that there is not just one paradigm, but many divisions reflected in the aims and methods (May, 1997, p. 34). For example, Denzin and Lincoln (1998) describe five historical 'moments' in the development of *qualitative research*. This describes how a particular approach, which itself was a paradigm shift (a progression historically and philosophically) from a position that is called *positivist*, can also be subject to development and change.

Methodological approaches

What is emerging is a complex use of terms that require some further exploration. Before we provide this it is important to conclude the brief discussion of paradigms by highlighting that basically what will be discussed are different paradigms – not 'competing' or 'warring'.

Table 5.1 *'Competing' approaches in social research*

Empirical (or data driven)	Theory driven
Positivist	Constructivist
Objective	Subjective
Deductive	Inductive
Realist	Interpretivist
Quantitative	Qualitative

Problems do arise when one paradigm is held up as superior, the 'gold standard' against which other ways of thinking about knowledge and undertaking research are compared, or even worse, judged negatively.

Having said that, Table 5.1 deliberately sets up some of the terms used in discussing social research in opposition to each other. Each column includes terms that are often grouped together and are seen to have some coherence or similarity, and are often set in opposition to the terms in the other column. Setting them in this way illustrates why they are described as being 'at war' (see Hammersley, 1995, Chapter 1) or more positively in dialogue (Guba, 1990). Looking at them in contrast to one another helps to identify the strengths of the different contributions and how they can contribute to the research design.

Empirical/theory driven

An explanation of the differences between *empirical* and *theory driven* was given in Chapter 1, but to recap:

● Empirical: involves the collection of facts and, based on the assumption that 'the facts speak for themselves, offers propositions on the basis of the facts.
● Theory driven: starts with a theory, a provisional explanation or a broad framework of concepts and ideas that can provide a framework for interpreting the world, or that part of the world that is being considered. However, to illustrate how the ideas and processes complement each other and work together theory can also be used to interpret empirical research: to start answering the 'why' questions

What follow are very brief and beginning definitions that try to capture the significant aspects of different ways of knowing. Each of them has been the subject of extensive discussion and there are also other ways of describing, defining and analysing different approaches to social research (see examples in Denzin and Lincoln, 1998; De Vaus, 2001; Ritchie and Lewis, 2003; Gilbert, 2008).

Positivist/constructivist

- Positivist: seeks to explain behaviour in terms of cause and effect and assumes that truth is dependent upon pre-existent knowledge and that this can be discovered and utilized by generalizing, predicting and controlling in research design. What is observed in research becomes the definitive answer and it is assumed that by using 'objective' measures this is not influenced by the researcher or the research process.
- Constructivist: starts from the position that all knowledge is constructed and that social phenomena and social reality are created out of the actions and interpretations of people during their social relations. Researchers have to develop approaches to find out how people construct or make sense of their reality and their reason for behaving in the ways that they do.

Objective/subjective

- Objective: such approaches attempt to emulate scientific method when researching the social world. They involve a process of deduction that leads to laws of human behaviour based on samples involving generalizations about the behaviour of populations. Researchers are non-involved and utilize ways of reducing their influence on the process of the research. Objective ways of undertaking social research include: sampling populations; anonymizing responses; undertaking 'double-blind' tests. The ultimate scientific approach is the random controlled trial. Such research is also more likely to use statistical tests to interrogate the integrity, validity and generalizability of the findings.
- Subjective: recognises that that both researchers and those who are the focus of research are trying to make sense of the world, whatever methods of enquiry they use. This acknowledgement is used to interpret the world, but also to critique claims-making in research, whatever approach is used.

Deductive/inductive

- Deductive: such an approach involves starting with a supposition, a theory that can be turned into a hypothesis, which can then be tested.

Data collected is linked to certain questions, which in turn are linked to the hypothesis.

● Inductive: this approach involves trying to 'get at' the meaning that people in social situations give to those situations. This at a basic level means generating concepts and theories out of data rather than theories guiding the collection of data. In an inductive approach the data collected is not prescribed and the emergent information or 'findings' lead to tentative theories.

Realist/interpretive

● Realist: involves an acceptance that there are some central organizing or underlying structural mechanisms or frameworks operating in the social world. The researchers' task is to discover these and to explain why we behave in certain ways. This is more than observation and description. It involves explanation of what is found within an organizing framework identified by the research.

● Interpretive: interpretivism suggests that knowledge is concerned with interpretation, meaning and illumination. Human action is given meaning through interpretation and researchers have to attempt to achieve an understanding of how people make sense of the world.

Quantitative/qualitative

● Quantitative research is often defined as being based on deductive, objective approaches: there are facts 'out there' to be known. It involves measurement through collecting and/or analysing numerical data through the use of questionnaires, tests, interviews or existing databases. The data collected and the analysis can be subject to tests to demonstrate its representativeness and/or reliability.

● Qualitative research invariably involves description and emphasis on context and process, which produces emergent theories and concepts. It is therefore based on an inductive approach and draws on a consuctivist philosophical approach. Methods for collecting information/data are subject to different 'tests' such as credibility, transferability and confirmability.

What becomes apparent from this very brief analysis of different approaches is that there are overlapping ideas that reinforce the idea that they are describing ways of knowing. Moreover, there are indications that what might be opposing approaches can be used together. The knowledge gleaned from each approach can influence, or help to formulate, how other approaches can be used to produce different and complementary knowledge/information about social situations.

Bridging the gap

The above definitions illustrate that social research is complex and contested, by which we mean that for every description and definition given there is probably a different and/or opposite one. Moreover, what happens in social research is rarely based on the either/or principle. Researchers are constantly looking for the most effective ways of gaining information about situations in order to understand them and this often requires more than one way of looking at the world, and finding out about it.

There are a number of ways in which the gap between the approaches can be bridged. One is what has been called critical research; the other is to use a mixed methods approach. In critical research the researcher stands outside the mainstream approach and offers different dimensions to the way the world is understood. Feminist approaches to research are often given as illustrative of critical research.

Feminist approaches

It is often assumed that feminist research concentrates only on the experiences of women and uses only qualitative methods (see Orme, 2004, for discussion). This is because early feminist texts in research drew attention to the way that social research was undertaken predominantly by men. The research did not overtly focus on male experiences, but because there was no thought that the experiences of women and men might be different, or that the experiences of women might be more important than those of men, little or no attention was paid to the experiences of women in research. Early feminist researchers argued that this research was 'gender blind'. By this they meant that statistics were collected and no distinctions were made, no description given of how women and men figured differently in the statistics. This initial criticism led to more detailed analysis of how research made women (and people from black and ethnic minority backgrounds) invisible and how research conducted on the experiences of non-disabled white men was assumed to describe the experiences of everyone.

The first response was to draw attention to this phenomenon, pointing out that research that was not rigorous in its analysis was not good research. This led to the process of what has become known as 'add women and stir'. That is, women became just another variable in the sample but little attention was paid to the implications of results that showed that, for example, more women than men lived in poverty.

These deficits in social research led to work in the 1980s that included critiques of the methods of social research used (Stanley and Wise, 1983). Feminists then began to focus on different ways of undertaking research to address women's experience (Roberts, 1981). Research undertaken building on this critique focused on women's experiences, which often involved analysing very private and personal aspects of their lives. This meant that methods had to be found that were sensitive but were also rigorous (see Ungerson, 1987). Because of this feminist researchers often drew on qualitative methods. Because women are in the majority on social workers' case loads (Orme, 1997) and the areas of women's lives being researched (poverty, caring, and domestic violence) are issues that social workers are dealing with, links between social work and feminist research were forged (Orme, 1998, 2008).

However, just as there are many strands to feminist theory (Humm, 1992, provides an overview) so there were many approaches to feminist research. The first was a strong strand of feminist thought that outlined a specific and different approach to research to be undertaken by feminists. This was associated with standpoint approaches that had emerged from Marxist critical theory. Researchers held firmly to the view that feminist research should be from the perspective of women: 'on women, by women and for women'. This approach enabled the development of research methods that focused on women's lives, which challenged the mainstream/malestream commitment to positivism and science. It also held firmly to the view that because 'the personal is the political' findings from research, no matter how small the sample, should be used to bring about changes in policies and practice. The purpose of some feminist research was a form of 'praxis'. That is, researchers did not just study the world, they used research findings to change it (Stanley, 1990).

Interestingly, Harding (1987) points out that early feminist approaches were also aligned with empiricism because the aim was to find evidence or 'proof' of the social conditions experienced by women. Feminists can count and 'hard' facts have their place. Debates about domestic violence, for example, led to calls for large-scale surveys to try to identity the levels of domestic violence experienced (Mullender, 1996).

Another, and very different, feminist approach came about as a result of feminists engaging with postmodernism. In challenging universalist claims and/or grand theories postmodernism could be seen to challenge the very idea of feminist approaches. However, postmodern feminist approaches accept that all theories provide different perspectives and, more importantly, challenge the notion of binary opposites such as male and female. Recognizing that the category 'woman' or female can include diverse groupings (based on age, race, colour, physical and mental abilities etc.), postmodern feminism argues that making universal claims from research on some women about the experiences of all women could be as oppressive as research that ignored women altogether. It also recognizes that feminist theory has relevance to society as a whole, and that men can be the focus of feminist research. This is particularly important in social work where the behaviour of men has a significant impact on social work practice, as research in the area of child protection demonstrates (Featherstone and Lancaster, 1997; Scourfield, 2002).

This very brief overview demonstrates that current feminist approaches to research do not involve mere methodological individualism, nor are they concerned only with focusing on women. They help to bridge the gap between the approaches that had been set in opposition to each other by being prepared to combine methods to undertake the particular project, which is to use feminist lenses to understand the social world, and to acknowledge the diversity of those inhabiting that world. Not surprisingly, the emergence of different ways of approaching research associated with feminism precipitated criticism (McLennan, 1995). Hammersley (1995), for example, in his chapter 'On feminist methodology' acknowledges that feminism makes a contribution to the social sciences, but is reluctant to see feminist approaches as constituting a new paradigm for social research.

The fact that Hammersley (1995) also rejects approaches to research based on anti-racism means that it is no surprise that he rejects the idea of critical research. Sarantakos (1998), on the other hand, argues that because of the way it views the world (in a critical manner) the whole theoretical and practical organization of critical research is tuned to a different environment and to a different level from that of positivist and interpretive, or constructivist research (Sarantakos, 1998, p. 60). He argues that critical research is directed towards breaking down taken-for-granted concepts and building new entities (Sarantakos, 1998, p. 65). Hence while feminist approaches to research might develop new methods, they also use methods employed in positivist and constructivist research. What distinguishes them is their focus and purpose. Feminist approaches combine ways of understanding the world and use different methods to:

● acknowledge the pervasive influence of gender as a category of analysis and organization;
● address understanding of gender through its interrelationship with other oppressions and other identities;

- deconstruct traditional commitments to truth, objectivity and neutrality;
- adopt an approach to ways of knowing that recognizes that all theories are perspectival, and are open to critique and debate;
- acknowledge the involvement of the researcher and those who are the focus of research in the creation of knowledge.

Feminist approaches, as well as providing vital research on the experiences of women and others who are the recipients of social work services, also offer perspectives on knowledge that resonate with the values and practices of social work. This makes feminist approaches particularly relevant to developing research based social work practice.

Mixed methods

Another way of bridging the gap is by merging or mixing methods. De Vaus (2001) has suggested that ways of knowing should be related to what is needed to be known. He describes research as being either descriptive or explanatory. These two different approaches answer different questions: descriptive approaches seek answers to the question 'What is … ?' and explanatory research attempts to find answers to the question 'Why is it … ?' But these are not necessarily separate. For De Vaus 'good description provokes the "why" question of explanatory research' (2001, p. 2).

As has been said already, it is important in social work to know the details of social issues that impinge upon the lives of those who need services: the levels of poverty; the number and characteristics of families living in poverty; the number and characteristics of people providing informal care; the number and characteristics of people offending. These data are helpful in describing how certain social conditions impact differently on people because of their age, gender, colour, race, physical and mental capacities and other diverse characteristics. However, it is also vital to know how individual circumstances are influenced by, or impact upon, the particular set of circumstances: 'the person in their situation'. This can be achieved by using a mixed methods approach.

A mixed methods approach does not mean that researchers can pick and choose the methods that they want to use, or that anything goes. At their simplest, 'mixed methods investigations involve integrating quantitative and qualitative data collection and analysis in a single study or programme of enquiry' (Cresswell *et al.*, 2004, p. 7). However, achieving that integration is not always simple. It has been argued that rigorous research has to be designed in order to answer the particular question, or address a particular issue, so methods cannot be mixed just by arbitrary choice. Mixed methods help to provide layers of understanding achieved in different ways but their use has to be justified and the 'mixture' has to permeate the whole of the research process. O'Caithin (in a presentation to a Researcher Development Initiative workshop) suggests that it is important to justify the use of mixed methods on the basis of confidence (this is the right design for this research question), comprehensiveness (this will cover more aspects of the issue being researched than a single method design) and increased 'yield' (a mixed methods approach reaches the parts single methods studies cannot). To be effective it is important to think mixed methods throughout the design, rather than thinking individual methods and then trying to bring them together, for example, in the discussion.

Integration can take a number of forms. Some research projects gather statistical data, and then devise methods using qualitative approaches to answer the 'why' questions that arise from the data. But approaches are not always used sequentially, one after the other. Qualitative and quantitative methods can be used concurrently. In approaches such as grounded theory (Glaser and Strauss, 1967), for example, different approaches are brought together by researchers, making no assumptions about what they will find and analysing each piece of data as they collect it to identify themes. Once themes have been identified and found to be present in other sets of data/information, the analysis moves to a much more 'positivist' or statistical phase.

Another approach is for research to be designed where there is an iterative process. That is, one approach informs and influences the other throughout the research process. Statistics provide descriptions of social conditions that lead to why questions. These can be examined further using qualitative methods that provide more explanatory material. This can then lead to more questions that require statistical data collection that gives further description. A key aspect of integration in all these approaches is that there is no hierarchy: no one method of collection and no one set of data is privileged over another.

Finally, a quote from Brannen (2005), one of the leading exponents of mixed methods in the UK, serves as a good footnote to the discussions in this chapter. She sees mixing methods as logical because she does not accept the distinctions made between qualitative and quantitative research:

the claim that qualitative research uses words while quantitative research uses numbers is overly simplistic. A further claim that qualitative studies focus on meanings while quantitative research is concerned with behaviour is not supported since both may be concerned with people's views and actions. The association of qualitative research with an inductive logic of enquiry and quantitative research with hypothetic-deduction can often be reversed in practice; both types of research may employ both forms of logic. That qualitative research lacks quantitative research's power to generalise is moreover only true if generalisability is taken to refer only to statistical inference, that is, when the findings of a research sample are generalised to the parent population. Qualitative findings may be generalised in a different sense; they may be generalised to other settings or contexts or they may involve theoretical generalisation, where findings are extrapolated in relation to their theoretical application. (Brannen, 2005, p. 175)

Conclusion

If social work is to develop a rigorous research base to inform practice then consideration of the ways in which knowledge is generated and understood has to permeate the research that is undertaken. Theories that underpin methodological approaches inform that understanding, while descriptions of methods used and how they relate to those theories are important to ensure that the research is 'fit for purpose': that is, the methods chosen address the issues to be investigated.

It is therefore important to try and keep an open mind: to avoid what Hammersley (1995) refers to as 'methodolotary' and theoretical arrogance. Methodolotary involves obsession with one technical approach, implying that the methods drive the research rather than the research question. This is not to say that researchers should deny that they hold a particular world view and that different ways of producing knowledge produce different kinds of knowledge.

Discussion of critical research illustrated by the description of feminist research and a mixed methods approach illustrates it is at times necessary to be open to the different contributions that can be made. These are particularly relevant to social work research, where it is necessary to understand both the conditions that impinge upon people's lives and the way that individuals experience and interpret those conditions: the person in their situation.

---

putting it into practice

Think of a piece of research with which you are familiar – or which you have found interesting. If you cannot bring to mind a specific piece of research then go to the website of the journal

Qualitative Social Work: Research and Practice:
www.qsw.sagepub.com.

This journal has articles that discuss and describe research projects. Many discuss the project from a particular methodological approach or describe the use of different methods – such as using art, literature or photographs in the research process. Find an article that interests you.

As you read the article make notes along the lines of:

- What is the specific issue being researched?
- What methodological approach has the author(s) described – if any?
- What methods are used?
- What are the reasons given for these choices?

Then think about the answers and perhaps read the article again and try to decide whether:

1. The article has given you enough information.
2. If it has, do you think that the methods chosen in this piece of research were 'fit for purpose'.

And of course in doing this you should note, if you do think it is fit for purpose – why? And if you do not think it is fit for purpose – why not? How would you have answered the particular research question or addressed the particular research issue?

Recommended reading

Brannen, J. (ed.) (1992) *Mixing Methods: Qualitative and Quantitative Research*. Aldershot, Ashgate. A useful text for those who want to know more about mixed methods.

Stanley, L. (1990) '"A Referral Was Made": Behind the Scenes During the Creation of a Social Services Department "Elderly" Statistic', in L. Stanley (ed.) *Feminst Praxis: Research, Theory and Epistemology*. London, Routledge. This is a very readable chapter that illustrates some of the issues around doing research in social work.

6 | Statistics and quantification: how numbers can help

Introduction

Having dealt with underpinning knowledge, values and the preparatory processes for research, in the following chapters we provide much more detail about different methods that can be used in social work research. As we have said, it is important for researchers to be clear about the methods used and how those methods can help to produce useful knowledge and information about the social factors that concern social workers and the situations in which they intervene. However, it is also important for practitioners, managers and service users and carers to have an understanding of the principles of the methods to help them to critically evaluate research to enable them to decide whether it is appropriate to use the results to inform their practice.

This chapter focuses on quantitative methods because social workers have always tended to be wary or even suspicious of them. Their reactions range from indifference to fear, and even hostility. In one sense, it is not surprising that they prefer qualitative approaches in social research; after all, many will have rejected the 'sciences' (especially maths) when making choices between subjects at school. But, in the main, it is not necessary to understand maths to make sense of quantitative methods and almost no knowledge of statistics is required to appreciate their potential or to critique the work of quantitative researchers.

One problem with rejecting quantitative methods out of hand is that social work practitioners are likely to become progressively more isolated from the research community because quantitative approaches already dominate social work research in the USA and in parts of Europe. They also are used in health research and policy research in the UK dealing with topics relevant to social work. Another problem is that, as we have indicated repeatedly, if social work is about understanding 'the person in their situation' then researchers and practitioners need to have comprehensive and accurate information about social situations that impinge upon those who use services. It is important for researchers and practitioners to understand how statistics and databases are compiled and analysed so that they are aware of the relevance of the results.

This chapter will give you the keys to unlock the potential of quantitative methods in social work research. By the end, you will be able to understand what is going on when such methods are used and you will be able to read with more confidence relevant articles using both established and contemporary quantitative and statistical techniques. The style adopted in this chapter is slightly different, in that it is more didactic because it contains concepts that you may not have been taught, either on qualification or on post-qualification programmes. Because of this, we have assumed you have little knowledge of the statistical ideas discussed. Even if that is not the case, it is useful to reflect on the practicalities of the chapter in the light of the ideas and arguments that have been discussed so far; namely the contribution that these methods can make to the development of a research base for social work practice.

When and why are numbers useful? If we take domestic violence as an example, social work practitioners can refer to qualitative research to shed light on and 'voice' the experiences of women who live with violent men. But they should be also aware of quantitative findings about the prevalence of domestic violence, or the chance of a new intervention working successfully with male perpetrators, or perhaps the effect on a child's social and emotional development if they have witnessed persistent violence at home. The incorporation of both qualitative and quantitative research offers much to social work practitioners if a *both/and* rather than an *either/or* approach is adopted.

Knowledge of statistical principles depends on an intuitive grasp of probability, which many people freely admit they find tricky. Here is a way to 'test' yours. Assume you have been a regular aircraft traveller for the past ten or so years. A friend of yours tells you she has read that the chance of losing your luggage is around 1 in every 30 flights (we made this up!). You have not lost one bag in over 50 flights. She then tells you that you are much more likely on the next flight to find your bag appearing at the wrong airport. Is she correct?

The answer is that you stand exactly the same chance of losing your bag on the next flight as you do on any flight; that is, 1 in 30. There could, for example, be a party of children on board who have never flown before: theirs and your chances of losing baggage are the same: 1 in 30 – it doesn't matter how many times you or they have flown.

Now try this example: if you have thrown a die three times and got a six each time, what is the chance of you getting one on the next throw? The answer is … 1 in 6 (the same as it is on *any* throw of a die; the same as it is, in fact, for any *number* on the die). But … you would, in reality, not put a large bet on your chances of getting a six four times in a row. There is a branch of probability – called Bayesian theory – that takes account of the intuitive 'reality' in such situations. We cannot go into detail here but Bayesian probability has considerable potential for social work practice because it is designed specifically for situations involving uncertainty. If you are interested in pursuing this further, read the article by Wooff and Schneider (2006).

'Easing' the distinction between quantitative and qualitative methods

As we discussed in Chapter 4 many writers now conclude that the dichotomous, and often oppositional, distinction between 'quantitative' and 'qualitative' methods has become unhelpful, partly because it is an inaccurate depiction of what is actually going on when research is undertaken.

The following example illustrates the danger of separating too sharply qualitative and quantitative approaches. We make no apologies for choosing our example from the classic studies of Durkheim (1951), and then Douglas (1967): they are timeless examples of the overlaps between quantitative and qualitative methodologies. What may appear at first sight as a detour will eventually show that seductive binary distinctions between qualitative and quantitative methodologies are nothing like as sharp as they might seem. The example also offers support to our contention that choice of method ideally should be 'fit for purpose'; that is, based upon the nature of the research questions posed, not the epistemological predilections of the researcher.

We also explore this example because it exemplifies why we need to approach research findings with an open mind … but not an empty head! The research-informed social work practitioner needs to be confident enough to question research findings, but not so naive as to think this can be done without the benefit of honed and sharpened critical appraisal skills.

Example: 'Why do people take their own life?'

At the turn of the last century Emile Durkheim opened up a series of debates about the nature and causes of human behaviour, which eventually crystallized into what we now understand as the 'sociological imagination'. The idea that the society in which we live can affect an individual's actions, thoughts, feelings, hopes and expectations is pretty much taken for granted today but in the early 1900s this notion was not just contentious, it was virtually unheard of. People were seen as acting in the way they did because of basic flaws in their personality, or as a result of predisposing features in their make-up (i.e. 'genetics'). Thus, 'criminals' were seen as 'deficient' in fundamental ways and were thought to have been 'born that way'. Durkheim took the unprecedented step of arguing that culture, politics and social structures influence our behaviour significantly by focusing on one of the most individual of behaviours, namely 'suicide'. He proceeded to argue that social forces produce different levels and 'types' of suicide. What Durkheim did was compare the 'rate of suicide' per million, over different periods of time. That is, on the basis of the available statistics, how many people in any given million might commit suicide. If, he argued, suicide is the archetypal 'personal' act, conducted in private, then why were the rates between countries so markedly different?

What he noticed immediately was that the numbers of suicides were very different and yet seemed not to be the result of individual characteristics, predisposing factors, stressful life styles etc. On the contrary, people were more or less likely to commit suicide depending on which part of the world they lived in. Individuals living in West Germany were roughly six times more likely to commit suicide than those living in Japan, for example. These figures astonished and unsettled those who had hitherto held the more comfortable belief that suicide was the result of a 'fault' in an individual; a matter of the mind, not a feature of society. But how exactly can the country we live in lead us to take our own life? For Durkheim it was far more complex and he went on to explore other dimensions of social life that he thought might explain what was happening. The point is that he was using a set of statistics from apparently incontestable data to back up his hypotheses and draw out meaning.

But Durkheim still did not have a theory to explain these results. This conundrum is rather similar to a situation that arose in the 1930s and 1940s relating to child development. It was noted that 'height' and 'infant mortality' were found to be negatively correlated (i.e. when one is 'high', the other is 'low', and vice versa), but no one knew or could establish *why*. It emerged later that another variable, initially defined as 'social class', was thought to mediate the effect but the key factor eventually found to be responsible was 'food nutrition' (i.e. shorter, 'upper-class' mothers were not 'nutritionally deficient', whereas 'working-class' mothers were, and this led to constricted pelvis size, thus placing the baby in danger during birth).

To return to the question of suicide: by considering different combinations of the 'rates' of suicide data, Durkheim identified two different features to explain the results. He did this by using an iterative process similar to that used by qualitative researchers, drawing upon the principles of grounded theory (see Chapter 8). He argued that a dynamic interaction existed between the levels of 'integration' and 'regulation' in societies, which led to differential rates of suicide. Too little integration leads people to feel isolated, akin to Albert Camus's notion of the 'Outsider', a person who cannot connect with people, accompanied with a desperate feeling that they don't belong to anything or to anybody. This state is seen by some to typify the chronic individualism and alienation in some contemporary societies, which is seen as having a marked effect on suicide rates among younger men, which are soaring in many Western societies. Too *much* integration, on the other hand, and we begin to see an erosion of individuality in favour of the group. This can occasionally lead people to take their own life to benefit their affiliative group, as an ultimate act of altruism. Older members of Inuit communities, for example, have been known to commit suicide when food is very scarce.

Durkheim's second factor was 'regulation'. Too little and people experience an emerging state of social deregulation – which he termed *anomie*, to describe a state of growing 'normlessness', eroding people's expectations about how they are expected to behave with each other. But too *much* regulation – for example, life in a prison – and individuals may contemplate taking their own life because it feels progressively pointless and meaningless and outside the individual's orbit of influence or control.

So Durkheim had skilfully interpreted the data to produce a plausible theory capable of explaining why suicide rates were different. Or had he? We will consider this again in Chapter 8 where we will discover that Douglas (1967) questioned the whole basis of the existence of 'rates of suicide', arguing powerfully that because they relied almost entirely upon the judgements of coroners to determine whether or not a death should be classified as a 'suicide', fundamental doubts were raised about the 'fact' of suicide.

There is a cautionary tale here in that we can see how a set of ideas can be powerful and persuasive, making it even more important for social workers to develop the critical tools with which to analyse complex findings, arguments and propositions. As we have argued in previous chapters, this requires a deeper understanding of the epistemological – the rationale upon which 'truth claims' are made – basis behind quantitative research; and this requires some relevant knowledge of number and statistics.

What do we need to get by?

In what follows, we have tried to outline the basic information and building blocks to help practitioners make sense of research that uses statistics.

Two fundamental concepts: means and standard deviations

Imagine you are about 14 and back at senior school. You are choosing your options for GCSE and one of your favourite subjects is history. You really like both teachers who take the history class and because the head-teacher is fond of you, she says she will, on this occasion, allow you to select which class to attend. You decide to ask the headteacher to tell you the average mark for each of the two teachers' results from the past five years' GCSE exams. She agrees and you learn that they both achieved an average of 50 per cent. How do you decide?

The answer is that you need more information. Specifically, you need to know the spread within each teacher's set of marks. Let's take a simple example. Suppose each teacher only had three students each and their results were:

Teacher A: 49, 50, 51 per cent
Teacher B: 15, 50, 85 per cent

Both have an average (or 'mean') of 50 per cent but with this additional information you are now in better position to decide: if the pass mark is 40 per cent you might well opt for teacher A, because everyone passed. On the other hand, if you think you are *really* talented at history, you might opt for teacher B, who could be better at developing the brighter students.

In statistical terms, what you have learned is that 'measures of central tendency' – in our example, the 'mean', depicted by a variety of symbols, including $\bar{x}$ ('x bar') or simply 'M' – are not very helpful without a measure of the dispersion (or spread) of the results. There are quite a few measures of dispersion available, including the range, the semi-interquartile range (or middle half) and one with which most social workers will be familiar, the centile (i.e. where 1 per cent of a population, often children, fall). Centiles are often used by health professionals to compare children – so 'the child's weight was in the third centile' means that it was very low, because only 3 per cent of children of that age and circumstances weigh less. But the most important measure of dispersion in statistics is the 'standard deviation' (depicted by the Greek lower case letter sigma 'σ' or, more simply, SD – and sometimes even just plain 's'). We are guessing that you will *not* want to see a formula for calculating the standard deviation but here is a simple description of how it is obtained: in our history example, first find the mean for the marks given by each teacher, by adding together each individual's score and then dividing by the number of students whose work was marked by that teacher. Now calculate the numerical distance between each student's individual score and your mean score. Next, add these up and divide by the number of students. But, if you *actually* did this, you would find the answer would be zero, because all the scores above the mean would cancel out all the ones below. For example, if the scores were 2, 3, 4, 5, 6, 7 and 8, the mean would be 5 and the difference would be –1, –2, –3, 0, +1, +2 and +3 respectively, giving a summed total of zero. So what we do is rather ingenious (or 'cheating', if you prefer!): we square each of the differences (if you've forgotten doing that at school, it involves multiplying a number by itself, e.g. 5 'squared' – written 5^2 – is 5×5). Doing this is acceptable provided we adjust the answer by eventually performing the reverse procedure on our final answer. You may or may not remember that the reverse process to 'squaring' a number is finding the 'square root' or '$\sqrt{}$' (you probably thought you would never to see that again!). For example, the square root of 49 – written $\sqrt{49}$ – is 7 (to be entirely accurate, it is also –7). The result is called the 'standard deviation'. If you look at the three sets of data in Table 6.1 you will see that although the mean is the same (M = 15.5), the SD is very different and we hope that by its being presented it in this way you can see why (this is an example regularly used in teaching – see, for example http://homepages.ius.edu/SRAUSC01/Chap03.ppt).

The other important thing to know is that most data are what is called 'normally distributed', indicating that there are relatively few scores at the high and low ends, with most falling somewhere around the middle. You can appreciate this from our classroom teacher example: in the real world, most of teacher A's students will not get exceptionally high marks and most won't fail; most will tend to get between 45 and 65 per cent. But here is the clever bit: if data are normally distributed, then we immediately know that roughly 95 per cent of the scores will automatically lie between 2 SDs either side of the mean because this is a constant property of normally distributed data (i.e. data looking like a bell shaped curve). For example, if the mean age of placement for 100 adopted children is 2 years and the SD is 3 months then 95 children will have been placed between 1.5 (2 × 3 months = 0.5) and 2.5 years of age. The chance of a child being placed outside the range is statistically unusual. How unusual? Only 2.5 per cent will be placed younger than 1.5 years of age and only 2.5 per cent will be placed above 2.5 years of age.

Table 6.1 *Comparing standard deviations*

Data A

					*						
					*						
*	*	*			*	*	*			*	Mean = 15.5
11	12	13	14	15	16	17	18	19	20	21	S = 3.338

Data B

				*	*						
				*	*						
			*	*	*	*					Mean = 15.5
11	12	13	14	15	16	17	18	19	20	21	S = 0.9258

Data C

*									*		
*									*		
*	*							*	*		Mean = 15.5
11	12	13	14	15	16	17	18	19	20	21	S = 4.57

Let us look at another simple example but, first, bear in mind that the standard deviation is always measured in the same 'things' as the mean (i.e. history test scores in our earlier example). Assume we have a group of 25 fathers taking part in a parenting class. You are interested to see if 'parenting capacity' increases as a result and you have a 'measure' of parenting capacity that the parents have completed before (often called T_1) and after (similarly, T_2) attending the class. Leave aside criticisms of the positivist assumptions behind the idea that 'parenting capacity' exists as a measurable phenomenon and let us also assume that there is a control group of some kind who are not receiving any intervention as, without it, we won't know if any resulting changes in parenting capacity scores would have happened anyway, without attending the classes. Assume that our 'measure' consists of a number of statements about parenting capacity, which are rated on '1 to 5' scale – called a Likert scale, after Rensis Likert, its originator – with 1 meaning 'not like me' and 5 'completely like me' (we will be considering such scales, inventories and questionnaires more fully in the next chapter). Now assume that you have a mean of 3.0 for the pre-test and 3.5 for the post-test. You want to know whether your difference of 0.5 is something important that you can get excited about (a 'significant' result as statisticians call it) or whether it was just a fluke, often due to 'sampling error', the effect of which means that it only occurred through chance, not the intervention itself: run the sessions again with different groups and the results could well be reversed . . . but, again, only due to chance and not because there is anything *really* different happening as a consequence of attending the parenting class.

So how do we know if our difference of 0.5 is statistically significant or not? We need to know the standard deviation of the scores. Let us now assume that, for our parenting classes, the standard deviation is 0.2. From what we know about normally distributed data, our parents' scores on the measure of parenting capacity *are* likely to be normally distributed. This is an easy thing to examine, but to explain it now is unnecessary and would only get in the way – we know that 95 per cent of the data lie within two SDs of the mean, i.e. 0.4 (2×0.2). So we now know that 95 per cent of the scores lie between 2.6 and 3.4. And this now tells us what we wanted to know: to get a difference of 0.5 *by chance* is *unlikely*: to be more precise, it is more than 95 per cent *unlikely*. Researchers have devised a quick way of expressing all of this. They use the sign for probability '*p*' and reverse the logic: if 95 per cent of results lie between two standard deviations of the mean, then that implies that less than 5 per cent lie *outside*, which they write as '$p < 0.05$' ('<' means 'less than' and 0.05 is 5 per cent written as a decimal – again, forgive us if you knew all this!).

You would actually see the result of our study into parenting classes written something like this: 'A significant improvement was noted in a study of 25 fathers who were tested on a five-point Likert scale using a measure of parenting capacity before and after attending parenting classes ($T_1M = 3.0$, $T_2M = 3.5$, SD = 0.2, $p < 0.05$).

Here is an example from a study of family group conferences (Mutter *et al.*, 2007, p. 265):

Numbers of males and females in the study were 26 (87%) and 4 (13%) respectively. Ages ranged from 10–18 years (mean = 14.7, standard deviation = 1.40). Most of the young offenders were on either an Action Plan Order, or a Supervision Order.

You can now deduce that 95 per cent were aged between 11.9 and 17.5 (use a calculator and see how we did this – check your answer at the end of the chapter).

Here is another example, this time from Howe *et al.* (2001, pp. 338–9), concerning 'age of placement and the experience of being adopted' and focusing on people who decide to search for a birth parent (see if it makes sense):

The mean age of searchers when they first contacted the adoption agency for information about their adoption and birth relatives was 32.3 years for men (SD = 8.9) and 29.8 years for women (SD = 9.3). Interestingly, the mean age at contact of those approached by a birth relative (the non-searchers) was similar to that of the searchers: 33.3 years for non-searching men (SD = 9.3) and 29.3 years for non-searching women (SD = 8.0).

Looking for differences in the data

It is only a very short step from this knowledge about means and standard deviations to understanding significance testing, depending upon the way the data is constructed and the type of variable under consideration (i.e. whether dependent or independent). Think of an independent variable (IV) as being the 'input', with the dependent variable (DV) the 'outcome'. So, you might want to study the effect of solution-focused therapy (IV) on depression (DV); or poverty (IV1) – as measured by, say, income – *and* alcohol (IV2) on the frequency (DV1) and level (DV2) of domestic violence.

A beguiling variety of tests is available to the quantitative researcher. So we have *t-tests*, *F-tests*, χ^2-*tests*, *analysis of variance* (ANOVA) and *multiple analysis of variance* (MANOVA) – and lots more! – but they all operate using the same principle we have outlined above. Results are significant if they lie outside the 95 per cent range of scores (or, as you will see it written, $p < 0.05$). Thus, we can see how to interpret the following example (from Howe *et al.*, p. 344):

Investigating connections between key variables and the age of placement involved performing a number of non-parametric tests – chi-squared (χ^2) – which do not assume normally distributed results. The following, including some variables already examined above, prove to be statistically significant:

- gender ($\chi^2 = 70.28$, $p < 0.05$);
- person felt s/he was given all the information ($\chi^2 = 123.81$, $p < 0.05$);
- experienced a feeling of belonging to adoptive mother ($\chi^2 = 227.17$, $p < 0.05$);
- felt loved by adoptive mother ($\chi^2 = 275.38$, $p < 0.001$);
- felt loved by adoptive father ($\chi^2 = 259.02$, $p < 0.001$);
- number of siblings ($\chi^2 = 190.83$, $p < 0.001$).

The authors have already explained that when data are not normally distributed in this example the test is called 'non-parametric' – because statistical tests that assume normally distributed data are called 'parametric' tests. The data were not normally distributed because this was a study of adopted adults who decided to search, significantly more children aged under one year were placed for adoption compared with any other age group, and very few children were placed aged over ten years. This might well be different today; if so, it would be termed a 'cohort effect'.

To make sense of the narrative it is not necessary to take account of the *actual* test value, given beside each χ^2 statistic. Instead, it is the '*p*' value that contains the important information. You will note here that we have two: (i) '$p < 0.05$', which you already know means 'the result is less than 5 per cent due to chance'; and (ii) '$p < 0.001$', which, using a little arithmetic, means 'the result is less than 0.1 per cent due to chance' (another way this could have been expressed is 'we would only have expected to obtain such a result purely by chance in one case in every 1000'). In other words, some very significant results were obtained.

Try interpreting and making sense of this extract, again from Mutter *et al.* (2007), which refers to levels of re-offending in the family group conference study:

> In all statistical results, a paired samples *t*-test was carried out using the full data set, unless otherwise stated. The drop in general attitudes between T_1 and T_2, indicating a lower risk of re-offending, is highly statistically significant (paired $t = 3.20$; $p = 0.004$). . . . Although mean scores for drug use show a gradual increase from T_1 through to T_3 (in both sample sets), these increases are not statistically significant. . . . The reduced levels of 'serious and persistent offending' scores of the young people in our sample between T_2 and T_3, were just short of statistical significance (paired $t = 1.92$; $p = 0.082$). The net decrease in seriousness and persistence of offending by young people who attended FGCs, from T_1 to T_3, is also slightly short of statistical significance (paired $t = 2.03$; $p = 0.067$). Those young people who re-offended after FGC, were more likely to have reduced the persistence of their offending rather than the seriousness.

We are told the test used – a *paired samples t-test* – but, again, we do not need to worry about the actual value. The precise value of the '*p*' value is stated in this extract and this reflects a growing trend in reporting, because there is something rather arbitrary when $p = 0.049$ is significant, whereas if $p = 0.051$, then it is not. It is important *not* to reject a potentially significant result by mistake. This is called a type II error; a type I error occurs when a finding is accepted as significant when it isn't.

As social workers you might be interested in some of the following questions, each of which would involve the use of statistical tests of significance to address it:

1. Investigating whether vulnerable adults are affected by the personal-
ization agenda by comparing outcomes of service users using direct
payments and a control group.
2. Exploring differential outcomes of risk-taking and intervention using
three different approaches: cognitive-behavioural therapy, solution-
focused therapy and parenting classes.
3. Investigating differences between two different interventions with
men who are violent to women.

A word about the use of 'significant', as there is often misunderstanding
about what it means. Just because a set of results is statistically significant doesn't necessarily mean that they are particularly important in
terms of their impact, or 'effect size' as statisticians call it. This can often
occur when very large samples are drawn from a given population.
Significant findings can emerge but they may not reveal much by way of
information about the phenomenon under consideration. This is why a
current trend in quantitative research is to concentrate more upon choosing an 'accurate' sample, rather than adopting a 'blunderbuss' approach.
An illustrative example is seen in a large European study, which looked
at, among other things, differences between attachment styles according
to gender (Schmitt and 130 members of the International Sexuality
Description Project; $n = 17,804$ in 62 cultural regions, 2003). Although
some significant results were found, they were often in the order of little
more than 0.1 or 0.2 on a scale continuum of 1–6, hence it was the sheer
size of the sample that had produced the results. This is why in contemporary research the 'effect size' is measured, using a statistic called 'eta
squared' (ε^2). (Whether the value of 'eta squared' is 'small', 'medium'
or 'large' will usually be explained and interpreted by the author(s) of the
article).

Looking for similarities

Up to this point we have focused on single variables, describing their
central tendency (the mean) and their dispersion (the standard deviation), e.g. 'How many people receive a home care service in Wales?' We
have also looked at differences between the means of two variables, e.g.
'What differences exist between men's and women's attitudes to direct
payments?' Just as often, however, it is interesting to look at similarities
and connections between the data, the usual term for which is 'correlation': how are the data co-related? Often research will seek to do both –
look at differences and similarities – and both can be built into the design
of the study.

How can we explore mathematically the association between two variables? This is more difficult to explain than with means and standard deviations, so this time we will use a graph, because correlation is easier to visualize. Suppose we have a measure of hot chocolate consumption (not too difficult to devise, and accurate if respondents are honest!) and a measure of happiness (much more difficult to do!). We could then ask 100 people to tell us how much hot chocolate they drink per day (but we would need to distinguish between all the different types and strengths) and then ask them to complete our 'measure of happiness'. Let's try a novel approach: rather than ask them to complete a self-reported Likert scale, we could measure their cortisol levels from a swab containing their saliva – a low reading could be thought to indicate low stress and, hence, more happiness (we accept there are lots of assumptions there – but we are only using this example to illustrate the statistics). If we were to plot each person's reading on the graph it might look something like Figure 6.1.

What does this begin to tell us? First we can 'eyeball the data', which is what statisticians call looking at the graph to try to discern patterns. This shows that, generally speaking, the more hot chocolate you drink, the 'more happy' you are (or is it 'feel'? – but let's not get side-tracked). The reverse is, in the main, also true: the less happy you are/feel, the less hot chocolate you drink. You have probably heard the term 'positive correlation' to describe such an association ('high on one variable' means 'high on the other' and vice versa: 'low on one' means 'low on the other'). Negative correlation occurs when one variable is high when

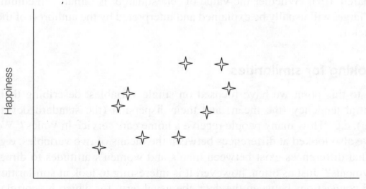

Figure 6.1   Scatter diagram

the other is low (and vice versa). Notice that we are hedging our bets by using terms like 'generally speaking' and 'in the main'. What we need is a measure that conveys something of the *strength* of the association. Many exist, and they are called correlation 'coefficients' (a mathematical term for 'number'). The important thing to know is that they are always calculated in such a way that they can only take values between −1 and +1. The reason for this is to let the researcher know whether the direction of the association is positive or negative. Something that confuses most people is that a correlation coefficient of 0.8 doesn't always indicate a greater level of association than (say) 0.6, because it all depends on the sample size and some other features of the design. So how *do* we know whether one coefficient indicates more concordance than another, given that this is pretty much the whole point of calculating correlations? The answer is revealed by knowing what the '*p*' value is (which, as you already know, *does* take account of sample size etc.).

You will often find correlations expressed in what looks at first sight to be a complicated table – the *correlation matrix* – but with a little deciphering it is relatively easy to make sense of what is going on (and it is infinitely quicker to comprehend than trying to narrate the information contained with in it). Table 6.2 provides an example.

Here we have a matrix that shows the correlations between six different people on a measure of attachment. What you will notice is that there are a series of what are called 'perfect correlations' (i.e. 1.00) along the diagonal and this is because they show each person correlated with themselves! You can also see that there are four correlations that are significant at $p < 0.05$ (i.e. those italicized and with an asterisk). For example, there is a significant *negative* correlation between person 1 and

Table 6.2 *Correlation matrix of scores between factors*

	1	2	3	4	5	6
1	1.00					
2	0.10	1.00				
3	*-0.35**	0.08	1.00			
4	0.18	0.29	-0.02	1.00		
5	*0.42**	*0.38**	-0.14	0.34	1.00	
6	-0.37*	0.20	0.21	0.17	0.04	1.00

* signifies a result at $p <0.05$

person 3 (i.e. −0.35) and a significant *positive* correlation between person 2 and person 5 (i.e. 0.38). And we are 95 per cent sure (because *p* is less than 0.05) that these correlations are not due to chance.

Social life rarely consists of just two variables – 'bivariate' correlation, as it is called. Fortunately there are other techniques available to explore more complex situations about which researchers are interested or in which they find themselves involved. We use a social work-related example to illustrate 'partial correlation'. Assume we are interesting in exploring connections between *time spent in foster care*, *gender* and their effects on *number of GCSEs obtained at 16/17*. What partial correlation allows us to do is hold either *time spent in foster care* or *gender* constant, while varying the other one. The expression you will often see to describe this is 'controlling for', as in 'we investigated the relationship between the number of GCSEs and time spent in foster care while controlling for gender'.

It is important to remember that because two or more variables may be correlated, it does not mean one *causes* the other. Many studies, for example, have shown that ice cream sales are correlated with children's accidents around or in swimming pools. But which variable is 'causing' which effect is likely to be complicated. For example, eating more ice cream could lead to more people swimming, and therefore to more accidents; or, an increase in children experiencing a swimming accident could lead to an increase in adults buying an ice cream for a child to calm them if it was their friend who had the accident. More likely, however, is that both variables are actually 'caused' by an increase in hot weather: more sunshine leads to more ice cream AND accidents and this makes it appear that these two variables are associated directly when they are not. Much correlational research is confusing and under-analysed because the effect of mediating, moderating and confounding variables is not explored.

More complex correlational research enables us to do something important, namely to predict how a number of independent (remember: 'inputs') variables are related to an outcome variable. An example given by Andy Field (2009) in his excellent book on the use of the *Statistical Package for Social Sciences* (SPSS) provides a simple but effective way of explaining 'multiple regression'. He provides data on 200 boy bands for (i) the actual of volume record sales, (ii) the amount spent on advertising/marketing, (iii) the amount of airtime on Radio 1 and (iv) a rating by a large number of fans of the 'attractiveness' of each band. Before we look at how to predict the effects of the three independent variables on the dependent variable, try to identify what the dependent variable is. The answer can be found at the end of the chapter.

Multiple regression allows us to investigate the differential effect of a number of independent variables on one dependent variable. In the boy bands example, we want to know how much influence each of the three 'inputs' (the amount spent on advertising/marketing, the amount of Radio 1 airtime and the overall 'prettiness' of the band) has on what really matters here: the number of records sold.

Regression analysis produces a 'scatterplot' (like the one above) and produces a line through the points in such a way that the total distance of each point on one side of the line is 'balanced' by those on the other side. This is called a 'line of best fit' or *regression line*. In our example of the hot chocolate consumption and happiness the regression line appears as in Figure 6.2.

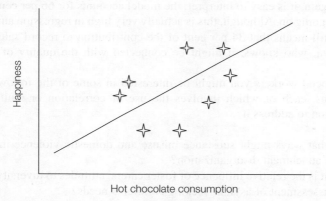

Figure 6.2   Scatter diagram with regression line

What it conveniently allows us to do is read off *any* level of 'happiness' given *any* level of hot chocolate consumption (and vice versa). We won't frighten you with the idea that, given that it is a straight line, the relationship between the two variables can be expressed by an equation, but the importance is that it contains what are called 'beta coefficients', which indicate the relative strength of the independent variable on the dependent variable. From Andy Field's example, the beta values are respectively:

0.511: advertising
0.512: Radio 1 airplay
0.192: attractiveness

This is straightforward to interpret, if we round them up (or down) as follows:

0.5: advertising
0.5: Radio 1 airplay
0.2: attractiveness

This means that the added value of the advertising is the same as the amount of airplay and about 2.5 times the effect of trying to improve the attractiveness of the band (in other words, don't spend a disproportionate amount on clothes and hairstyles!). What we don't know is *how much* of what is going on in this situation is accounted for by the model. But with regression analysis, this can be found from the calculation of a statistic called R^2 (you guessed it, the square of the correlation coefficient – don't ask why!). In the Boy Bands example, the value of R^2 was 0.66. Again, it is easy to interpret: the model accounts for 66 per cent of what is going on. Although, this is actually very high in regression analysis, it still means that 34 per cent of the contribution to record sales is unknown: who knows, it might be connected with the quality of the music!

As social workers you might be interested in some of the following questions, each of which involves the use of correlation or multiple regression to address it:

1. In what ways might substance misuse and domestic violence influence attachment disorganization?
2. What is the relative influence of foster carers' attitudes to diversity on the assessment of asylum-seeking children's needs?
3. How are early upbringing and childhood biography associated with later parenting capacity?

Conclusion

We have covered a lot of ground in this chapter. It is intended that this will enable you to make a lot more sense of articles and research reports using quantitative methods and statistics. Our overall advice is to try studying such articles; you should find that you are not so fazed by them. It also illustrates how much the data collected and the interpretation of that data is contingent – that is, it is dependent – upon a number of factors. Hence it is difficult to draw absolute conclusions or make absolute predictions. As we said in Chapter 2, the only way to know that all swans are white is to look at every swan. This chapter has shown how statistics can save a bit of time and effort by giving us a workable hypothesis: that is, to be able to claim that 'on the basis of the information we have so far . . . it is likely that all swans are white . . . '!

answer to question posed on page 104

2 SDs are 2.8 (1.4 x 2) and the 95 per cent range is found from 14.7 − 2.8 (i.e. 11.9) to 14.7 + 2.8 (i.e. 17.5).

answer to question posed on page 110

The dependent variable is the 'volume of sales'; the others are all independent variables, because they are each thought to contribute − make an *input* − to the outcome.

putting it into practice

Here are two examples for you to try your hand at:

(The reference to '*F*' is to a specific significance test.)

Example One: A two-way between-groups ANOVA was employed to explore differences in levels of violence between men and women in three age groups (group 1: <24, group 2: 25–34, group 3: >35). There was a statistically significant main effect for age (*F* = 4.21, *p* = 0.03); however, the effect size was small (eta squared = 0.02). Comparisons between age groups indicated that the mean score for age group 1 (M = 20.21, SD = 3.55) was significantly different from age group 3 (M = 31.96, SD = 3.29). Age group 2 (M = 22.40, SD = 3.55) did not differ significantly from groups 1 or 3.

Example Two: Multiple regression revealed a model accounting for 56.6 per cent of the variance in men's aggression (R^2 = 0.566, *F* = 214.5, *N* = 325). This model comprised attachment security and perceived level of self-control, and independently accounted for 35.4 and 16.3 per cent of the variance respectively (correlations = −0.64 and −0.78).

Recommended reading

Field, A. (2009) *Discovering Statistics Using SPSS*, 3rd edn. London, Sage. This has everything you need to know about statistics and SPSS, written in an accessible style with lots of examples. Also try his website at Planet Andy (http://www.statisticshell.com/dsus.html).

Goldacre, B. (2008) *Bad Science*. London, HarperCollins. An extremely readable, entertaining book but with a serious message.

7 | Samples and surveys

Introduction

In Chapter 5 we saw that there is no assumption about the methods to be used in any particular research design. The choice of methods should be made to ensure that the best possible information is gathered to answer the question. The next two chapters therefore discuss certain methods or tools in more detail.

This chapter specifically looks at how to improve the ways we ask people their views on topics. It is designed to help those who might want to undertake some kind of survey by introducing terms and concepts. It also provides discussion about the interpretation by researchers of surveys conducted they conduct. This is to help practitioners and others to critically evaluate such surveys.

The chapter also looks at the growing use of scales and inventories in social work and social research. While these have been devised for a variety of purposes, the chapter looks particularly at those aimed at measuring complex psychosocial phenomena such as 'self-esteem', 'attachment' and 'motivation to change'.

Asking questions

In thinking about asking questions it is necessary to consider a number of factors, such as: what to ask; who to ask; how to ask; and how to make sense of the answers.

Questions may take the form of precise, closed, pre-determined items in a questionnaire or they may involve an open-ended, unstructured interview in which the researcher merely prompts the interviewee in certain directions (in biographic-narrative research, they may simply ask someone to 'tell their own story' in respect of the research topic of interest). Obviously in the first kind of questions there is need for greater precision than in the latter.

There are numerous examples of poorly worded survey questions. This means that the information that they provide is of limited value and it is hoped that after reading this chapter you will be able to spot them. One example of a questionnaire aimed at canvassing the views of professionals attending child safeguarding conferences when family members were invited contained the following item:

> On the five-point scale below, how well did you think gender and culture were addressed by the chairperson with family members before and during the conference?
>
> | 1 | 2 | 3 | 4 | 5 |
> |---|---|---|---|---|
> | Poorly | | | | Very well |

If a respondent circled '2', this could mean four different things! To complicate matters, none of the respondents could possibly answer the part about what the chairperson did before the conference, because it involved a meeting with family member(s) that professionals did not attend!

Similarly, the following question was seen recently at London's Charing Cross station: 'Does the idea of a pension bore you to death or frighten the life out of you?' Of course, this was not intended to be an impartial, survey question: it was a deliberately biased question, aimed at persuading readers to purchase a pension scheme from a specific advertiser.

Survey and questionnaire design is thought by many to be fairly easy to do but this is not the case. Consider a topic that often appears in the media: 'Should parents be allowed to smack their children?' Now consider the complexity of 'simply' trying to find our 'How many parents actually smack their children?' Who do you ask: parents ... or the children (but, given that most smacking takes place below the age of three, this would be difficult)? What about asking the children to reflect upon their childhood experience, later as adults (i.e. were you smacked as a child)?

We will also need to establish how large the sample will need to be for us to be confident about the generalizability of the results. An additional problem with these methods is that they rely on people's honesty (and memory) about actions they may wish to deny. There are also definitional problems: what do we mean by 'smacking'. We will need to distinguish between a 'clip' and serious physical assaults, which few parents are likely to admit. We will also have to ensure not just confidentiality, but full anonymity, because identifiable offences would have to be reported to the police and/or social services. Unless we repeat the survey over a number of years it will be impossible to address a question such as 'Do parents smack their children more nowadays?' (which begs the question 'more than *when*?'). Cultural practices will need to be taken into account and we may wish to take account of gender, education, whether a parent using corporal punishment was smacked as a child etc., but questions aimed at enumerating these independent variables will be difficult to pose given the need for anonymity (the dependent variable, by the way, is 'smacking'). Finally, there are always people who, having been smacked as a child, will retort with 'Well, it never did *me* any harm'. You will already appreciate that to explore questions aimed at examining outcomes is even more complicated.

Our brief examination of this apparently straightforward research question – 'How many parents smack their children?' – was not introduced to put you off surveys; the discussion was raised to illustrate dangers, pitfalls and challenges facing the survey researcher and the difficulties of understanding the outcomes.

Clarify the nature of the research problem, objectives and key questions

We cannot stress enough how important it is for researchers to be precise about the question(s) they hope to address in the study. So often, even with experienced researchers, the actual research question is omitted or merely expressed in vague terms such as 'We were interested to find out the views of adult children about caring for a parent'. The focus needs to be crisper and clearer than this. Here is an example of what we mean:

How do three relationship factors:

- attachment organization
- perceived closeness, and
- feelings of respect

affect adult sons' and daughters' intended willingness to care for an ageing parent, if the latter became less independent?

In this example we should begin with how to specify what we mean by 'relationship factors'. For example, we might specify the following four independent variables: the 'adult children's attachment organization', the 'ageing parent's attachment organization', 'felt closeness' and 'felt respect'. The last two factors will be examined from the perspective of the adult child towards the parent, not vice versa (it is important to recognize in research that you cannot do everything). Finally, one dependent variable will be included, namely a measure of the adult child's 'willingness to care'. At this stage it is also important to ensure that constructs central to the study are operationally defined (such as 'family violence', 'abuse', 'neglect' etc.).

Having decided what to ask we now outline briefly some of the considerations in deciding who to ask.

Selecting a sample

Sampling theory is complicated but basically boils down to an articulation of the methods by which a given number of people is selected from a *target population*. The target population refers to everyone who would be theoretically eligible as a member of your study and the *sampling frame* is everyone you would invite if you had the resources to do so. It is a list of all the people you could feasibly contact. So if you wanted the views of a random sample of 100 newly qualified social workers in the UK, the target population might be 'all final year social work students in the UK', with the sampling frame comprising all final year students in (say) three universities. But how might you choose the universities to avoid possible bias when doing this?

Types of sample

One way that biases can be avoided or acknowledged within the design of the research is in the way that samples are chosen. This involves determining the sampling approach, sample size and expected response rate. There are different types of samples to choose from depending on what you want to achieve. **Probability-based sampling** uses some form of random selection, whereby every member has the possibility of being selected, each being representative of the larger population. Such a sample enables the researcher to assess possible bias and error.

Probably the most well known of these is the **simple random sample**, which can now be selected relatively quickly and easily with computer-generated random number tables (assuming that a complete list of the *target population* is available). The advantage of this kind of sample is that it is straightforward to administer and is compatible with the assumptions of many statistical tests. Another way of achieving a random sample is to divide the number of names on the list by the estimated sample size and then take every *n*th name from the list, but it is essential to *randomly pick a place to start*. This called a **systematic random sample**.

A **stratified random sample** uses subgroups of different/similar sizes in the exact proportion to those in the general population. So, in our study about 'hitting children' we would need to sample mothers, fathers, cultural group and ages of the children in exactly the same proportion as they occur in the UK. **Cluster random sampling** is similar and involves selecting a certain number of groups/areas instead of a random sample from the population. So, for example, you may wish to gain the views of all social workers in a locality but select an equal number working in 'children and families', 'mental health' and 'adults' teams. As you might expect, these methods can be combined and this is called **multi-stage sampling**. So, for example, we might first use cluster sampling, then obtain a list of names of the selected clusters and finally take a simple or systematic random sample from the clusters.

It is quite common nowadays, especially in psychosocial research, to see the use of **convenience sampling**, whereby students themselves are the research subjects (hence the word 'convenient'). This would not be appropriate if, say, 'intelligence' was being investigated. On the other hand, much research into 'attachment' is done with university (often psychology) students because, provided the samples are large enough, the main attachment organizations will be represented.

Similarly, **purposive sampling** is also now routinely used but you should be on the lookout for assumptions made in the 'results' section of research reports if generalizations are made to the wider population, because purposive samples do not permit this. Three examples of purposive sampling are: (i) **critical-case samples**, which select examples of particular importance (for example, children who have been the subject of a Serious Case Review – the procedure in the UK whereby an independent review is carried out if a child dies in suspicious circumstances or who has been subjected to serious abuse and/or neglect); (ii) **snowball sampling**, which describes the situation when one informant refers another to the researcher and is often used in research into recreational and problematic drug use; and (iii) **theory-based sampling**, in which subjects are selects who theoretically fit a particular construct (in attachment-based research it is often necessary to include each of the three main attachment styles – 'secure', 'avoidant' and 'ambivalent').

Although we will look at qualitative research in more detail in the next chapter, the idea and practicalities of sample selection are different to quantitatively based samples. Such samples are called **non-probability samples** and are used when the emphasis is on *settings*, *actors* (not the same as '*people*'), *events* and *processes*.

Sample size

The question 'how large should a sample be?' is not quite in the category of 'how long is a piece of string?' because it depends on the precise nature of the main research question. Taking account of **design sensitivity** means ensuring that an effect, if present, is detected, bearing in mind that the overall ability to discover significant differences is determined in part by the amount of variability in the dependent variable within the sample: where there is less variability, greater sensitivity is required and vice versa. This also means, as we saw in Chapter 6, that a larger sample size produces *less* variability in the dependent variable; conversely, a smaller sample, if selected carefully, produces more variability in the dependent variable. As we saw, a smaller sample can increase the 'effect size' of the results from significance testing.

This knowledge means we can be reasonably confident about the guide to sample sizes given different research designs provided in Table 7.1. Additionally, the following rules apply to quantitative surveys (http://www.testscoring.vt.edu/questionnaire_dev.html):

- For large populations, if you knew you could obtain a 100 per cent return, a random sample of 400 is usually sufficient for statistical operations. Naturally, if a 50 per cent return rate is 'expected' (but the problem is you never know!), you will need a sample of 800.
- A random sample of 132 from a population of 200 is needed to achieve the same accuracy that a random sample of 384 will provide for a population of 1 million (clearly, you might as well consider asking the whole 200 in this case). This is why general election polls are often based on what appear to be small samples.

Once the sample has been decided, decisions about the 'what' and the 'how' of gaining information have to be considered.

Table 7.1 *Table of sample size related to research design*

Type of design	Minimum sample size
Correlational	About 30 per group
Multiple regression	At least 15 per variable
Survey	100 per major group; 20–50 per subgroup
Causal-comparative	About 15 per group (whether experimental or quasi-experimantal)

Critically appraising a questionnaire

In addition to the wording of questions a researcher needs to pay attention to question sequence as well as the overall length of the questionnaire and the placing of sensitive questions. Similarly, the capacity of respondents to understand and answer the questions will need to be taken account of (age, educational background, vocabulary, prior experience in completing questionnaires etc.). Attention should be paid to the appearance of a questionnaire, not because style is more important to content, but because the accessibility of the questions in terms of size of font and ease of filling in boxes etc. makes it more likely that people will complete it.

The availability of on-line versions of questionnaires makes their completion more interesting (and easier to return to the researchers than in the past, which, of course, improves the return rate, not to mention saving postage on reminder letters). However, as has been said, this does have implications for the sample.

Types of question

In *quantitative* surveys, unless there are compelling reasons to include them, the advice is always to keep to a minimum the number of **open-ended questions** such as:

- What are your views on Internet dating?
- What do you think of UK airport security?
- Why do you think people drink Red Bull?

While these allow respondents freedom of response, the data produced is in narrative form, which can be time-consuming to complete and difficult to code, and leads to the possibility of researcher bias in interpretation during analysis. This is not to say that open questions are not important (their use is recommended in social work interviews); we are merely pointing to their pragmatic limitations in *quantitative* research.

With **closed questions**, decisions need to be made between the following types, depending on the research question(s) being explored:

- **Single answer**: 'Did you check your email this morning? (tick *Yes* __ *No* __)'.
- **Multiple answer**: asking people to tick a box to describe their level of income.
- **Rank order**: asking people to place a series of items in order of preference – but try to avoid more than five or six items.

- **Numeric**: asking people to specify how many of something, e.g. 'How many children do you have?'
- **Likert-type**: using a spaced scale – often 1–5 – to indicate, say, agreement/disagreement.

Another type of closed question is the **semantic differential**, used a lot by marketing firms in attitude measurement. A set of adjectives is devised that incorporates three dimensions:
1. Evaluative, e.g. good–bad.
2. Potency, e.g. weak–strong.
3. Activity, e.g. tense–relaxed.

For example, we might ask two members of a social work team to rate the following dichotomized adjectives on a five-point Likert scale in respect of the Director of Social Care Services:

- unfavourable–favourable;
- weak–strong;
- active–passive.

If we then found that one social worker's rating was unfavourable/weak/passive, while the other scored unfavourable/strong/active, it would be fair to assume that this measure of their attitudes would probably produce markedly different behaviour from the two people towards this senior manager.

When is comes to the wording of questions always avoid **double-barrelled** questions such as 'To what extent do you agree or disagree with the following statement: "The last social worker I met was friendly and informative"?' If the respondent scores 4 on a five-point scale (from low to high) we don't know what they mean: was the social worker 'friendly', 'informative' or both.

Response items should not make **assumptions**. For example, if we ask 'How would you feel about putting your mother in a residential home?' this assumes the respondent's mother is alive and discounts the possibility that the respondent's mother isn't already living in a residential home (this question would have been acceptable if the sample only included people with living mothers *not* living in a residential home).

Generally speaking it is prudent not to ask people questions that rely on **memory** – for example, 'What is your GSCC registration number?' – or unnecessary calculation, such as 'What proportion of your team's budget is spend on out-of-area placements?'

If potentially **difficult** or **embarrassing questions** need to be asked – such as those containing demographic questions – consider putting them at the end. Full anonymity may help to increase candour but this is not always possible or desirable.

It helps to reduce 'questionnaire boredom' by using a mixture of question formats. Don't restrict the questionnaire, for example, to Likert items only. Remember also that 'ordering effects' mean that some questions may need to be placed later in the format than others. Positive experiences tend to end up even more positively perceived by the end of a questionnaire, and vice versa with negative ones.

Finally, cast a critical eye over a questionnaire that over-uses the response option '**other**', especially if it contains lots of responses with few recorded against the forced-choice items.

Item wording

Paying attention to **vocabulary** and **grammar** is especially important when children and young people are involved. With very young children you can use 'pots and beans' – 'put one bean in the pot if you really do not agree and five if you really do' – or smiley faces to represent different positions on a Likert scale.

Ambiguity, **confusion** and **vagueness** are probably the greatest cause of questionnaire responses proving fruitless. With a questionnaire you only get one chance to ask the respondents' viewpoint; if they don't understand your question, unlike in an interview, you can't clarify it for them. For example, in 'Do you read social work journals regularly?' what does 'regularly' mean?

If we now turn to specific areas to look for when assessing the merits of a questionnaire, it is important to be aware of the pitfalls of **position bias**. In the following example the order of questions is crucial (reversing the order removes the bias):

1. How important do you think parental drug abuse is as a contributing factor in child maltreatment?
2. What factors do you think are important contributors to child maltreatment?

It might seem obvious to stress the need to avoid **emotional language** and **leading questions** – for example, 'What should be done about despicable paedophiles who threaten the safety of our children?' – but many questionnaires contain items (perhaps less obvious than this one!) that clearly betray the researcher's bias or viewpoint.

Finally, it is important to avoid the use of **negatives** (especially double-negatives). A question such as 'It is not a good idea not to undertake an assessment before implementing a plan of action' will probably lead to confusion and then impatience on the part of the respondent, both of which should be avoided.

Categories

Turning to **response categories** themselves, Likert scales are normally anchored from low to high intensity but to minimize **acquiescence effect** – the tendency for respondents to answer questions in the way they believe is 'required' – it is worth varying the polarity of responses ('high' becomes 'low') or wording the question to indicate the opposite meaning – the item 'Overall I feel happy at present' rated on an agree/disagree scale could be changed to 'Overall I feel unhappy at present'. (The effect of the reversal is then adjusted for when entering the results into SPSS, but we will not dwell on this because it is not the purpose of this book.) Similarly, if at all possible questionnaires should avoid **mid-point response categories** (simply because respondents sometimes prefer to sit on the fence).

Survey questionnaires must ensure that **Likert** or other scaling **anchors** address the full range of feeling or experience implied in the intended affect. For example, the categories moderately happy/somewhat happy/very happy leave no room for an absence of happiness (or the experience of *un*happiness).

Surveys that fail to reduce **scale point proliferation** – such as (1) Never, (2) Rarely, (3) Occasionally, (4) Fairly often, (5) Often, (6), Very often, (7) Almost always, (8) Always – will end up with confusing results.

Finally, it is advisable, if at all possible, to avoid **category proliferation** such as:

Marital status:

1) Single (never married)
2) Married
3) Widowed
4) Divorced
5) Separated

(This may not be possible, however, if the study is aimed at exploring these specific categories.)

Before we look at the growing use of scales and inventories it is worth bearing in mind that *the questions we ask are not necessarily the ones respondents are answering!* In a fascinating study, one question in an attitude survey included the following statement:

> People who have AIDS get much less sympathy from society than they ought to get.

The authors continue:

> [Our analyses] convey the general idea that the question being asked is along the lines of 'Do you agree that there is something about AIDS or AIDS victims which causes people to be less sympathetic about those with the illness than they should be?' This could be regarded as a reasonable interpretation of the question. However, about a quarter of respondents interpreted the question as 'Do people with AIDS get a fair go?' or 'Are people with AIDS victimised?'; about 10% thought the question meant 'Should people with AIDS get more sympathy?'; and the remaining 13% had a variety of interpretations, including 'Should we feel sorry for people with AIDS?', 'Do people with AIDS expect to get more sympathy?' and 'Is the AIDS issue understood by the general public?' Clearly these respondents misunderstood the intent of the question. (http://marketing-bulletin.massey.ac.nz/V5/MB_V5_A1_Gendall.pdf)

This is why piloting the questionnaire is essential, ideally by conducting interviews with a small number of respondents to ask them what was going through their mind when answering each item (in order to check out what they thought *you* meant).

The growing use of scales and inventories

There is a growing interest in the use of scales and inventories in social work practice (as distinct from research). Consider the following list of nine scales, questionnaires and inventories, which the Department of Children, Schools and Families recommends are used by social workers when undertaking core assessments as part of the Common Assessment Framework for Children and Young People:

● the Recent Life Events Questionnaire;
● the Alcohol Scale;
● the Family Activity Scale;
● the Home Conditions Scale;
● the Parenting Daily Hassle Scale;

- the Adult Well-being Scale;
- the Adolescent Well-being Scale;
- the Strengths and Difficulties Questionnaire;
- the 'Home' and 'Family' Assessments.

If we consider Robert Goodman's modified Strengths and Difficulties Questionnaire (SDQ, see http://www.sdqinfo.com/b3.html), for example, it consists of 20 items as follows:

- emotional symptoms (five items, e.g. 'Nervous and clingy in new situations');
- conduct problems (five items, e.g. 'Often has temper tantrums or hot tempers');
- hyperactivity/inattention (five items, e.g. 'Constantly fidgeting and squirming');
- peer relationship problems (five items, e.g. 'Rather solitary and tends to play alone').

(Items are scored using a three-point Likert scale: not true/somewhat true/certainly true.) Using a scoring key the four separate scales are turned into a 'total difficulties' score relatively quickly and easily (see http://www.sdqscore.net/).

There are also five prosocial behaviour items (e.g. 'Readily shares with other children'), which also produce a score. As with all scales and measures, however, there is little point in simply producing a score: it is the use that is made of the score – and the process of completing the scale – that is far more important. (Researchers can now get the items scored by visiting http://www.sdqscore.net/.)

Earlier we looked at the research question 'What relationship factors are likely to affect adult sons' and daughters' willingness to care for an ageing parent, if the latter becomes less independent?' It was also mentioned that each of the four independent variables ('adult children's attachment organization', the 'ageing parent's attachment organization', 'felt closeness' and 'felt respect'), along with the dependent variable ('willingness to care'), would be measured using existing scales, inventories and tests. This is because each variable is a 'construct': it is of a different order to seeking someone's views on (say) how much job satisfaction they feel they experience at work. Questionnaire items are more concerned with the measurement of opinions and demographic details. When working with psychosocial constructs such as 'attachment', 'self-esteem', 'felt closeness' etc. it is important to use established psychometric measures because they will have been examined from the point of view of their 'validity' (does it measure what it sets out to measure?) and 'reliability' (does it measure it accurately and consistently?).

Like most ideas in social science the notion that a researcher can use a scale to 'measure' something as complex as 'depression' is contestable. Remember that one of the most famous kinds of scales is the intelligence test, but there are still many psychologists who argue that all IQ tests do is measure a person's ability to do an IQ test and get a good score: this is not the same as claiming that the score measures the person's 'intelligence'. It is generally accepted too that the most sensitive IQ tests only tap into about a quarter of what psychologists would consider as comprising intelligence. For example, IQ tests tend not to take account of emotional intelligence: how many people do you know who are clever, but lack common sense; how about people who might not be very 'educated' but have considerable quantities of 'savvy' and are immensely street-wise and, hence, tend to cope well in situations when 'intelligence' is needed.

How do you know if you 'are' depressed (or not) by completing a depression scale? In a well developed test, we would have many questions, and we would ask hundreds of people to take the test. By analysing people's responses, we would be able to determine the composition of low, average and high scores. We now examine the principles governing the creation of sound psychometric measures.

Scale construction

The first step in the process of *scale construction* is to *operationalize* the construct. Take attachment, for example. A large number of possible statements are taken from the relevant literature. In the Close Relationships Scale (CRS), for example, 482 were found initially, which were then tuned down to 60 and then *factor analysed* to find major organizing components in order to find out the smallest number of explanatory concepts. In the CRS there were two: *attachment avoidance* and *attachment anxiety*. These were then each expressed as one of two axes to produce four quadrants, each one corresponding to the four adult attachment organizations – 'secure', 'preoccupied', 'dismissing' and 'fearful'). On this basis it is now possible to calculate someone's attachment score by asking them to complete all the scale items and then compare their score with a set of norm-referenced statistics (by looking at means and standard deviations) from the results of administering the scale to a very large sample in the past.

Here are the first five items of Experiences in Close Relationships-Revised (ECR-R), a more recent self-reported measure of attachment (considered now to be the most reliable and accurate scale).

1. I'm afraid that I will lose my partner's love.
2. I often worry that my partner will not want to stay with me.
3. I often worry that my partner doesn't really love me.
4. I worry that romantic partners won't care about me as much as I care about them.
5. I often wish that my partner's feelings for me were as strong as my feelings for him or her.

There is an on-line version (which you can complete and which gives you your own score and personalized explanation: http://www.web-research-design.net/cgi-bin/crq/crq.pl).

We have seen that it is especially important to use reliable and valid measures, but what do these terms mean?

Validity

Central to the notion of validity is whether the scale or inventory is 'capturing' what it is supposed to measure. There are various ways of doing this, the first being to investigate whether it *looks*, at first sight, both to lay people and to 'experts', as though it is likely to address the overall phenomenon of interest. In the ECR-R, the first question is 'I prefer not to show how I feel deep down'. To most people this would seem to have something centrally to do with close relationships, so it has high **face validity** (if the item had read 'I like Rice Krispies for breakfast', it would have had low face validity!).

But face validity is only the start. If possible, we need to investigate whether the scale is positively correlated with other psychometrically 'sound' measures. This is called **concurrent validity**. In our example, we would look for other measures of close relationships – typically, existing measures of adult attachment – give both measures to a large random sample and then investigate their level of association using correlation tests (see Chapter 6). Another way of doing this is to see if the scale is *negatively* correlated with psychosocial features that are known to be negatively related to close relationships. Some may be more obvious than others, so, for example, a measure of 'preference for independence' would be expected to be negatively associated with high scores on the ECR-R. Sometimes the tests used to investigate validity might be more subtle. For example, if we wanted to devise a measure of 'views on diversity' we could investigate its validity by comparing scores from a large random sample with their scores on an established test of 'conservatism' (where we would expect a negative correlation). On the other hand, if we also compared their scores on the 'diversity' test with their scores on the Marlowe–Crowne Social Desirability test – which reliably measures the tendency of individuals to project favourable images of themselves during social interaction – we would expect a positive correlation. Thus, if eating Rice Krispies for breakfast *was* (but for some reason unknown to us) correlated with preferring close relationships, then this item could have been included in the scale. We would report that it has 'high concurrent validity but low face validity'.

Reliability

At the heart of the notion of reliability is the need to ensure that, unless there is an *a priori* reason to suspect that respondents' scores will change from one 'reading' to another, they will stay reasonably constant. This is called **test–retest reliability**. Suppose we are researching grandparents' feelings of relational closeness to their grandchild(ren). We would expect this to stay relatively constant from one month or year to the next. On the other hand, if we wanted to gain an insight into memory retention, this might change between different measures, especially over longer periods of time.

If a scale is not completed by the respondent but, instead, behaviour is rated by others, we need to be able to depend upon the fact that different raters will arrive at tolerably similar scores. As you might expect, this form is called **inter-rater reliability**.

There is a third measure, known as **internal reliability**. With longer inventories and measures people tend to lose concentration and sometimes get bored (this is one reason to keep questionnaires as short as possible). Psychometric designers attempt to increase the internal consistency by using the Cronbach split-half *alpha coefficient* statistic, which simply means correlating a number of halves of the questionnaire. To do this they calculate the correlation between the first and second halves of the scale with the odd and even items, and then finally the association between the first and third quarters, and the second and fourth quarters are included to complete the calculation. A high Cronbach alpha (measured from –1 to +1, because it is a correlation coefficient) is an indication of good internal reliability – which tells researchers that if their respondents 'switch off' a little when completing the questionnaire, the results should not be affected significantly.

From this discussion, we can see that the three forms of reliability cover three different aspects: test–retest reliability focuses on *stability*, split-half internal reliability addresses *homogeneity* and inter-rater reliability tackles *equivalence*.

We now give an example of some work in preparation, which brings together many of the ideas discussed in this chapter. The main research question is:

> How do three relationship factors – attachment organization, perceived closeness and feelings of respect – affect adult sons' and daughters' intended willingness to care for an ageing parent, if the latter became less independent?

The aim of the research is to see how willing a group of middle-aged (45–65) people *believe* they would be to provide care if their ageing parent (over 70) became dependent. An obvious criticism of this study is that one of the measures – the Willingness to Care scale – involves a hypothetical situation: the adult son's/daughter's intentional state concerning what they *say* they will do if their parent became less independent. Provided, however, that this caveat is borne in mind during the design, reporting and dissemination of the results, the findings are likely to be of use to social care managers and planners, as well as to practitioners in the field of social care. We now explain the background and design by drawing on the psychometric knowledge and terminology used above. If you feel a bit rusty, it will be easy to return to an earlier paragraph in this chapter, where a particular concept that has escaped you can be revisited.

The Willingness to Care study: a brief outline of the design of a work in progress

The aim of the study is generate a *non-random convenience sample* ($n = 200$) of university students who had at least one surviving parent *and* at least one surviving grandparent (memories about deceased grandparents are not included as to do so would introduce bereavement dynamics into the research, which would then act as a *confound*). The usual justification given by attachment researchers for the use of student samples is that key attachment processes – especially what we do when separated from and reunited with attachment figures – are 'universal', in that they operate relatively independently of occupation and, in most respects, age. Gender and culture, however, do affect attachment processes and, hence, the sample needs to be *stratified* and *cross-sectional* to take account of diverse demographic features. You will notice, however, that the students are not involved directly in the study: they are simply the conduit through which the instruments are conveyed to their parents and grandparents.

We want to examine three relationship factors: *attachment organization* (parent and grandparent), *perceived closeness* and *feelings of respect*. As we saw in the previous chapter, these are our *independent variables*. Our research question indicates that we are interested in examining the relationship between these four IVs and our dependent variable 'willingness to care'. We consider each of our measures in term.

Each of the four scales used has high published internal reliability (Cronbach's alpha) and test–retest reliability, as well as sound concurrent validity.

IV1 Attachment organization

In terms of attachment organization we want to investigate the bi-directional nature of the relationship: we are interested in the way the adult son/daughter is attached to their parent(s) as well as how the parent attaches to their son/daughter. We used the ECR-R for this purpose but had to modify items to take account of the following combinations:

● father about grandfather and grandmother;
● mother about own father and mother;
● grandmother about son and daughter;
● grandfather about son and daughter.

Here are the first five items of the 'Student's Mother-to-Own Mother' (i.e. 'Student's Grandmother') version (research design often gets this complicated).

The ECR-Revised: Experiences in Close Relationships Questionnaire (Fraley *et al.*, 2000) contains 36 items on two attachment dimensions: 18 on 'avoidance' and 18 on 'anxiety', which participants are asked to rate on a seven-point Likert scale.

Please circle the number that best summarizes your view.

1. I prefer not to show my mother how I feel deep down.

Disagree strongly   1   2   3   4   5   6   7   Agree strongly

2. I worry about being abandoned.

Disagree strongly   1   2   3   4   5   6   7   Agree strongly

> 3. I am very comfortable being close to my mother.
>
> Disagree strongly   1   2   3   4   5   6   7   Agree strongly
>
> 4. I worry a lot about my relationship to my mother.
>
> Disagree strongly   1   2   3   4   5   6   7   Agree strongly
>
> 5. Just when my mother starts to get close to me I start pulling away.
>
> Disagree strongly   1   2   3   4   5   6   7   Agree strongly

IV2 Perceived closeness

Here we asked both parties – adult children and their parents – to complete the ISOS: Inclusion of Self in the Other Scale (Aron *et al.*, 1991). This measure of perceived closeness uses an unconventional technique that nevertheless possesses sound psychometric properties. The respondent is presented with seven Venn diagrams, and asked to pick the one that best captures how close they feel to the other person. (This scale has high *concurrent validity* with other measures, so it can be used safely as an alternative; it is also commented upon favourably by participants as 'being more fun' to complete than a 'standard' scale or inventory.) The rubric is shown in Figure 7.1.

IV3 Respect

Moving back to a more familiar scale layout, all participants are now asked to complete the RfPS: Respect for Partner Scale (Frei and Shaver, 2002). It has 20 items on a seven-point Likert scale and here are the first five items of the 'Father to Grandmother' version:

> With the statements that follow, please indicate your level of agreement or disagreement.
>
> 1. My mother shows interest in me, has a positive attitude, is willing to spend time with me.
>
> Disagree strongly   1   2   3   4   5   6   7   Agree strongly

'With each of the pairs of circles below, one represents *YOU*, and the other represents your *MOTHER*. Please select which pair best "captures" how close you feel your relationship is with her *now*'.

PLEASE CIRCLE YOUR CHOICE: A   B   C   D   E   F   G

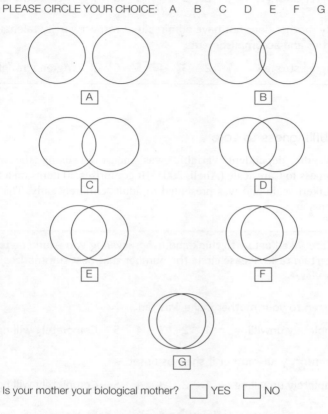

Is your mother your biological mother?   ☐ YES   ☐ NO

Figure 7.1   Example: inclusion of self in the other scale

2. My mother does not respect my views and opinions and insists on her own wishes.

Disagree strongly   1   2   3   4   5   6   7   Agree strongly

3. My mother is helpful, supportive, present when needed and tries to fulfil my needs.

Disagree strongly   1   2   3   4   5   6   7   Agree strongly

4. My mother is sensitive and considerate to my feelings.

Disagree strongly   1 2 3 4 5 6 7   Agree strongly

5. My mother does not have admirable or respectworthy talents, abilities and accomplishments

Disagree strongly   1 2 3 4 5 6 7   Agree strongly

DV1 Willingness to Care

Finally, the dependent variable was measured using the WtC: Willingness to Care scale (Abell, 2001). It comprises 30 items on a five-point Likert scale and was presented to adult 'children' only. The first five items are:

You are asked below to think about *how willing you would be* to do certain tasks. Please circle the number that best summarizes your view.

1. Listen to your mother if she was sad.

Completely unwilling   1 2 3 4 5   Completely willing

2. Comfort your mother if she was upset.

Completely unwilling   1 2 3 4 5   Completely willing

3. Help your mother deal with anxiety about the future.

Completely unwilling   1 2 3 4 5   Completely willing

4. Hold your mother's hand if she was afraid.

Completely unwilling   1 2 3 4 5   Completely willing

5. Encourage your mother if she felt hopeless.

Completely unwilling   1 2 3 4 5   Completely willing

Proposed analysis

It is always important to think about the nature of the analysis to be performed when designing a research survey. This point may seem obvious but it is surprising the number of researchers who, having collected the data, then ask 'What kind of statistics or graphical representation is best to address my research question?'

In our Willingness to Care design we plan to use two relatively recent analytic procedures. The first is called *dyadic data analysis* using a procedure called *actor–partner interdependence method* (APIM). It is particularly relevant to social work because it treats *aspects of the relationship between two people as the independent variable*. We need to return to some ideas from Chapter 6 to explain this.

Suppose you want to look at the level of closeness between two people – as we are in the 'Willingness to Care'. As we have seen above, we propose using the RfPS: Respect for Partner Scale. We will end up with a score from 1 to 7 for the sample of sons/daughters and a score for their parent. In most statistical analytic procedures we then calculate means and standard deviations across each sample. Inevitably, we will find differences, so we the use an appropriate test of significance (e.g. the '*t*' test, the '*F*' test, ANOVA). But the results we obtain are always restricted to the *group* of adult 'children' and the *group* of their parents. What dyadic data analysis (DDA) enables us to do is make comparisons about *each separate family pair*. Taking a simple example, suppose the results of three son/mother pairs are as follows:

RfPS SCORE

	SON	MOTHER
Pair 1	5.3	3.4
Pair 2	3.8	5.3
Pair 3	4.2	5.9

Dyadic data analysis treats the differences (respectively +1.9, −1.5 and −1.7) as the independent variable (you might be wondering why this needed a new statistical programme but this is because it is actually more complicated than this). This enables a much more congruent 'fit' to be made with actual relationships than aggregating scores across the sample; more accurate 'real-life' connections, associations and differences can be made because the data now refer to what actually happens between the *specific individuals* concerned. As before, the dependent variable is the Willingness to Care score, and, using APIM, the analyses will be comparing the difference between each pair against each individual's WtC score.

Conclusion

This 'work in progress' has illustrated some of the key concepts articulated earlier in the chapter. We have stressed throughout that samples and surveys are only appropriate methods to explore certain types of research questions, namely those aimed at quantifying responses, attitudes and behaviour. Many of the examples are drawn from psychology and/or research undertaken in the USA. This is because the use of social scales to quantify and/or catalogue attitudes and behaviour has not really developed in UK social work (apart from in the field of criminal justice: see McNeill *et al.*, 2009). However, with more emphasis on 'evidence' for practice globally and with work in the USA on the development of what are known as 'intervention studies', it is likely that the use of such scales in all aspects of social work practice will increase. It is therefore important that social work researchers engage with such research to ensure the scales that are devised reflect social work values and to provide an informed critique of the methodological developments.

In the next chapter we explore methods that are more usually associated with qualitative approaches and that give different kinds of information when addressing research questions and therefore inform practice in different ways.

---

putting it into practice

Find two or three questionnaires from the web and print them out (try to avoid a very well known survey or marketing organization such as MORI).

- Use the checklists earlier on pages 00–00 to critique the design of the questionnaire as well as the item wording.
- How could you improve on them?

Now find two articles in a peer-reviewed journal such as the *British Journal of Social Work, Health and Social Care in the Community, Child and Family Social Work* etc. – one of which has used a survey questionnaire (designed by the author(s)) and the other of which has included a scale or inventory.

> ● From what you have read in this chapter, reflect on the extent to which the usage of these research instruments conforms to our good practice guidelines.
>
> Finally, find a study that has taken a sample of service users and reflect upon the following questions:
>
> ● How explicit was the sampling method?
> ● Was the sample size and composition adequate for the study?
> ● Were the claims made in the conclusions warranted from the sampling method?

Recommended reading

Bradburn, N.M., Sudman, S. and Wansink, B. (2004) *Asking Questions: The Definitive Guide to Questionnaire Design*. Chichester, Wiley. A clear and practically based text.

Groves, R. M. *et al.* (2004) *Survey Methodology* (Wiley Series in Survey Methodology). Chichester, Wiley. A thorough-in-depth and comprehensive textbook.

8 | Talk and discourse

Introduction

In this chapter we continue to look at different methods in greater detail to give a sense of the rigour needed to produce a useful research base for social work practice and to help practitioners, managers and service users to be discerning about the research with which they come into contact. We have arrived at the point where we focus on what are loosely called 'qualitative methods'. This term covers a range of different approaches including grounded theory, discourse analysis, narrative analysis and conversation analysis, as well as ethnographic, biographic and visual sociological methods. In the space available we concentrate on two frequently used qualitative methods: grounded theory and discourse analysis. As with the previous two chapters we are not attempting to show how to use these methods but explore examples to help you to appraise critically qualitative research studies.

These examples illustrate how certain approaches to data collection are 'qualitatively' different. As was discussed in Chapter 5 they are used to explore the question 'why?' and to provide rich data to add dimensions to understandings of social situations and/or interventions over and beyond the descriptions provided by quantitative approaches.

It is because of this emphasis on communication and relationships that these approaches are often thought to be more relevant to research for social work; it is argued that they explore the complexity of social life, concentrating on process rather than essence. As was discussed in the first part of this book the distinctiveness of social work research is because of its interest in encounters and the process of encounters: between individuals; between individuals in groups and families; and between individuals and professionals.

Context

Let us return to our discussion on Emile Durkheim's insights about 'suicide rates'. We were left in Chapter 6 with a question as to whether he had actually discovered key social and cultural reasons to explain marked differences in rates between comparable nations. Following Durkheim's analysis Douglas (1967) devised ingenious ways of exploring suicide by studying coroners' reports using qualitative methods. By doing so, he raised questions about 'rates of suicide', which, he argued, relied heavily on the *judgements of coroners* to determine the classification of a death. He discovered that suicide was not a 'fact', merely a reflection of coroners' values and interpretations of *some* of the biographical details preceding or surrounding the event of the death. For example, one coroner's report referred to the biography of the deceased, in which a (supposed and assumed) crucial factor was described thus: 'there's a classic pattern for you: broken home, escape to the services, nervous breakdown, unsettled at work, no family ties – what could be clearer?'

It is worth noting that in undertaking this analysis Douglas (1967) used as 'informants' not people, but their written reports. This is partly because of the difficulties of obtaining first hand reports of motivation for suicide. However, written material – for example, court reports or social workers' records – are an important, but different, source of information about issues and situations in which social work is involved. It is just as important as interviews in providing insights and more in-depth description of situations, people's actions and different perspectives on these. For this reason the study of narrative in social work research is a developing area (see Hall, 1999).

So, to return to the coroners' documents, it is highly likely that a large number of actual suicides are not recorded because they don't conform to such a 'classic pattern': some people commit suicide by driving their car into an object (such as another car) to cause their own death but to create the illusion of an accident, thus sparing family and close relatives the guilt of not responding to the deceased's cries for help. To confuse matters further, another potential source of documentary evidence, suicide notes, were the exception rather than the rule, and even when they do exist, they may not provide a reliable indication of motive. Unless, therefore, there is unequivocal evidence that a person did indeed take their own life, the notion of a 'suicide' could well exist only in the individual and collective minds of coroners, and it is therefore the product of complex social, historical and cultural processes.

Douglas (1967) was exploring 'beyond' – or 'beneath' – the numeric data to find out what might be 'going on'. Like Durkheim he was asking the 'why' question of the data provided by the quantitative descriptions, but using different methods. He concluded that the basis of Durkheim's claims was flawed because, ultimately, there was no such thing as a 'suicide rate'. For him 'suicide' could only be studied with reference to the experiences of those involved – friends, relatives, loved ones, coroners – and, of course, the deceased person's accounts would reveal far more than 'numbers of deaths per thousand' across different countries. The question is, in terms of the different sources of data, whether this 'simply' results in a collection of individual, personalized and poignant accounts, but without any potential for generalization beyond the particular group in question.

Developing qualitatively derived 'abstracted common attributes'

All methods embody one key feature: they seek to find 'abstracted common attributes' from people immersed in the phenomenon of interest; they aim to find 'resemblances', 'typicalities', 'uniformities' and 'regularities' within and between accounts. If this is sounding overly theoretical, an example should help.

Some years ago June Thoburn (a Professor of Social Work) was studying how adoptive parents who had their own birth children treated their adopted children. One of the mothers said that she knew her adoptive son was truly part of the family when she started to 'lick his spoon' when feeding him. She went on to describe how this turning point had occurred unconsciously, without thought or premeditation. This notion of 'licking the spoon' of another person usually resonates with most people (whether or not they have children) as striking at the heart of what it is to be intimate and close to another human being. It is unlikely, for example, that we would 'lick the spoon' of a baby we didn't know well or to whom we were not related. What is noticeable about this powerful example is that the epistemological status (remember: the basis of a 'truth claim') of the concept of 'licking the spoon' does not depend on the number of people who refer to such an abstracted idea. It does not rely upon any level of quantification; it was not obtained by surveying a large number of people and then calculating the average number of people agreeing with a suitable worded statement (as we saw in the previous chapter). Indeed, it is doubtful whether the notion of 'licking the spoon' would have occurred to a researcher designing and piloting a survey questionnaire. It is therefore an excellent example of the kind of knowledge that is held by people who are in actual situations that are being researched and highlights the challenge for social work research to use and develop methods to try to access this knowledge.

Intensive or 'depth' interviewing can reveal such ideas when people are encouraged to 'tell their story'. Other methods that are used in social work research to enable people to tell stories include focus and other kinds of group discussions. Researchers are also developing methods that include the use of writing, art and photography to help people describe their situations or their feelings.

Emerging concepts and constructs, such as 'licking the spoon', then raise other questions, which may not necessarily have been explored by in formal interviews, such as 'Do people who are related by birth always want to "lick the spoon"?' 'Can these feelings be reversed, for example if the parent becomes dependent later in life?' 'Do we always tend to "lick the spoon" of *anyone* whom we grow to like and love, or do they need to be biologically related in some way?' 'Does the idea of "licking the spoon" happen naturally or does it need to be "worked at" (and, if so, what might accelerate the process)?' Thus, what people say can lead to a series of mind-maps or 'thought experiments', which the researcher may decide to pursue in more depth in subsequent interviews (or different methods to help people express themselves) or simply reflect upon theoretically in subsequent analysis.

Encouraging 'talk'

It is rare, however, for such concepts to 'jump out' like this, to be handed to the researcher on a plate, so to speak. One method of developing concepts from interviews is 'grounded theory' (see Glaser and Strauss, 1967). Grounded theory, as process, is 'inductively derived . . . it is discovered, developed, and provisionally verified through systematic data collection and analysis. . . . One does not begin with a theory, then prove it. Rather, one begins with an area of study and what is relevant to that area is allowed to emerge' (Strauss and Corbin, 1990, p. 23).

Data is often obtained from interviews or, as they are more likely to be called – and, more appropriately, perhaps – 'guided conversations' (Rubin and Rubin, 1995). The key difference between an 'interview' and a 'guided conversation' is that the latter is more concerned than the former with encouraging the interviewee to talk at considerable length about aspects of the topic that the researcher is interested in exploring (hence the term 'guided' conversation). Good interviewing 'technique' avoids 'Why . . . ?' questions in favour of 'What . . . ?' or 'What happened next . . . ?' questions.

For the purposes of research the interviews or conversations are usually recorded so that the meanings of the words, the silences and the intonations can be studied. This is usually done by writing up the data on the tape as a 'transcript'. This encourages what the philosopher Gilbert Ryle (1990) termed 'thick description', the preferred form of an eventual transcript, because it enables a researcher to work on the text in ways we shall examine. It is relatively easy to see whether this has been achieved in practice by examining a transcript: if the interviewer's text is, overall, taking up more than 5–10 per cent of the space, something has gone wrong!

Although 'interviewing' is the primary vehicle for data collection in qualitative research, texts, documents and 'naturally occurring talk' can also be the medium. For example, you can try your hand at looking for themes within the personal columns in a newspaper or periodical. What do people decide to mention about themselves? What do they stress? Are there discernable gender differences?

Returning to data generated from interviews, let us consider an example, deliberately chosen as an emotive area for study: suppose we wanted to explore birth mothers' experiences of losing their child to the care system, and specifically their views on the way they were treated by the social worker. It would not reveal very much to ask a question such as 'What did you think about the way you were treated by the social worker?' ('How did you feel . . . ?' would probably be even less effective at getting the person to talk about the very thing you are actually interested in, namely their 'feelings'). A more productive approach would be to ask them to recall where they were in the house when the social worker arrived and then ask 'Can you describe what happened next?' and, depending on what they say, 'What happened after that?' Generally speaking, asking 'What went through your mind?' is preferable to 'How did you feel?' as it tends to produce more by way of 'talk' about the topic from the person involved in the research, which, we should not forget, is the main purpose of qualitative interviewing.

Virtually all qualitative analytic techniques are aimed at moving beyond the mere description and/or reorganization of quotes, placed under headings that have been selected by the researcher *before* the study has been undertaken. Unfortunately, 'cherry-picking' the tapes and transcripts, merely to find quotes to place under prearranged themes, along the lines of 'Person A put it this way . . . whereas Person B expressed it thus . . .', is rather too typical of some qualitative research.

Grounded theory as an analytic method

So how does the use of analytic methods help to overcome this tendency? One approach is called 'line-by-line' coding, the aim of which is to generate conceptual categories that go beyond the actual words used by the interviewee. This is vital because simply to use the words of the interviewee is unlikely to take the analytic process very far.

Broadly speaking the 'technique' is to think of a noun to describe as accurately as possible, and without any predetermined standpoint, *what* is 'going on', and then to decide on one or two adjectives that capture as accurately as possible the *way* it is 'going on'. So, for example, if in the course of describing how they feel about having an illness someone says:

One day it's this tablet and the next day the pain moves somewhere else and it's like people think you are a hypochondriac.

A researcher might code this as

Interpreting images of self given by others.

You might like to reflect upon the extent to which this process is similar to processes in social work. Because the researcher is forced to 'get under the skin' of the interviewee, to see things from *their* perspective, they are using a form of empathy. This technique is sometimes used in supervising practice when a supervisor might try to identify what is going on for a student in a given situation.

It is not always necessary to use 'line-by-line' coding. Sometimes the researcher may wish to take a whole paragraph (or more) as a unit of analysis, called 'open coping'. Consider another example, taken this time from a study into later life filial attachments (see Shemmings, 2006). The participant is talking about the way in which she 're-stories' her past in order to make it seem more acceptable (i.e. less painful) to her. At the end of the excerpt below, it could be argued that she uses the re-storying tactic within the interview itself:

When growing up I was often unhappy but I would tell myself that 'life was idyllic'. I wanted to say 'as far as childhood goes it was really very nice'. And we *did* have a very nice house overlooking the beach . . . and lots of friends, lots of company, lots of goings-on in all directions, so it *was* really nice, in a way . . . wasn't it?

Using the method outlined above this excerpt was coded '*Conscious positive reframing*'. It could have been labelled '*Deliberate optimistic retelling'* – or indeed with any other combination of words provided by a good Thesaurus – but the meaning should be (virtually) the same, whatever code is used. Notice that to have coded the above extract as *'life was idyllic'* or *'had lots of friends'* would have achieved little more than a paraphrase of the original text. It is important to stress here that *'conscious positive reframing'* is not an interpretation: it is simply an accurate depiction of what is 'going on'. Later, the researcher may wish to interpret the concepts from a particular perspective (e.g. feminist theory, Marxist theory, attachment theory) or even develop new 'middle-range' theory around the phenomenon of interest, but during early coding it is important to 'stay close to the talk'. This should be the case whatever method of qualitative research is used.

The purpose of these analytic methods is to move towards a conceptually 'higher' level of conceptualization (sometimes called 'axial coding'). Think of the first levels – what we considered in the above 'line by line' example – as 'bananas', 'apples', 'pears' etc. At the next level of abstraction we might arrive at 'fruit' as a unifying construct. En route we may encounter examples that don't easily fit the emerging category, such as a 'tomato' – is it a fruit, or a vegetable, or is it salad? – which may necessitate refining the category or the creation of a new one. Using our 'fruit' example, the researcher may go on to derive other abstracted concepts, such as 'food' or 'nourishment' and so on. As consumers of research, you should find it helpful to distinguish in the write-up between informative and illuminating qualitative research and the merely representational through the existence of such conceptual analysis.

As soon as categories begin to emerge, researchers usually articulate them using a process known as 'memoing', whereby the underlying meaning behind a concept is described and explicated. Memos eventually form part of the write-up (typically a report, an article, a chapter of a book or a thesis). Here is an example using the code 'Deliberate optimistic retelling'.

Deliberate optimistic retelling

(Date and time of interview)

Brief description

- Idea that the explanation is that, when reflecting on their early childhood memories, some adults include accounts which suggest that they are telling the story in such a way as to think

about it and present it in a more positive light than it may
have been experienced at the time (and possibly in the present
too)

Location of examples

- Interview 5: line 14
- Interview12: lines 27–28

Software (such as NVivo) make this analysis a lot more manageable
nowadays but, as you will no doubt appreciate, qualitative research is an
immensely time-consuming, intellectually taxing, absorbing and fascinating process, and is not in any respect a soft option compared to quantitative research. Researchers who have experience of both approaches
often say that quantitative approaches are 'easier' than qualitative
methods. It is probably more accurate to conclude, however, that the
design of a quantitative study is complex whereas the data *analysis*,
especially when using SPSS, is relatively straightforward, in the sense
of it being predetermined. On the other hand, the *interview stage* in
qualitative research is usually more straightforward than the analysis
stage, which, as we have seen, is often intricate and dense (but usually
engrossing!).

The sheer practicalities of undertaking qualitative research need to be
factored into the design. Furthermore, 50 interviews of around an hour
each would be likely to generate verbatim transcripts of over 400,000
words, i.e. about four averaged sized novels; a prospect not for the faint-
hearted, clearly! Some types of transcription take considerably longer
because they involve recording the length of pauses, two or more people
speaking at the same time, as well as conveying the stresses and other
paralinguistic features of 'talk'.

In Chapter 7 we considered the idea of 'appropriate sample sizes' in
quantitative research. Is the same consideration possible (or necessary)
in qualitative research: can we say how large a sample should be?
Provided the interviewees are fully immersed in the phenomenon in
question, a 'rule of thumb' guide is that around 25–30 people are likely
to lead to what is called 'theoretical saturation' (i.e. the point beyond
which another interview is unlikely to add much by way of new codes
and categories). Even at this point it is important to engage in 'theoretical sampling', by which is meant the deliberate selection of interviewees
thought likely to represent 'unusual' or minority views (interestingly, in

quantitative research these are referred to as 'outliers' and need to be avoided!). For example, we might be interested in research to seek the views of parents who, when separating or divorcing, refuse to see their children. We decide to select a broadly equal sample of 20 mothers and 20 fathers. What we may well find is that none of the mothers refuse, whereas some of the fathers do. In quantitative research (if the sample had been selected randomly and had been considerably larger) the actual differences would be subjected to significance testing, but in qualitative research such differences are non-generalizable, due to small sample size and selection bias. (As an aside, one way to spot 'poor' qualitative research is to look for the use of *quantitative* metaphors such as 'more than half the sample', or 'a significant proportion said X': such notions are inappropriate in a qualitative study). In the situation when there is an 'absence of viewpoint' it is important that the qualitative researcher deliberately seeks out someone who will express such a perspective: in the separation/divorce study, we need to find a mother who *doesn't* visit or see her child.

Discourse analysis

Grounded theory is a qualitative analytic method that concentrates upon the *content* of 'talk'. A different approach is *discourse analysis*, which focuses more exclusively on the way language is *used*, often subconsciously, to convey messages that may appear 'hidden' within the text.

Discourse analysis can involve the analysis of both text and language. It is a qualitative analytic method predicated upon the notion that language use is 'designed not merely to *represent* the world, but to do specific tasks *in* the world' (Wooffitt, 1993, p. 297). Narrative analysis is a specific aspect of discourse analysis that focuses on a particular form of communication: story telling. Social work researchers have been accused of treating all communication as narrative but Riessman and Quinney (2005) warn against this. In their review of narrative research they provide exemplars of how rigorous narrative inquiry can provide new knowledge for practice. For them, rigour involves: systematic observations; attention to sequence and consequence; analysis based on transcription; and attention to epistemological and methodological issues.

Discourse analysis stresses that, while it may be an unconscious activity, language usage is active and performative, never passive. Consequently, speech is considered to be non-haphazard, designed to accomplish specific tasks. Speech, in other words, is a cipher of personal but possibly unacknowledged meaning. In this fashion, Wooffitt (1993) asserts that '. . . any description or reference is produced from a potentially inexhaustible list of possible utterances, each of which is "logically" correct or true. So when we pose the analytic question "why this specific description?" we need also to ask "what *tacit practical reasoning* informs the design of this specific description?"' (original emphasis, p. 297).

Because language both structures and is a vehicle for socialization, a research interview obtained in the form of a guided conversation is a 'place where culture and "the social" happen . . . in which social organisation is accomplished in talk' (Wetherell, 1998, p. 391). The study of participants' discourse and their preferred linguistic repertoires, through which metaphors and figures of speech reflect specific attitudes, offers insights into the ways in which events and beliefs are organized to construct particular versions of the world. Unlike grounded theory as a qualitative data analytic method, in discourse analysis the content of the tapes is of much less importance than the manner in which language is used.

To illustrate this practice, we refer to Wooffitt's (1993) example of discourse analysis from research into a young person's account of 'violent incidents' at a rock concert. A key excerpt contains the phrase 'after one or two wee scraps' to describe the behaviour of the group with which the interviewee was affiliated. It continues,

> of all the ways which could be used to describe what happened – 'fighting', 'violence', 'a punch-up' – the word 'scrap' clearly minimises the seriousness of the incident. Indeed 'scrap' evokes images of schoolboy tussles in the playground. (Wooffitt, 1993, p. 297)

Similarly, the use of the phrase 'one or two, provides the most minimal characterisation of "more than one"' (p. 298). Wooffitt also notes, first, that the speaker does not say 'one' or 'two' but 'one or two', thus indicating that he does not know the precise number, and, second, this also suggests that the display of 'not knowing marks the precise number as not *requiring* clarification' (p. 298). Wooffitt concludes thus:

> So, although the speaker does reveal that indeed there were some violent incidents at the concert, he does so in such a way as to portray the more than one incidents as minimally as possible, while at the same time registering the relative insignificance of these events. (p. 298)

We now illustrate the use of discourse analysis by focusing on the actual transcribed tapes.

An example of discourse analysis: self-efficacy talk among looked-after children

This project was interested in discovering ways in which the young people used metaphor, figures of speech and other devices as part of their linguistic repertoire when they spoke about 'self-efficacy'. (The research was conducted by Steve Walker (1999) for a postgraduate thesis in social work.) Given the focus on the young person's sense of self-efficacy, extracts were selected for analysis if they included such discourse. Interestingly, nearly half (44 per cent) the total length of the 49 tapes contained 'self-efficacy talk'.

The young people interviewed used language that indicated they felt some events in their lives were the result of fate or other people's actions, while some occurred as a more direct result of their own influence. But we noticed that they often recalled such events using a markedly *active* mode of expression. An *inactive* or passive mode might have included silence or minimal interaction – 'I don't know' or 'I don't care' – but after listening to the tapes we were struck by the considerable efforts made by the young people to regain some control *with the listener*. Although they may not have experienced feelings of self-efficacy when trying to exert control over important decisions in their lives, in the interview itself they regularly used metaphors and linguistic repertoires containing 'self-efficacy talk'. Consider the following example, about the timing of a 'Looked after children' review:

> They say 'If it's convenient to you' and I say 'I've got football training that day'. They then say 'Oh well, you'll have to miss it' . . . but they say 'Is it convenient?

In this example, the use of *reported speech* brings *temporal immediacy* and the preference of the *present over the past tense*, evident in using 'say' (four times) instead of 'said', transports the event into the 'here and now'. These linguistic devices can be seen as enabling this young person to offset his felt lack of efficacy in the actual encounter by subsequently having an impact on the interviewer. Further, by appealing to the interviewer's (presumed) sense of fairness, the speaker deploys some of the dramatic techniques of a prosecutor's summing up speech to a jury. The interviewer is thus recruited into the conversational equivalent of a courtroom drama. Now consider the young person's deployment of a familiar technique, often used by public speakers, of constructing arguments in *three-part lists*: 'If it's convenient' . . . 'I've got football training' . . . 'Then you'll have to miss it'. The effect felt like the lead-up to the punch-line of a joke and, as Wooffitt (1993) reminds us, these structures are regularly followed by applause when used by politicians. In discourse analysis, the grouping of ideas in threes is sometimes referred to as *occasioned co-class membership* (see Wooffitt, 1993), the word 'occasioned' used to stress that these devices are intentioned (however unconsciously).

Placing ideas in three-part lists 'conveys the general class of object to which the speaker's activity has been directed' (Wooffitt, 1993, p. 299). Thus the young person is not just talking here about 'convenience': he is conveying subtextually his thoughts about fairness and unfairness. The word 'convenience' returns, however, in the final '. . . but they say "Is it convenient?"' Its effect is to lasso the listener back to the opening gambit, but it is noticeable that, now, the original statement is reframed as a question, a far more powerful way of drawing attention to the irony of the interchange. The extract represents a quite sophisticated effort to regain efficacy from an earlier situation during which it had, arguably, *not* been experienced by the young person.

Additional linguistic devices are deployed in the next extract:

> Now actually if I've got something to say, I say 'Oh b . . . r what's socially acceptable, excuse me but this is my f . . . ing review here so will you just shut the f . . . up'. Now that does tend to raise a few eyebrows, but it works. It may not be very nice but it works and I must say I do try being civil first; I'm only uncivil if civility doesn't work.

Here we see the same use of reported speech to achieve the effect of temporal immediacy, but this time the discourse is infused with what Timor and Landau (1998) refer to as a *mixture of sociolects*, in this case the 'civil' and the 'uncivil'. But we are not just told by the speaker about the difference, we are treated to a first-hand example of the *un*civil discourse, rendered powerfully in an *un*civil manner by the speaker. This sophisticated organization of what, at first sight, might appear merely as descriptive sequences is accomplishing a considerable amount of 'work' for the speaker to achieve the specific social product of persuading listeners to comprehend how he is (re?)discovering the experience of self-efficacy. The speaker even manages to conjoin the two sociolects – civility and incivility – into the single phrase 'Excuse me, but this is my f . . . ing review'. By combining a discourse marker of civility – i.e. politeness – with a discourse marker of incivility – i.e. swearing – the young person uses irony in a similar way to that deployed in the first example.

He uses another linguistic device, namely that of deploying *dismembered physical attributes* – 'people' become 'eyebrows' – when he says

'Now that does raise a few eyebrows, but it works.' This illustrates how he decides to treat his audience as a 'group' in order to get them to listen. A sign that he may be learning to trust his own ability to make others listen is evident in his deployment of the phrase 'but it works', twice in a short space.

Both examples also illustrate the use of *paired contrasts* to accomplish performative tasks, but the next extract demonstrates the same device more directly. Asked in the interview how she makes decisions – choice of placement, contact with her parents etc. – one young person replied, in a manner suggesting some irritation with the interviewer,

> Look, I don't know. How did I decide what to wear TODAY? I don't know! I **don't know** (shouting)!

The first half of the paired contrast illustrates how she juxtaposes the apparently straightforward notion of deciding what to wear with more complex decisions about the future, the effect of which is aimed at gaining and holding the attention of the other person. The second half of the paired contrast comes soon afterwards: when asked about the degree of choice she had experienced in a recent placement with new foster carers, she said:

> I didn't **decide** that I wanted to go, I just thought I'd give it a chance.

It is easy to dismiss this as evidence of passivity and a *lack* of self-efficacy, but it is also possible to hear this as a deliberate and active, albeit pragmatic, approach to decision-making. Only a more detailed knowledge of this particular young person would clarify this point. Thus care is needed when interpreting the use of active and passive speech modes with short extracts, as it not always clear what the speaker intends.

In discourse analysis, *extreme case formulations* (Pomerantz, 1986) – such as 'never', 'brand new', 'nobody', 'completely innocent' – 'serve to portray the maximum (or minimum) character of the object, quality or state of affairs to which they refer' (Wooffitt, 1993, p. 298). What purpose do they suggest? In the following example, the term 'really big question' is used to point out to the interviewer the inappropriateness of asking such an important question in a large, formal meeting.

> You was about 11 weren't you (*name of brother*)? . . . and I was about 9? And there was all those people there and they put all this pressure on you and they are looking at you with all these eyes and they're just asking you this really big question and expecting you to answer it there and then. I mean like some

of those questions you need to answer by yourself or sometimes me and
(*name of brother*) speak about them in bed when we're not allowed!

The phrases 'all those people', 'all this pressure', 'all those eyes' and
'really big question' are examples of *extreme case formulations*, and can
be 'heard' as pointing strongly to things that matter considerably to the
speaker.

In the next extract, the need to have an impact and make a difference,
albeit with nearly tragic consequences, is clear both from the content
itself and from the use of a number of linguistic devices:

> Yeah, she said, 'Give it a couple of days, see how you feel, get yourself settled
> in and see how it goes'. Well, after a couple of days I hated it even more so I
> phoned her up and said 'I want to move'. She said 'Well you can't move just
> like that; we'll try and make it work'. So I said 'I can't, so there'. Anyway, I
> took a couple of overdoses there, and she eventually moved me after a month.

Here again we have the familiar rhythmic sequence of occasioned co-
class membership – 'see how you feel, get yourself settled in and see
how it goes' – but one of the potent consequences of using reported
speech here is to claim authenticity: this is what the social worker *actually said*, so it is less amenable to challenge. Because it is not possible to
verify whether the other person *did* use these words, the use of reported
speech is a powerful way for the young person to increase self-efficacy.
The version as stated becomes *her* version. Whether the young person's
veridical account of what the social worker said is accurate is not of
concern here; instead, 'we are interested in the descriptive resources that
are used to construct this version, and to sketch what dynamic and func-
tional properties this function has' (Wooffitt, 1993, p. 297).

What specific discourse accomplishments might be intended in the
above excerpt? She seems to want the listener to agree that, by expect-
ing her to stay in a place where she was unhappy, the social worker was
being unreasonable. She then strongly contests the idea that she can
'grow' into a new placement; for her, first impressions count for more,
and she wants to be able to act upon them quickly. She also betrays a
certain impatience with her social worker for being disingenuous by the
way she introduces the phrase 'a couple of days'. Most people would see
the term 'a couple of days' as meaning an 'insignificant amount of time'.
So when she uses the 'actual', reported speech of the social worker –
'Give it a couple of days' – the discourse conveys the message that, if the
young person does not feel comfortable after a very short period of time,
she will be found somewhere else to live. By using the *repeated phrase*

'a couple of days' – in 'Well, after a couple of days I hated it even more' – she expresses her frustration that when she asked the worker to honour her promise, the worker's response was to change the meaning of 'a couple of days' by extending the time period considerably. This use of *linguistic symmetry* enables her to use paired contrasts to expose, as she sees it, the way in which language can be used by those with power to mean what they want, when it suits them. Tragically, she reminds the listener that she too has power; the power to threaten to (or actually to) take her own life. Perhaps it is not too fanciful to suggest that she reintroduces the word 'couple' in the phrase 'Anyway I took a couple of overdoses . . .' to indicate that she too can use 'couple' in a misleading way by suggesting an 'insignificant amount of a significant action'.

A feature of this part of the extract is the way in which the last phrase tails off, in this case by minimizing the attempted suicide. This could be seen as indicative of psychosocial denial, a key to which is the use of the word 'anyway'. But it could also be interpreted as a way of increasing the self-efficacy of the speaker: 'I too have power and I could/would use it if all else fails'. Thus, ironically, the use of *de-intensifiers* may be designed to leave a lasting impression in the listener's mind. A less dramatic use of a de-intensifier emerges in the next example, when the occasioned use of the word 'simple' is considered:

> . . . if he (dad) doesn't want to send me a birthday card, I don't want him to come to my review, simple.

Here, the linguistic 'trick' is found in the attempt to make an emotionally complex psychosocial event appear straightforward. If accomplished, it achieves two tasks simultaneously: keeping others at arms' length, while persuading oneself that the event actually *is* simpler than it feels. Either way, the use of the device suggests an attempt to persuade the interviewer that the young person has some control over events.

Sometimes the frustration of young people, when they feel that what they say or do makes little difference, leads to the creation of an *idealized or hypothetical active state*. This can be inferred from the next two examples:

> Why can't she talk about it with my social worker and then like get my social worker to talk to me?

> I would have asked about the meeting if I didn't know about it.

In each example we see how speakers refer to the kind of service or decision they would have preferred by formulating idealized and preferred responses to the one they received. Both contain examples of self-effi-cacy talk.

Finally, there was some evidence within the responses of *metacogni-tive thought* (Crittenden, 1998) – i.e. the ability to 'think about thinking' – alongside *reflective functioning* (Fonagy *et al.*, 1998) – i.e. the ability to consider and reconsider one's own and others' actions from different perspectives. Both are evident in the last excerpt, and each points to a sophisticated and developed sense of self-efficacy:

> I think the other thing is also to look how, for example, some of the kids here (a residential home) . . . if they can't get their point across they break down into either doing something delinquent or just sitting there swearing their f . . . ing heads off or being really, really abusive towards somebody. And that's just dismissed as being childish. . . . If it comes down to it, at the end of the day I will win because if I flatly refuse to honour any decision that's made in my absence, then there is f . . . all they can do about it. So I hold a few cards if I choose to play them.

The irony is that the decision he has been fighting for is to stay another year in care, until he is well over nineteen. Hence, perhaps the main reason why he concludes that 'kids' who 'swear their f ... ing heads off' are seen as 'childish' is that he feels childish too; which may suggest why he expresses his own complex construction of self-efficacy with such vitriol.

Overall, the amount of 'self-efficacy talk' in the tapes was striking, especially considering that the interviewer was unknown to the young person. But what are some of the implications for professional practice? There is clearly an important role for social workers and others to listen carefully to what young people say but also – and sometimes more importantly – to the way in which they say it.

The practice-related implications of our re-examination of the tran-scripts are considerable because they suggest strongly that recognizing self-efficacy when young people speak is not straightforward; it emerges only after patient observation by professionals, and sometimes the frus-tration, rage and despair in which it is communicated can easily confuse an adult not tuned in to its wavelength. Because developing resilience in children is a key role for professionals working in family support systems, and because 'warm, supportive secure relationships' (Howe *et al.*, 1999, p. 242) are crucial to effective interventions, they will need to listen actively for self-efficacy talk (including its absence) as an indica-tor of such resilience, and then respond to it, or try to create the condi-tions for it to develop.

The detail given of this study is intended to convey both the complexity of the method and the value of the information obtained from this approach to research. It has concentrated on discourse from interviews but there are other forms of discourse, including what Potter (1997) refers to as 'natural occurring talk'.

In social work the study of discourse from observed situations such as case conferences, team meetings and interdisciplinary ward rounds has been undertaken by researchers such as Sue White.

Conclusion

At the outset of this chapter we suggested that narrative and discourse approaches are well suited to providing a research base for social work practice, and have sought to illustrate why. However, it is important to recognize that this is not without its challenges. The increasing emphasis on certain kinds of 'evidence' as the basis for social work described in Chapter 2 is making it more difficult to get funding for the kinds of research described in this chapter. Riessmann and Quinney (2005) point out that narrative and discourse approaches are much more a feature of UK social work research than they are of US social work research. Their explanation provides further warnings. They suggest that the particular definition of science in the USA has excluded perspectives and assumptions of much qualitative research. The fact that research councils in the UK do give some funding to these approaches, especially for interdisciplinary research, is seen to provide an opportunity. If social work researchers can demonstrate rigour and expertise in such methods then they will be able to influence other social science researchers and define a place for distinctive approaches in social work research.

And finally, to conclude this chapter we return to our epistemological discussion about the meaning of suicide. You may have asked yourself this question: persuasive as Douglas's critique is of Durkheim's work, does it explain fully the reason behind the differences between suicide rates in different countries (acknowledging that the notion of what constitutes 'the rate of suicide' may well be problematic)? If 'suicide' is a social product of the collective experience and interpretation of coroners, then why are Japanese coroners so different from German coroners? To tackle this we have to step back from the specifics of 'method' and adopt more of a 'helicopter view' over the relevant literature *as a whole*, as we did in Chapter 4 when we identified the need for the analysis, synthesis and critical appraisal of a complete body of findings, rather than the somewhat partial view offered by a few studies. We shall revisit to the question of critical synthetic appraisal in Chapter 10, when we consider the dissemination of research studies, findings and results.

putting it into practice

Have a look for two articles that have used two different methods for undertaking qualitative research.

- Do the authors make it clear why the methods were chosen (and does this make sense)?
- Do the authors clarify and justify why they selected their chosen methods over other methods (in other words is sufficient attention paid to epistemological concerns)?
- If grounded theory is used, does the analysis go beyond 'cherry-picking the transcripts' for quotes that merely serve to support the authors' arguments?

Print out an article in *Community Care*.

- Select a short extract and then try line-by-line coding it.

Recommended reading

Letherby, G. (2003) *Feminist Research in Theory and Practice*. Buckingham: Open University Press. An important theoretically based approach to talk and text.

Paltridge, B. (2007) *Discourse Analysis: An Introduction*. New York, Continuum. Gives more detail on discourse analysis.

Rubin, H. and Rubin, I. (1995) *Qualitative Interviewing*. London, Sage. A good introductory text with lots of examples.

Strauss, A. and Corbin, J. (1998) *Basics of Qualitative Research Techniques and Procedures for Developing Grounded Theory*, 2nd edn. London, Sage. Gives more detail on grounded theory.

Part 3 | Implications of Social Work Research

9 | Who owns the research?

Introduction

To develop research based social work it is necessary to have a substantive body of rigorous research and for that research to be meaningful and useful to those in practice. This means not only that the topics have to be relevant to practitioners, managers and service users and carers, but also that the way the research is conducted has to be mindful of the values in social work. Finally, the research has to be disseminated in such a way that it is available to practitioners and able to be used by them. The chapters in this last part of the book therefore focus on these aspects of research and the relationship between the research process and the practice that it is intended to investigate and inform.

This chapter discusses who owns the research. While it might seem straightforward – the person doing the research owns it – this is not always the case. Ownership involves issues of funding, but also issues of power. When research is commissioned, or paid for by an outside body, there are frequently clauses that control both the process and the dissemination of the outcomes. Undertaking funded research can mean that the research proposal determining what is researched and how is controlled by the funding body. Such constraints have implications for the way research is managed but also illustrate some of the issues of power and ownership in the research process.

These issues permeate all research whether it is funded or not. Practitioners who undertake research as part of their employment or as part of their individual staff development not only have to negotiate with their employers for the time or resources to undertake the research, but might also be expected to research topics that are meaningful to the agency rather than a topic that is of particular interest to themselves. This will have implications not only for what is researched, but also for what happens to the results of such research. Similar constraints might apply to service users who are involved in agency-based research.

Underpinning all this, as was indicated in Chapter 3, are the ethical implications of 'ownership' in the research process. When people participate in the research process, especially in social work related research, they give a commitment of time and effort, but they also give of themselves – their opinions, details of their personal life that can involve their emotions. This is well illustrated by ethical considerations in cross-cultural research. In New Zealand, for example, research ethics are informed by the principles of the Treaty of Waitangi, which respects Maori culture. More information can be found on websites such as http://www.maramatanga.co.nz/ and http://www.manu-ao.ac.nz/. The principles of participation, partnership and protection are paramount. When a researcher seeks knowledge this may be considered tapu (sacred or sacrosanct) by the respondents. Knowledge can include that which has not been made public and is not usually available to outsiders, and can be held by living respondents or contained in personal documentation. It can involve anonymized statistical data about communities as well as more personal and qualitative data. The implication is clear – the knowledge belongs to individuals, tribes and communities, and cannot be shared (not even with the examiner of a PhD thesis) without the agreement of any or all of those people. While other cultures might not have such specific requirements, they are an important reminder that those who participate in the research process do not do so for the good of the researcher, they own the knowledge that the researcher wishes to access.

This analysis of ownership of research highlights the responsibilities involved in conducting research and ensuring the process is managed in a way that has integrity for all those involved and for the findings and the knowledge claims.

Conducting research

The notion of conducting research is a useful one because no matter how large or small the research project it will have a number of components that need to be 'orchestrated'. That is, they need to have appropriate attention given to them as individual aspects of the work, but they also have to be seen to make a distinctive contribution to the project as a whole. Moreover, as in a piece of music, the order and timing of the process is important. We have learnt that it is vital to undertake a litera-ture search at the outset to identify other research in the area and help to clarify the focus of the particular research project. Similarly, decisions about methodology and method have to be made at an early, or 'design', stage. However, as in music, research is not a totally linear process, there is always the need to go back and repeat and develop different parts of the process. For example, as new areas come to light more reading will have to be done. Moreover, developments in the research process might cause researchers to revisit their methodology. This might involve reasserting exactly what the research is focusing on. This is vital as it is very easy to 'lose one's way' by being side tracked into subsidiary research questions that are very interesting, but not central to the main research question.

An example of this is the evaluation of the social work degree in England that was commissioned by the Department of Health. This was a three-year evaluation of a specific innovation in social work education and training. The evaluation involved identifying whether a degree level qualification made a difference in social work education. However, the introduction of the degree coincided with many other policy changes. The evaluation also gave the opportunity to access student feedback in ways that had never been done before. This raised all sorts of interesting questions about social work education and training, but the research team had to remind themselves that what they were funded to do was evaluate what difference degree level education made to social work training (Orme *et al.*, 2007; DoH, 2008).

Commissioning

This example indicates one of the positive aspects of undertaking funded research – it helps to keep the focus on the initial research question. Undertaking funded research usually involves having a reference group, steering group or small group of people to whom regular reports are made. This might take the form of written reports but usually involves some face-to-face meetings. These provide a useful sounding board for discussing the material that is emerging, but as has been indicated it also helps to provide a brake or keep a sense of direction to the research.

However, this is also one of the limitations of commissioned or funded research. Funding is usually made available for research and evaluation by organizations and agencies because there are specific questions to which they want answers. This means that those who are writing research proposals in order to undertake the funded project can be constrained by the perceptions of others. For example, the methodology might have to be chosen in order to give the kind of information necessary to answer the questions posed, in the way that the question is posed. Ungar (2005), for example, undertook a review of experiences of attempting to gain funding for social work research in the USA and Canada. He describes how the criteria from the funders seemed to be at odds with the best research design. This does not mean that the outcomes of the research are dictated or pre-empted by those commissioning the research; it means that the researcher does not necessarily have the freedom to make the kinds of philosophical decisions that were discussed in earlier chapters. Ungar (2005, pp. 268ff) suggests that techniques such as 'dressing up' and 'sleeping with the elephant', 'search but never find' and 'table scraps' are successful strategies in grants applications

Having said that, not all funded research involves such constraints. Organizations such as the Joseph Rowntree Foundation and the Nuffield Foundation fund projects under categories that they identify, rather than specifying the research question. The ESRC is an independent research funding body that encourages researchers to bring new ideas for research by providing a variety of research grants. Its grants cover a whole spectrum of researchers and over time have become more relevant to social work. For example, the ESRC postgraduate awards for doctoral training are one way for social work practitioners to achieve funding for research. While there are some issues around agencies being prepared to support practitioners in achieving doctoral qualification (Orme, 2003), the increase in the number of collaborative studentship is encouraging. These are offered and managed by a collaboration between universities and non-academic organizations and therefore can contribute to developing a research base for social work. While the research issue is identified by the organization, joint supervision allows wider exploration of how to undertake the research.

Increasingly students and practitioners are being encouraged to undertake research projects as part of qualifying and post-qualifying education. While this is to be encouraged, it is apparent that the scope of such projects is limited by the resources available, in terms of both time and money. Such projects are not commissioned in the formal sense of there being a contractual arrangement, but as has been said such projects are often linked to an agency agenda. In such circumstances it is vital that agencies have an appropriate infrastructure to support the project. This might not be as formal as the reference groups and steering groups set up to monitor commissioned research but needs to represent the agency and, where appropriate, the education institution where the study is taking place. In this way students can be given support, assistance with access and a forum to discuss the project. Such arrangements illustrate one aspect of the organizational excellence model for research infrastructure described by Walter *et al.* (2004).

Reference has already been made to the methodological constraints created by research questions posed by organizations and agencies who commission research. However, another constraint is the level of funding. This can be crucial in determining the actual methods used. For example, an electronic questionnaire can reach more people for less money than a questionnaire that is administered by individual researchers, or even one that is sent out by post. However, using electronic questionnaires can influence the kind of questions that can be asked, or more accurately the kinds of questions that will be answered. It might also limit respondents to those who have access to computers. In terms of numbers this might not be as limiting as using interviewers to administer questionnaires – but it might influence the 'sample' of people who are accessed and reply.

Negotiating access

The discussion of different methods of accessing those who might participate in research is crucial to the process of conducting research and has implications for ownership. In social work it is sometimes assumed that those who are in touch with social work agencies and/or information about them are readily available to researchers. The Data Protection Act 1998 gives some protection but raises challenges for social work in developing research based practice. If, as has been said, it is important to raise research questions from practice, the process of identifying an issue, checking to see to what extent it is experienced by other service users and then researching it can be sensitive, not least because until the research is undertaken the number of people receiving a particular service or experiencing certain social conditions might be very limited. The increasing recognition of the different impact of social conditions or practice interventions on people from diverse backgrounds or with diverse needs means that 'populations' might be small and more able to be identified.

Consent

This is not to say that such research is not possible, but that the ramifications for those who might be involved in research need to be thought through. Guidelines exist associated with codes of ethics discussed in Chapter 3 about confidentiality and anonymity and ways of gaining the consent of those being asked to participate. Often this is covered by a letter or form to be completed by participants, and ethics committees require copies of such material. There are legal definitions and guidance given to deal with situations where permission is sought from parents, guardians or carers who give consent on behalf of others. While it is vital to adhere to these, it is not enough to follow the letter of the law. It is recognized in social work research that certain groups – for example, those with difficulties in communication – have been denied their own voice. Traditional methods often mean that research has been done 'on' them, or other people have spoken for them.

One such group is children. The need to have a rigorous research base for working with children is paramount and support is given for such research by governments in all countries that support the UN Convention on the Rights of the Child (1989). However, this need to have research *on* children does not always recognize their right to be involved in research. As Balen *et al.* (2006) point out from their analysis of research in England and Australia, existing gatekeeping systems for research construct children as dependent and in need of protection. This is evident in systems and ethical codes that require parental consent for any involvement of children in research. But this can get in the way of enabling children to be participants in research. Balen *et al.* (2006) describe how in research children cease being 'active beings' and become 'human becomings'. This does not have to be so. Organizations such as Barnardo's, the National Children's Bureau (2003) and Save the Children (2004) issue guidelines for both researching children and involving children in the research process. There are also descriptions of how to involve children and young people in the research process, giving them a voice (Broad and Saunders, 1998). Research involving children and young people includes studies of very sensitive situations of domestic violence (Mullender *et al.*, 2002) and children with complex needs (Watson *et al.*, 2006). Watson *et al.* suggest that the best way to proceed is to assume that everyone can communicate irrespective of age and/or disability but to have resources to help children (and especially those who cannot communicate well verbally) to communicate their ideas and feelings. It is important to be flexible, to recognize that barriers will be put in the way – and that mistakes will be made during the process of working out the most effective way for children to be involved in research. Like all researchers, if children and young people are to undertake aspects of the research they will require training and advice about issues of confidentiality. McLaughlin (2007) discusses the advantages and disadvantages of involving children and young people in research, but some of the overwhelming arguments are that it treats children and young people with respect, gives them a voice and therefore produces research that is more meaningful to the lives of other children and young people – and is therefore of greater use to practitioners.

Considering issues of ownership and power therefore means that attention has to be paid to the needs of all potential research participants in negotiating access, gaining permission and deciding on methods to be used. This includes finding ways of directly enabling them to give consent, or not.

Remuneration

Issues of negotiating access have also been influenced by user participation in services and research. Some years ago it was thought unethical to offer incentives for people to be involved in research because doing so might influence their motives, and their responses. However, demands for service users and carers to give of their time and resources to research processes, such as in repeated interviews or involvement in focus groups, are increasing. There is now an assumption that there will be some remuneration for time spent.

The impact of this is complex. 'Consultation costs' was the slogan of disability rights groups trying to draw attention to the fact that researchers were either taking it for granted that service users and carers would be involved or, even worse, assuming that service users and carers would be grateful for the opportunity to be involved. However, the fact that some kind of remuneration is expected means that resources have to be found, which can curtail the research undertaken by students or practitioners who do not have access to such resources.

The nature of the remuneration can also be problematic. For example, if financial payments are given to research participants who are in receipt of benefits the monies paid might affect their entitlement to benefits. Some researchers are concerned that with certain groups, those who are known to be dependent on drugs or alcohol, for example, giving financial rewards might be counterproductive or even be seen to condone illegal behaviour.

This raises the question of whether all research participants should be given remuneration. This question arises not because some are unworthy of it, or will abuse it, but because the nature of the involvement might not seem to require it. Filling in an on-line questionnaire, for example, does not take much time, and the practicalities of remunerating people who do complete such a questionnaire are difficult, not least if the questionnaire is completed anonymously. Sometimes the remuneration is not in cash or goods (such as store tokens) but in terms of services – those involved in research might get access to facilities.

Apart from issues of practicality and questions about the motivation of those who will only participate if there is a reward or an incentive, the notion of remuneration raises interesting questions about who owns the research. To pay people to be involved in research whether it is in cash or in kind suggests some kind of contractual arrangement whereby the researcher has then completed a 'deal' or contract with the person, and the information then gleaned belongs to the researcher. This would certainly not be acceptable to Maori cultural norms, and has implications for methodological approaches where the knowledge development comes from a process of sharing and reflecting on emergent findings with participants.

Impact of research

The discussion of payment for and shared approaches to research highlights that the question of ownership has to be revisited at different stages in the research. One important reason for doing this is because the process of being involved in research can have an impact on those who participate in it. Apart from the emotional impact of researching sensitive topics discussed in Chapter 2, there are also issues of definition. Researchers often 'problematize' issues and situations that might not accord with the views of research participants experiencing them. To be included in a research project or invited to participate in research that negatively labels part of your identity or experience can be salutary. Moreover, being asked to participate in research that looks at resources or services can unduly raise expectations or anxieties unless the research is presented appropriately.

This is illustrated by research into practitioner workloads. In 1978 the Home Office undertook a study of the workloads of probation officers. This involved workers logging their activities every 15 minutes. There was such suspicion that this study was to demonstrate that they were not working hard enough, doing enough in a given time frame, that the officers stopped taking meal breaks and comfort breaks in order to demonstrate how over-worked they were.

One major conundrum is how to research or evaluate actual practice rather than practice which is undertaken in certain ways because the participants know they are being observed. That undertaking research can influence the practice being observed is recognized in the Hawthorne effect, which suggests that if people know they are being studied as part of research they will change their behaviour. Ethical research requires that when negotiating access the researcher has to explain clearly what is being undertaken in order to gain the full consent of those participating. The notion of 'covert' research – that is, undertaking research without informing those being researched, or describing one aspect of the research to be undertaken while at the same time preparing to gather other data – is therefore ethically problematic.

Covert research highlights the potential for power imbalances within research. Once there is an agreement from a person to participate it is vital that researchers continuously reflect on the research process and to what extent it is keeping within the parameters agreed by the participants. The examples of medical research where agreements given for the use of body parts in research have been breached are the more extreme examples of how researchers, often with the best of motives, can abuse the power given to them through access to people and data. In social work examples might not be so dramatic, but situations that involve access to case records, for example, raise issues of ownership. While the record is held by an agency, the information is about a person and therefore could be said to 'belong' to them. Researching residential care raises similar issues. While staff and managers might give consent for researchers to access residential establishments, they are effectively the homes of residents who should also be asked to give permission.

Publication

The point at which ownership becomes even more complicated is when research is in the public domain. Neither researchers nor participants have influence over the way that research is interpreted and used by those who have access to the findings. The responsibility of the researcher is to ensure that the final document and any reports or publications based on it are is as clear as possible about the findings, their implications, interpretations and limitations. Even when this is done there will be some research that presents challenges. For example, the findings of a research project evaluating interventions in the area of domestic violence (Orme, 2001) were presented to a news conference. The research came to the tentative conclusion that men in the research project who had been convicted of offences of violence against their partner had unrealistic expectations of what constituted 'feminine' behaviour. It was difficult to present these results without being seen either to excuse the behaviour of the men, or to blame women for that behaviour.

This example raises many issues about dissemination, but also about ownership. The fact that it was piece of research conducted independently means that it was possible to share the findings at a conference or a news conference without gaining the agreement of a steering group or a representative of a funding organization. The dangers of this are evident in the example. Discussion with such a group might have urged caution. However, sometimes such arrangements are experienced as censorship. This is particularly the case when research has been contracted by government organizations where the research findings might be sensitive, or the policy might have changed since the research was initiated.

In these situations the ownership of the findings is made clear in the contractual arrangements for the research. However, there are arrangements that are less well defined and care must be taken to ensure that the sensitivities of the material and the implications for those involved are respected. This is relevant not only to academics who publish journal articles on the basis of projects undertaken for agencies, but also for students who present their findings as a report, dissertation or thesis for an academic award. There has to be commitment to, and acknowledgement of, those who have participated in the research, who have given of themselves in different ways – be that time or information. This respect includes, first, finishing the project to the highest possible quality and, second, devising ways of recognizing the contribution made. In terms of ownership research would not be possible without the cooperation of participants and appropriate ways need to be devised of acknowledging that with them, not just writing it in the preface to the document.

It is useful to end this section with the observation from Nutley *et al.* (2007) that some people are more likely to take notice of research if it is commissioned from official sources. Such research is seen as less influenced by the personal interests of the researchers and is more likely to be rigorous and balanced. As has been indicated, this is not necessarily the case, as those funding the research may have their own particular slant on the practices or policies. More importantly, if this situation prevails then it has implications for developing research based practice informed by research that has been undertaken by practitioners and service users and carers. Research that is commissioned by organizations is more likely to be undertaken by government researchers, academic researchers or those working for independent research organizations. Some, but not all, organizations and research funders insist that research bids from such organizations must involve service user and carer representatives in the research process, as consultants or members of reference or steering groups. The rigours of the tendering processes and the infrastructure of resources required to support the research mean that only a limited amount of user-led research is undertaken.

Stakeholder research

The question of ownership has been discussed above predominantly from the perspective of research being undertaken by 'outsiders' – that is, researchers from universities or research agencies. As has been said often in this text one aspect of developing research based practice is to encourage ownership of both the research findings and the research process. The next chapter will discuss dissemination of research findings but here we discuss the process of owning the research process from the perspective of two different groups of stakeholders: practitioners and service users and carers.

Practitioner research

The notion of practitioner research has many drivers, but the most significant one in the UK and the USA is that being involved in research by actually doing it might encourage practitioners to appreciate the relevance of research for their practice. Studies such as that by Nutley *et al.* (2007) identify ownership as being vital to the uptake of research. It is this finding that makes it especially pertinent to developing a research base for social work practice.

Resistance to research in social work was identified by Everitt and colleagues (1992, p. 5) who wrote 'At best practitioners experience research as irrelevant: at worst, as the process of being ripped off', arguing that the concern was that practice might be used for research purposes that might not necessarily enhance practice. This reaction is explained by Nutley *et al.* (2007, p. 312), who found that where implementation of research is received or perceived as a coercive process this can be counterproductive.

The situation may have changed somewhat, mainly through attempts to facilitate practitioner research. However, although Fuller and Petch (1995, p. 3) argued that 'Research conducted by practitioners is an idea whose time has come', the study by Walter and colleagues nearly a decade later (2004) found that practitioners made statements about the value of research-informed practice but there was very little unpicking of what this might mean and little evidence of ownership.

This might be because there is confusion in the profession about the relationship between practice and research. Shaw and Shaw (1997) suggest that over time social workers have been offered the choice of applying research, conducting research or applying forms of research-based practice. The aim of initiatives to develop a research base for practice includes encouragement to practitioners to engage with research at a number of levels. It is thought that this will increase ownership through appreciation of research processes and critical evaluation of the outcomes of research.

However, ownership of research through participation is not without challenges. There are those who have argued that practitioner research is suspect in some way. Having initially challenged the partisan nature of practitioners researching their own practice (Hammersley, 1995), Hammersley in a later article acknowledges that such work has a contribution to make, but that it should be considered to be 'enquiry' and not 'research' (Hammersley, 2003).

These distinctions echo earlier work in the USA by Thyer (1989), who argues that the goals of practice research are different and that the difference is between *application* and *implication*. Practice research, he argues, has applications to the delivery of social services, while what he calls 'science' studies are aimed at the development of knowledge that might have implications for practice.

Another distinction is around methods. One myth to be challenged is the assumption made by many writing about practitioner involvement in research that practitioner research is predominantly qualitative research (Fuller and Petch, 1995). Earlier chapters in this text have outlined the demands made on those undertaking research and have acknowledged that practitioners are likely to undertake small-scale enquiries. However, there is increasing scope for developments in methodological excellence in analysing large-scale databases, or working with practice agencies to collect quantitative data.

One set of arguments for practioner research is that practice and research share common characteristics (Gilgun, 1994, 2009). While in some ways this might seem to be encouraging ownership of research, it can also be problematic. It can lead to practitioners assuming that they do not have to address the complex questions and processes involved in research that have been discussed in this and other texts (D'Cruz and Jones, 2004; Corby, 2006; McLaughlin, 2007). Shaw and Shaw's (1997) argument in the UK that what are needed in practitioner research are new understandings and new methodologies are echoed in the USA in the work of Mullen (2002) at his centre for research practice.

Returning to the subject in 2005, Shaw drew upon empirical work to challenge both the criticisms and the claims that have been made on behalf of practitioner research. He found a striking degree of diversity in what passes under the 'practitioner research rubric' (Shaw, 2005, p. 1237). However, he identified that practitioner researchers were often marginalized. This suggests that 'ownership' is problematic at the level of the organization, as well as at the level of individual practitioners.

The discussion of the implications of practitioner research for ownership of research is therefore complex. On the one hand it is important to encourage practitioner involvement in undertaking research, but on the other the conditions required include both organizational support for the practitioner and openness to the critical nature of enquiry that might be the result of more focused and rigorous practitioner research. This would suggest that a culture change is needed in organizations: a move away from requiring merely descriptive research to a willingness to engage in critical evaluation of organization and interventions.

Another significant finding from Shaw's (2005) study suggests that other changes are necessary. The absence of user involvement in practitioner research might, according to Shaw (2005), be because practitioners operate with a service development and delivery agenda and/or because projects linked to higher education (and perhaps leading to a qualification) do not encourage multiple stakeholder involvement. As the imperatives for user and career involvement in research increase, important culture changes are needed to facilitate service user involvement in research.

Service user research

Throughout this text we have referenced the growing movement to have service users participate in research. This can be either as members of steering groups discussed earlier in this chapter, or as members of the researcher team. As was discussed in Chapter 2 the ultimate in emancipatory research is when users have the resources to direct and undertake research themselves. However, while this is an important goal, the nature of research and the politics of ownership sometimes make it difficult to achieve.

One example of user and carer involvement in research is SureSearch, which is a network of users and survivors of mental health services and their allies who have experience and/or an interest in mental health research and education. The network, supported by the Centre of Excellence in Interdisciplinary Mental Health at the University of Birmingham (http://www.suresearch.org.uk/index.html), aims among other things to increase the involvement of mental health service users in research and education, and to influence the quality, ethics and values of mental health research by linking with other local, regional and national partnerships in the mental health arena. This enables members either individually or collectively to respond to and take up opportunities for research, consultancy and education. Such initiatives are being spear-headed in the UK, where the involvement of service users in service delivery, research and social work education and training are much more advanced than anywhere else.

However, it must be recognized that not all service users will want to be so actively involved in undertaking research, but all research undertaken in social work should consider how a service user perspective can be incorporated into the design. This involves complex aspects of ownership. The principles of participation, partnership and protection identified earlier as being central to research with Maori communities might be helpful. The notion of protection could be thought to have overtones of paternalism, but in fact it is a guiding principle in the ethical base for all research: that it should do no harm.

On the other hand, if opportunities for ownership of research are to be open to all, then changes have to be undertaken to make it possible for service user groups to tender for research funding and for social work practitioners and researchers to be as open to being researched as they expect service user and carer groups to be. Suggestions that people with disabilities have increased control of disability research can be subject to the same critiques as practitioner research: as being partisan and unscientific. This has in the past been rejected by researchers because it was seen as a means of control and a restraint of academic freedom and a challenge to social work researchers' 'expertise' (Gibbs, 1999). Gibbs suggests that it is necessary to seek ways in which the two groups can work together: 'to seek examples where the objectives of researchers and their subjects converge in ways that preserve the freedoms of the one and advance the freedom of the other'.

This suggests that participatory research that involves dynamic partnerships between researchers and service users could work to the benefit of both, with the expertise of both being recognized and ownership being shared. However, achieving convergence is not always simple. As we said at the beginning of this chapter, issues of power are inherent in most arrangements for research and these do not go away and at times can be exacerbated during the research process. This does not mean that such research should not be undertaken, but all participants have to be prepared to critically reflect on the process and to learn, and to share the lessons learnt.

Conclusion

In reflecting on the implications of developing a research base for social work practice this chapter has discussed the arrangements for undertaking research and their implications for ownership of research. It has acknowledged that there are many forms of ownership and many stakeholders. Underpinning any arrangement are issues of power. These do not disappear with different arrangements for research, they become manifest in different ways.

It is therefore necessary for agencies and organizations, whether they are funding bodies or employers, to reflect on the arrangements for research. This includes which research is funded, with whom it is undertaken, who undertakes it and, as will be discussed in the next chapter, how the outcomes of the research will be disseminated to those who participated and to the wider social work community in order for them to be a useful resource for social work practice.

putting it into practice

A research project has been undertaken that involved a group of older people working with researchers from a university to look at how the care needs of older people in a particular city were met. The research focused on the services provided by a particular social work team and was funded from finances provided jointly from local and central government. Representatives from the funding bodies joined older people on the steering group, as did representatives from the agency that was the focus of the research.

The results of the research are critical of a number of organizations – from central government through to the local social services department. When the draft final report was presented to the steering group there was dissent:

- The older people members think that it should be released immediately and want local groups and the local press to be made aware of the results.
- The representatives from the funding bodies want the researchers to write another draft – toning down their criticisms.
- The representatives of the agency question the results of the research and are challenging the methodology.
- The researchers want their research to be published. They also want to be eligible to apply for future funding. However, they also stand by the rigour of their research and the results.

In your view what are the implications of this disagreement? Whose view should prevail? Why?

Recommended reading

Mullen, E. (1995) *Practitioner–Researcher Partnerships: Building Knowledge from, in, and for Practice*. NASW Press. A useful perspective on practitioner research from North America.

Smyth, M. and Williamson, E. (eds) (2004) *Researchers and Their 'Subjects'*. Bristol, Policy Press. This book discusses the relationship between the researcher and those participating in research in a number of disciplines, not just social work.

10 | Getting the message across

Introduction

The final stage in undertaking research is disseminating the results. Hence we address this topic in the last main chapter of the book. In academic research the end of the process is connected with the beginning: that is, publishing your research means it is available to be quoted by others and to be available when future researchers undertake their literature review. In terms of developing a research base for social work, disseminating results might be the beginning of other processes. These include informing practitioners and others about the results of the particular enquiry and encouraging them to critically review these results and the process of obtaining them. Doing this will also ideally lead practitioners to utilize the relevant research results to introduce positive changes into their practice. It might also stimulate thoughts about other, related research and how this might be undertaken. It is this joined up series of stages that can contribute the development of what we call *reflective practitioner researchers* (RPRs).

As part of the emerging infrastructure to develop research based social work practice there have been a number of initiatives to enhance dissemination and encourage utilization. In this chapter we reflect on some of these to consider the main principles underpinning good dissemination practice. In doing this we suggest that one of the distinctive aspects of social work research is that strategies for dissemination by researchers have little point unless individual practitioners and agencies can be encouraged to utilize research evidence. This does not mean that social work research always has to be empirical. It is just as important for practitioners to reflect on theoretical developments as it is for them to take note of outcome studies and evaluations.

Dissemination

In Chapter 9 we discussed how effective dissemination is an important aspect of encouraging ownership of research. If no one reads or learns about a study, it raises questions about its overall purpose. Good dissemination is a tangible and powerful way of securing and then demonstrating stakeholder engagement.

There are a variety of ways of disseminating research. The simplest is through various media and print forms. The advent of diverse electronic media permits faster, more accessible and, if designed well, more engaging ways to share the findings and implications of research, because most dissemination materials are presented in eye-catching and memorable formats. Prior to the explosion of electronic media, the only way practitioners and others could keep abreast of research was to read about it in books or journals, or to attend a seminar or conference on a particular topic of interest. Now, with blogs, discussion groups and dedicated webspace for the uploading and downloading of information, practitioners and service users can read, think about and discuss practice-related research at any time of the day or night, if they wish. They can read reports of research and policy-related material on-line within minutes of it having been completed.

The main forms of contemporary dissemination media for research therefore include the following.

User-friendly presentation of research findings

There are numerous examples of how organizations such as the Joseph Rowntree Foundation, NSPCC and Barnardo's make their research reports available in hard copy, which is also available in downloadable form from the Internet.

To assist the accessibility of research findings SCIE has developed the website Research Register for Social Care (RRSC) (http://www.researchregister.org.uk/). Researchers can register and add research to the website, which records social care research (which in SCIE includes social work research) that has been subject to independent ethical and scientific review. It includes current and completed research, and research carried out by students and practitioners. It can then be searched by anyone wishing to access details of research in a particular topic to obtain summary details of the individual studies and links to further information about them. In the USA the resources provided by SCIE can to some extent be found through organizations such as the Society for Social Work Research (SSWR) and the Institute for the Advancement of

Social Work Research (IASWR). The former is predominantly for academic researchers but the IASWR was founded in 1993 by five national professional organizations that represent the social work practice and education communities. Its aim is to strengthen social work research resources. Through its website and listserv (http://www.iaswresearch.org/) it makes available, among other things, information about conferences, publications and research findings.

Organizations such as Research in Practice and Making Research Count in the UK have been set up specifically both to make research accessible and to work towards practitioners making effective use of it. These initiatives have developed expertise at translating academic and technical findings into user-friendly summaries, aimed at a non-specialist audience.

Over and above the translation of the actual research findings, other mechanisms have been developed to increase their practical relevance by working closely with stakeholders to map potential areas of impact and gain feedback. Presenting and debating research findings at practitioner meetings, conferences and on-line discussion forums, before 'formal' publication, encourages both a practitioner perspective and service user involvement.

Face-to-face

Sometimes there is no substitute for face-to-face communication, using lectures and seminars to present and discuss research findings. Research in Practice and Making Research Count run a series of dissemination workshops based around new research studies and findings.

Many social work departments in universities have seminar series to which practitioners are invited. Much is gained by actually meeting and engaging in debate with authors of research. Hearing accounts, warts and all, can demystify the process of research and makes the research outcomes more comprehensible. In Scotland, through the work of the Institute for Research and Innovation in Social Services (IRISS) (formerly the Scottish Institute for Excellence in Social Work Education, SIESWE), dissemination has been enhanced by some research seminars being made available as podcasts to assist practitioners who are not able to get to the actual seminar (for examples see: http://www.iriss.org.uk/rss/podcast/sieswe.xml).

Thematic seminars are supported by the ESRC. Competetitive bids are made for funding for seminar series, which usually involve collaboration between more than one institution. The Theorising Social Work Seminar Series discussed in the Introduction to this text, which stimulated work around developing a research base for practice, was one such series. Another that has had impact was Health Inequalities; Gender and Family Construction and Equalities are other examples. However, accessibility is an issue. Even when the seminars are held in different parts of the UK, participants have to live or work near to a university, and have to find the time in busy work schedules to attend. Further, seminars funded by the ESRC are primarily for academics.

Engaging with research findings

In the UK the concern is that there are no systems for ensuring that what is learnt is absorbed and applied to practice, especially in relation to using research results. As we have frequently referenced, the study for SCIE by Walter *et al.* (2004) demonstrated differential arrangements for embedding research in practice. Surveys undertaken by SCIE (Fisher *et al.*, 2007) and IRISS (Miller, 2007) both indicate that practitioners have the will to access and use research, but often practicalities get in the way.

One practice to encourage engagement with research is the use of questionnaires to gauge the reaction and feedback on a set of research findings when specific information or viewpoints need to be ascertained. Such questionnaires can be web-based and interactive, and have the added attraction of offering confidentiality when needed.

Another use of feedback questionnaires for engaging practitioners with research has been developed in North America, where practitioners have to evidence their post-qualifying studies in order to remain registered as a social worker. Often journals will offer questions at the end of published articles. Practitioners complete these and obtain points towards their required quota for re-registration. In the UK the modernization agenda made registration mandatory for those wishing to use the title social worker. The requirement to undertake 90 days of Post Registration Teaching and Learning (PRTL) therefore encourages practitioners to engage in different forms of learning and training. Practices like those in North America are beginning to appear in the UK. Most frequently practitioners are given a certificate of attendance when they attend a seminar or a day course. New Zealand introduced registration at about the same time as the UK (Orme and Rennie, 2006). More rigorous assessments of what has been gained or learnt by participants are required in order to qualify for registration. Just as importantly, practitioners have to provide evidence that they are able to apply their learning to practice.

Barriers to practitioners engaging with research include the availability of literature, the accessibility of the descriptions of the research and time. Here technology can be of assistance both in making information available and enhancing communication. Examples include the following.

Network development

An obvious advantage of web technology is that it allows people with similar interests to stay in touch. Websites can be set up with an 'open access' public area as well as with 'restricted', password-protected space. A mixed strategy helps to maintain interest and engagement with specialist, opt-in, interactive areas on the website, along with both 'one-to-one' and 'one-to-many' communication media to alert website members to interesting and topical discussions, postings or opportunities. As with online questionnaires, eMedia can include demonstrable levels of anonymity to encourage candour in situations when confidentiality is judged necessary.

Expert classes

Another recent development is the provision of 'expert seminars', whereby a service user, practitioner, manager or researcher is invited to give a short presentation, which is recorded using a camcorder, digitized and then uploaded onto dedicated webspace.

An example of this is provided by the IRISS, which has established a Learning Exchange. This is a resource available to academics, practitioners and service users. While the main purpose of the Exchange is to provide 'learning objects' for use to enhance and inform teaching, these objects are frequently based on, or derived from, the results of research. As has been said, resources such as podcasts of research seminars, which can be downloaded at times convenient to practitioners, do make research more accessible. But practitioners have to be motivated to access the research, often in their own time.

Synchronous and asynchronous chatrooms

Alternatively, a group of different stakeholders can be invited to debate research findings 'on camera'. 'Live' discussions can be video- or audio-recorded using technology capable of producing downloadable files for subsequent transmission to laptops, Macs/PCs, iPods and MP3 formats. Synchronous and asynchronous chatrooms in which participants communicate 'live' and on-line can be pre-arranged to discuss topics hosted by an invited guest. Dedicated webspace can also host news items and other information through a linked homepage. All of these forms of dissemination permit discussions from blogs, chatrooms and discussion groups to be printed out as hard copies.

Although some of the above may be unfamiliar, it is likely that all will be routine and commonplace in the next five to ten years.

Utilization

In a report for the Joseph Rowntree Foundation a team from Barnardo's (Hughes *et al.*, 2000) pointed out that the volume of research produced exceeds its application. Their very practical advice tries to stimulate the utilization of research and has messages for researchers and practitioners and policy-makers. This recognizes that practitioners have limited time and should not be expected to use their 'free' time to access literature, websites and other resources. The recommendations for agencies included the need for:

● leadership and senior management commitment, which is crucial;
● organizational culture that recognizes the importance of developing evidence based practice;
● adequate training and development support for all staff;
● incorporation of appropriate research skills in basic and advanced courses;
● product or issue 'champions' who are enthusiastic and have credibility in the organization;
● resources linked to research and development;
● integration of the research and development component in job descriptions;
● managers ensuring that time is made available within the practitioners' work routines (Hughes *et al.*, 2000: http://www.jrf.org.uk/publications/linking-research-and-practice).

Barnardo's was part of the consultation group working with the SCIE-commissioned project to investigate research utilization in social work and care (Walter *et al.*, 2004). This study identifies three models of research use in social care:

1. *The research based practitioner model*: where the responsibility for keeping abreast of research rested with individual practitioners.
2. *The embedded research model*: research enters practice by becoming embedded in the systems and processes of social care.
3. *The organizational excellence model*: where leadership and management of the organization take responsibility for developing research-informed practice.

These models were found to be not mutually exclusive and the report concludes that a whole systems approach would build on the relationship between the three approaches or models. The authors also identify missing dimensions to the models. These are research commissioners and service users and carers who need to be included in any development of whole systems approaches.

This work illustrates that developing research based practice needs both organizational change and culture change. In trying to bring about such changes it is also necessary to avoid a sense among practitioners that systems are being imposed as part of a managerialist agenda.

Communities of practice

Innovations to bring about change in social work often focus on the concept of a learning organization. While the concept of the learning organization is a positive one and is associated with attempts to bring about culture change, its use in social work has limited application to disseminating research and encouraging the take-up of research findings. As such it can be associated with top-down initiatives, which carry overtones of a managerialist agenda.

There is emerging evidence that initiatives that have centred on the notion of communities of practice (Wenger, 1998) have had a more positive impact on developing practices that utilize research. Developing communities of practice involves bringing together like-minded people around a particular activity to help to permeate the culture of the organization. This avoids the need for individual champions who can be alienated and ignored in organizations.

Using the notion of communities of practice as a means of bringing about change in learning related to research can involve effective partnerships between agencies and providers of research, such as university departments. They can also involve more than one agency, or profession. Gabbay *et al.* (2003), for example, set up multi-professional groups to develop plans for improving services for older people. They documented how as these groups matured, they worked with various forms of evidence/knowledge dissemination to help to inform their plans and their practice.

As part of its work to disseminate and support communities of practice Barnardo's introduced a number of initiatives, including staff training and providing resources such as *The Evidence Guide* to help social care professionals to develop skills to find, judge and apply research evidence in practice (http://www.barnardos.org.uk/resources/research_and_publications/theevidenceguide) and the *Evidence Request Service* to assist access to relevant, reliable research evidence to Barnardo's services. These initiatives, alongside the appointment of a dedicated Evidence Based Practice Development Director, are part of Barnardo's commitment to becoming an evidence based organization. This strategy arose out of the recognition that to assist practitioners to use research, agencies must go beyond the dissemination of evidence and increase the focus on the application of evidence to practice.

Reflective practitioner researchers

We end this chapter with an example of perhaps the ultimate model of research based practice. This is when organizations become involved in disseminating research findings and setting up initiatives to ensure that they bring about changes in practice, or at least influence the way that practitioners think about their practice.

Work associated with an initiative called the Assessment of Disorganized Attachment and Maltreatment (ADAM) Project illustrates how an evidence-informed approach can be used right from the start of a project. Initially dissemination involved a number of traditional dissemination sessions given to over 500 social workers during 2008–9.

As a next stage a slightly longer version of the project information (see Appendix) was sent out to three directors of children and families departments in London (it was written in plain language in order to communicate complex research findings in an accessible way)

The three directors agreed to be involved in a different approach to dissemination. They nominated two or three of their most experienced social workers as *reflective practitioner researchers* (RPR) to the Project. The RPRs were subsequently invited to an inaugural workshop. They were e-mailed a link to a website containing a 'target article' (Bakermans-Kranenburg *et al.*, 2005) to stimulate discussion (http://www.temple.edu/devscilab/732_wiki/Bakermans.20051.pdf). A series of seminars was then conducted in the three London boroughs to brief as many teams as possible.

A total of ten RPRs across the three boroughs eventually comprised the ADAM Project team. Dedicated webspace with password-protected access was created at the University of Kent. The website hosts areas for RPRs to upload recent articles and they have right of entry to the university's on-line library (with access to over 40,000 journals containing over 35 million contemporary on-line articles). The website also offers chatrooms and discussion boards. RPRs can set up a synchronous chatroom, whereby all of the RPRs communicate 'live' at a pre-arranged time. Invited 'guests' have also hosted chatroom sessions at pre-arranged times. The Project Group of RPRs also meet 'face-to-face', roughly every three months.

The main aim of the RPRs during the first year of the ADAM Project was to draw on the available research to explore complex questions about the role of social workers and other professionals involved in the safeguarding of children, such as:

- At what stage in an investigation should these methods be introduced? (It was seen as important not to use them as part of a general 'needs assessment', for example.)
- What if a parent refuses to allow a child to be interviewed using these methods?
- Who should inform the parents of the results of an attachment-based assessment?
- How can social work values and sound practice be strengthened; how can parents and carers be fully involved in a transparent, open and sensitive way (thereby modelling what they may not be able to offer to their children)?
- How does attachment-based assessment of allegations fit in with and complement other aspects of safeguarding practice (such as working with families to promote safer and more sensitive parenting practice)?

RPRs were encouraged to publish findings, jointly or individually, in a variety of different outlets, including in journals and in the social work 'tradepress' (typically *Community Care*). At the time of writing a second phase is planned. During this phase RPRs will help to design the evaluation of the ADAM Project (see Appendix), which will also include family members and young people. They will be encouraged to undertake some of the evaluative work themselves – and to publish the findings – because one of the main aims of the Project is to share evaluation and research in ways that are accessible to practitioners and families, as well as to contribute to attachment-based research in the wider academic community. RPRs are also encouraged to present progress at conferences and to contact other key researchers in the field – as potential mentors – to discuss problems and challenges that emerge during the implementation stages.

The RPRs are 'champions' for the project and are involved actively in implementing the ideas behind it: they identify challenges with other practitioners, they discuss potential solutions and options with their supervisors (and managers, if necessary), and then they communicate their experiences with their colleague RRPs and the Project Directors (David and Yvonne Shemmings), using the various electronic media outlined above. The on-line notes, discussions and communications are incorporated with other research evidence as the basis for various publications and conferences. PowerPoint slides, seminar papers and lunchtime discussions are available to all staff in the three departments from another section of the website (which is not password protected).

The approach to innovation outlined in the ADAM Project (see Appendix) is itself based on contemporary research into the nature and effectiveness of change, particularly when the aim is to introduce new ideas requiring practice development and attitudinal shifts. It is derived from what Gladwell refers to as achieving a tipping point (see http://www.gladwell.com/tippingpoint/index.html), whereby lasting change occurs because it is 'caught', virally – the same way the common cold is transmitted – between people at the same level in an organization, rather than hierarchically (the metaphor of a 'trickle down' effect is used regularly to describe the latter phenomenon). The role of senior management is to create the conditions for the innovation to catch on and then 'stick' – precisely what the ADAM Project sought to achieve. This is where committed and knowledgeable RPRs can be instrumental: social workers change their practice because the RPR is a respected colleague, who they will listen to, rather than because management tells them to alter their practice.

Although the ADAM Project was initiated by an academic, there is no reason why it could not have been instigated, developed and maintained by one or more RPRs. Similarly, such projects do not need to involve more than one organization; they could be contained in one department. At the point of writing this book, initial reactions to the ADAM Project as an example of the role of the RPR are very encouraging, although they have not yet been formally evaluated.

Conclusion

This chapter has sought to describe processes for disseminating research results, and to reflect on these within the wider agenda of developing research based social work practice. It has highlighted that dissemination of results is not enough. The doctoral thesis that gathers dust on library shelves or even the journal article available through electronic access has limited value if practitioners are not aware of its existence, or do not have the time or motivation to seek it out. Dissemination has to be proactive. Researchers have to produce findings in accessible formats and create the means for these to be available to practitioners.

However, even when research results are in the public domain there is no guarantee that they will have any impact on practice. To ensure that research results are used – that is, they are reflected upon and the implications for practice or for further research are considered – it is necessary to have commitment from organizations. Arrangements need to be made both in the structure of organizations and in the culture. For example, even when research resources are available in organizations managers have to ensure that workloads are managed in ways that take into account the time taken by practitioners to access relevant research as part of their assessment of cases. Managers also have to ensure that in supervision sessions practitioners are encouraged to reflect on the information they have gathered from reviewing the research and the implications for intervening in this particular case at this particular time.

It is only when this becomes embedded in social work agency practices that social work can be seen to base its practice on research.

putting it into practice

In earlier chapters we have asked you to think about a piece of research that you might want to undertake relating to your own practice. In other chapters we have asked you to think about a specific project involving elder care. Choose to focus on one of these for this exercise.

Go to http://www.researchregister.org.uk/. Here you will find the SCIE Research Register for Social Care. Decide what information you might need to help you prepare to undertake your research in this area – what other research results you could draw on.

Using the access facilities as described on the website search and access the information that looks relevant and useful.

1. When you have done this reflect on how easy you found it to navigate the site.
    i. What were the benefits or positives of the site?
    ii. What were the difficulties or barriers to using the site?
2. Consider how useful the information is that you have been able to access.
    i. Is it written in a format that is easy to understand?
    ii. Are you reassured that the research is rigorous and has been reviewed?
3. Does the information that you have accessed cause you to:
    i. Rethink your approach to the research you would undertake?
    ii. Rethink the way that you approach this aspect of practice?
4. While you were navigating the site did you see other categories that interested you? Did you think that you might return to the site to find out more information about topics relating to your practice?

If you were planning to undertake this research you would need to do the same exercise with other sites, so you might like to try that now. For example:

Joseph Rowntree Foundation: http://www.jrf.org.uk/
Research in Practice: http://www.rip.org.uk/
Research in Practice for Adults: http://www.ripfa.org.uk/
Barnardo's: http://www.barnardos.org.uk/

Recommended reading

Ruckdeschel, R. and Chambon, A. (2009) 'The Uses of Social Work Research', in I. Shaw, K. Briar-Lawson, J. Orme and R. Ruckdeschel (eds) *The Handbook of Social Work Research*. London, Sage. This chapter explores the links between the production, use and dissemination of research based knowledge.

Conclusion

Introduction

Throughout this text we have been focusing on developing a research base for social work practice. In this conclusion we reflect on what we have learnt about the processes, structures and strategies necessary to develop such a research base. We stated in the Introduction that the text would not be a 'how to do it' guide to undertaking research but a synthesis of the arguments for a research base for social work and an examination of some core processes and practices. The structure of the book therefore helps us to identify three themes that have emerged that are distinctive, but not exclusive, to social work research.

Situating social work research

The first theme focuses on the need to situate social work research in the wider social sciences, and especially to identify links with social theory and critical theory. Doing this helps us to understand the complexities of knowledge production in what is usually described as social research. Understanding the epistemological arguments for approaches to social work research helps us to be realistic about the implications of findings but also ensures that social work research is rigorous and is based on more than anecdote or personal opinion. It will be able to withstand the scrutiny of researchers from other disciplines. That is not to say that it is necessary for all social work research to use particular approaches – quite the opposite! Knowledge gained from in-depth enquiry with a small number of participants can be just as meaningful as a large-scale data gathering exercise. But in both the limits of interpretation and significance have to be acknowledged.

Situating social work research in the wider social sciences also enables us to demonstrate that social work research is more than just the appliance of other subject areas. It offers opportunities to produce new knowledge and develop new insights into how individuals and societies operate. Social workers intervene in social situations that involve relationships between individuals and between individuals and formal and informal structures. These include highly complex interpersonal interactions. Social work research therefore has to find ways of exploring or investigating these situations. This raises challenges in terms of both the methods needed to gain knowledge and the ethical considerations raised by the often sensitive nature of the situations. Social work researchers have to work closely with practitioners and those to whom their services are offered, but they can also draw on skills developed in practice. Acknowledging this means that social work research does not merely draw on other social sciences for its methods and understandings; it can contribute to research undertaken by other disciplines. This contribution includes new methodological approaches and new knowledge about social situations that can provide new insights and new theories.

Developing the research base

The second theme develops from this position: that social work has something to contribute to the wider social sciences. To do this and to be useful to social work practitioners, social work must develop a research base comprised of projects that have been undertaken rigorously and are critically reflective in the presentation of their results. While it is important to increase the volume of social work research this should not be done at the expense of the quality of the research.

We have offered an insight into a range of methods that can be used in social work research. But this is only an indication of the wealth of approaches to enquiry that can be undertaken. In providing some detailed exploration of certain methods we have tried to indicate the level of knowledge that is required to undertake rigorous research. We have also attempted to show how different methodological approaches provide different kinds of knowledge for social work practice.

While not necessarily favouring any one methodological approach, we have explored the complexity of the situations researched by social work researchers and tried to indicate that an either/or approach is not always the most helpful in providing useful knowledge for practice. What is necessary is the use of methods that are fit for purpose, that answer the particular question posed. It is the question that has to be useful as well as the methods used to elicit answers if the knowledge produced is to be helpful for practice.

Starting from this position means that social work research should also be involved with colleagues from other disciplines in the development of methodological approaches that will provide important understandings of ever more complex social situations. Building up interdisciplinary and interprofessional partnerships can help to improve the status of social work research by, among other things, making other researchers aware of the extent and quality of the social work research base.

Embedding research in practice

The final theme recognizes that while it is important to increase the volume of social work research, there is little point in producing more research if it is not to be used by practitioners.

We have indicated above that the questions asked and the knowledge gained have to be fit for purpose: that is, they have to address concerns and puzzles confronting policy-makers, agency managers, practitioners and those who use the services. However, when such research is produced it is necessary to have structures and processes in agencies that enable it to be accessed by those who need it. Structures and processes also have to be in place to enable and encourage practitioners and others to reflect on the knowledge and information being produced and the implications of that knowledge for their own and their agency's practice.

This does not mean that practice has to change every time a new research study is published. Practitioners have to be discerning. They have to have the knowledge and skills to critically evaluate the research that is produced. This includes assessing the question posed, the methods used and the interpretation of the findings produced. To do this practitioners have to be both research minded and research literate: they have to consult the research as part of their overall assessment of situations but they also have to be able to discern whether the messages from research are valid.

Developing research based social work practice

The overview informs strategies for developing a research base for social work. In the UK the JUC SWEC research strategy (see Bywaters, 2008) provides one set of approaches, but this is predominantly from the perspective of social work academics. We conclude with some thoughts about the different components of developing a social work research base.

Educating for research

As indicated in the Introduction to this text, developments in social work education provide opportunities for the integration of research and practice. These opportunities are provided for beginning practitioners to be educated and trained in the basics of undertaking research to enable them to critically reflect on research findings. Evidence to date (Orme *et al.*, 2008) suggests that there is still some way to go before research is embedded in the curriculum of social work courses in ways that will prepare beginning practitioners to undertake the critique. Nevertheless, it is apparent that raising the level of the qualification and the length of training has enabled educators to address some of the deficits of previous qualifying levels that had been identified (Orme and Powell, 2008).

However, there are a number of caveats to putting all our research eggs in the qualifying education basket. The first is that it is unfair and unwise to expect students and newly qualified workers, probably the least powerful people in an organization, to bring about significant change in the culture of the organizations they join.

The second is that there is a constant and unhelpful tension between research and practice. Discussions about the content of social work courses at the introduction of the degree, and subsequent reviews in the light of child abuse enquiries (for information about the Social Work Task Force see http://www.dcsf.gov.uk/swtf/), often involve assertions from ministers and civil servants that the qualifying degree has to be about practice. At the same time there are repeated calls for practice to be evidenced-based. How can practice be evidenced-based if social workers are not able to access and evaluate the evidence that is produced? What kind of evidence will be produced if practitioners are not engaged with research by either raising research questions from their practice for others to investigate, or investigating the research questions themselves?

The split between research and practice has implications for the quality of education and training. There is evidence in the audit of research teaching on social work courses (Orme *et al.*, 2008) that little or no research teaching takes place in social work agencies. The amount of supervised practice required on the degree is also seen to limit the opportunities for teaching research methods. The emphasis is therefore on introducing students to the research evidence related to particular subject areas such as child protection or elder care. While this is important it does not necessarily lead to the skills development necessary to critically evaluate research and/or undertake rigorous research. This means that students might have to be self-motivated, or that the introduction to research methods teaching takes place at post-qualifying level.

Continuum across the professional life course

The need for introductory teaching in research methods could be seen as part of a continuum of education and training across the professional life course. In terms of developing a robust research base for practice this would involve practitioners progressing from being research minded and research aware; to becoming research informed; and ultimately being research competent and literate (Orme and Powell, 2008, p. 1004). Such a continuum needs to be embedded in arrangements for post-registration learning and teaching (PRTL). For this to occur effectively research would need to be included in all post qualifying courses, not just in specific courses on research such as a master in research (MRes). For example, to change the culture at qualifying level it is necessary for those involved in supervising and assessing students on their practice component to be aware of the need to critically reflect on research findings as part of thinking about assessment and intervention strategies. Courses preparing practitioners to work with students therefore need to equip participants with the means both to critically evaluate research and to develop structures and methods in supervision sessions to encourage and enable students to do this.

A joint Research and the PQ Framework issued by JUC SWEC and the General Social Care Council (GSCC) (http://www.gscc.org.uk/Publications/) recognizes the need for attention to research in post-qualifying training but does not go as far as suggesting that all post-qualifying courses should have a research training element.

Engagement of practice agencies

Such recommendations for training highlight the need for changes in the responsiveness to and engagement of social work agencies in the research agenda. In Chapters 9 and 10 we discussed a number of initiatives to encourage the use of research in practice. However, it is noteworthy that these have tended to take place in the voluntary and independent sectors.

There is some attention to research agendas in statutory agencies. However, in Scotland a *Preliminary Report on a Survey of Practice-related Research* (Miller, 2007, p. 7) found that there was considerable difference between the most research-active and the least research-active local authorities. This may be to do with organizational culture and how research activities are valued by key personnel within the local authority. It might also be related to pressures on agencies in terms of levels of personnel and resources. To give time to practitioners to investigate and reflect on research findings requires appropriate staffing levels and workload allocation. Allocating time to such activities might be seen to take practitioners away from direct work with service users. Here is the conundrum: if no priority, and therefore no time, is given to ensuring that practitioners use the best and most effective practice, then the time spent could be time wasted for both practitioners and services users.

Miller (2007) also found that there was a lack of clarity about who knows about and who is responsible for organizing research in local authorities. This suggests the need for clarification of roles concerning practice-relevant research and the managerial level at which the responsibility for research is recognized. There is no need to suppose that Scotland is very different from other countries. But as a result of the *Changing Lives* (2004) agenda there has been more active support for developing research in and for practice in Scotland. It was this that led to the survey being undertaken.

There is an urgent need for practice agencies to engage with the research agenda. Until agencies have the infrastructure to support research usage there will be little change in opportunities for students and practitioners to learn about research in practice. There will also be limited opportunities for practice to inform the research agenda.

Practitioner research

The most obvious way to ensure that the practice agenda informs the research agenda is for practitioners to be involved by undertaking research on topics that arise from their own practice, that of their colleagues and issues raised by service users. In other words they have the opportunity to become reflective research practitioners.

There is evidence of practice research. Miller (2007) found many examples of excellent and innovative research practices in Scotland that can be drawn upon and disseminated across the local authorities and across the different sectors. She concludes that there is a desire to develop research capacity within the local authorities. Shaw (2005), however, found that there was a tendency for practitioner researchers to be isolated within organizations.

Such initiatives obviously require that practitioners have a sound education and training base to enable them to undertake rigorous research. However, as has been said, practice can also enhance the development of approaches to research. Shaw (2005), for example, suggests that practitioner research needs to refashion the interface between methodology and methods of social work practice and research. Generating practitioner research capacity, he argues, would recognize the genuinely 'practical' agenda in practitioner research and promote critical practice (Shaw, 2005, p. 1245). Clearly what is needed is the reconfiguration of agencies to value both the use of research and the opportunities to undertake research. This would impact on the way agencies are structured, who has responsibility for research activities and how research fits within the wider mission of the agency. It could involve the creation of dedicated practitioner research posts (Bywaters, 2007) or the role of reflective practitioner researcher described in Chapter 10. Alternatively, or additionally, units within organizations could be created to coordinate practice research and support those undertaking it, providing supervision and access to resources as well as mechanisms for disseminating the findings and helping them to permeate practice. This approach is exemplified by Mullen's work in North America in establishing a Center for the Study of Social Work Practice (Mullen, 2002).

Conclusion

The climate in which this text is published is extremely exciting in terms of the opportunities to develop a research base for practice. There are a number of initiatives at local, national and international levels involving practice and policy agendas. This means that there are opportunities for all stakeholders in social work to inform these agendas.

In this text we have maintained that good social work practice requires a strong research base and that all practitioners should be research-aware and research-alert. We have also suggested that particular roles could be created to facilitate the research agenda for practice. This is because we firmly believe that developing a research base for practice is an iterative process: for practitioners to base their practice on research the research must draw on practice.

Appendix: Assessment of Disorganized Attachment and Maltreatment (ADAM) Project

Introduction

Many commentators believe we are at a critical point in the safeguarding of children and that tried and tested approaches, with a strong evidence base (see, for example, Bakermans-Kranenburg *et al.*, 2007), from other disciplines to the assessment of referrals and allegations now need to be considered. Recent developments in attachment theory and research offer such a prospect because, if certain assessment techniques are used, they focus on the way the mind of an abused or neglected child quickly betrays what is happening to them. The appeal for social work practitioners is that these methods are child-friendly, ethically sound and reliable (if used in conjunction with confident professional judgement and analysis). Mild separation and reunion experiences can detect the presence of disorganized attachment behaviour, an indicator of fear of (or fear 'for') a caregiver. Disorganized attachment, as Mary Main puts it, strongly indicates 'fear without a solution'; a child 'in harm's way'. The use of story stem completion exercises and attachment interviews can also identify catastrophic and disorganized narratives from the child's concluding accounts; and the analysis of children's drawings and artwork will expose similar patterns.

At present, professionals tend to rely on three approaches, either individually or in combination, to the investigation of abuse and neglect. First, they aim to develop a trusting relationship with children so that they will eventually feel safe enough to disclose. The problem with this approach is it can take too long, or it may never occur. Second, they hope that abusing carers will admit that they are placing a child in danger or failing to protect them. But, again, some carers cannot or will not accept such responsibility; indeed, recent high-profile tragic cases have also introduced a shocked public to the phenomenon of 'disguised compliance' and the highly manipulative parent (in the case of Karen Matthews, a mother who abducted her daughter, Sharon, in order to gain financially from the media coverage). The third way professionals investigate allegations of abuse and neglect is by the identification and risk assessment of 'signs and symptoms', but Marian Brandon presented at a conference in 2009 on the findings of two studies into over 350 Serious Case Reviews in the UK the following bullet point: 'Most cases were too complex for serious injury and death to be predictable' (see also Brandon *et al.*, 2005). Eileen Munro (2002) also explains why signs and symptoms can only rarely be used confidently to predict future harm or neglect to a child.

Aim

Attachment-based assessments offer a complementary way for professionals to investigate allegations of abuse and neglect. A series of discussions with practitioners and supervisors are planned as an action research project to apply attachment-based assessment methods to social work.

Using evidence-informed research into disorganized attachment

When a child is abused by a parent or caregiver, their brain 'creates a series of internal messages that, basically, conveys to them that 'this must be happening because I am unworthy and unlovable'. It is rare that a child being abused – especially in cases of sexual and emotional abuse – would actually blame the adult; not only do they suffer the abuse, they are very likely to believe it was their fault. But it is precisely such pernicious and powerful internal messages that, if the social worker is trained to understand them, can provide some of the evidence needed to protect the child (or at least raise other questions).

There are various ways of creating the conditions for understanding the operation of a child's mind. One is story stem completion. The child is told the beginning of an 'attachment-related' story – for example, one involving a mild separation experience as in 'Mummy and Daddy [this would be modified to suit the circumstances of the particular child] have gone out for the evening and you are going to be looked after by a [known] babysitter. Can you show and tell me what happens next?' A 'typical' story told by a securely attached child might be 'Well . . . I told Emma [the babysitter] that I am allowed to watch Dr Who – but Mummy doesn't let me! – so I got a bit scared and when I went to bed I thought I could see a monster on my wall – Emma said it wasn't really a monster but I still wanted the light on – then I could hear Mummy and Daddy come back and I thought I would get told off but instead Daddy read me a story and Mummy made me some hot chocolate and then I went to sleep.' Securely attached children can risk mildly frightening themselves, precisely because they believe things end 'happily ever after' – it is the basis of the enduring popularity of nursery rhymes, which are often quite violent. Children being abused or seriously neglected tell very different stories (if they tell one at all, because some refuse or become distressed – a signal in itself) involving catastrophic events and mysterious aliens, often with the child being abducted or imprisoned. No one rescues the child, who is invariably left abandoned. The manner of telling the story can sometimes be somewhat 'matter-of-fact'.

As it is virtually impossible for an adult to censor or coach a child to present or avoid certain themes or stories – they could only tell them not to cooperate, which would be an important indicator in itself – such methods offer a reliable way of finding out what may be happening to a child thought to be in need of protection.

Different techniques need to be used with children under 3–4 years of age because they do not possess the cognitive skills needed to make sense of the 'game'. With toddlers, certain behaviours need to be observed and watched for carefully in situations when their attachment system is mildly activated, such as a carer leaving the room temporarily and then returning or, more deliberately, observing a child's behaviour when in the close proximity of a suspected abuser. For example, sequential or simultaneous displays of contradictory behaviour (e.g. strong proximity seeking followed by marked avoidance, such as running away from a parent while extremely distressed) could be symptomatic of 'disorganized attachment', a pattern often seen in children who are frightened of, or frightened for, a parent (as in the case of the unpredictable caregiving given by a chronic and persistent drug-using parent). Similarly, 'freezing', along with slowed movements and expressions (e.g. no movement and a dazed expression), should raise questions in the professional's mind, as would direct indicators of unexpected or unwarranted apprehension of the parent (e.g. a startled or fearful expression when being picked up).

Range of assessment-based methods

In summary, the following range of methods will be included, some of which have general application, whereas others are age-specific:

- 'naturally occurring' observable behaviours (all ages);
- troubled 'reunion' behaviour when an abusing caregiver leaves the child for a short period and then returns (c.9 months to 3 years);
- use of story stem completion tasks and analysis of picture response attachment-related drawings (c.4–9 years);
- the Child Attachment Interview (c.8–15 years);
- the Adult Attachment Interview (adults and caregivers);
- Assessment of Parental Sensitivity (adults and caregivers).

It is important to stress again that the aim is not to train practitioners to use these assessment devices in their strict clinical sense, which aims at a more precise classification of attachment behaviour. Instead, professionals will need to acquire a deep sense of the theoretical principles of attachment underpinning the methods in order to observe, understand and analyse children's behaviour with a purpose. The results of these assessments will need to be incorporated into other emerging and accumulated evidence; it is unlikely, for example, that isolated observations would be accepted as evidence in a court.

References

Abell, N. (2001) 'Assessing Willingness to Care for Persons with AIDS: Validation of a New Measure', *Research on Social Work Practice*, 11(1): 118–30.

Alaszewski, A. and Manthorpe, J. (1993) 'Quality and the Welfare Services: A Literature Review', *British Journal of Social Work*, 23: 653–65.

Aldgate, J. (2001) *The Children Act Now: Messages from Research*. London, Department of Health.

Arber, S. and Gilbert, N. (1989) 'Men: The Forgotten Carers', *Sociology*, 23(1): 111–18.

Aron, A., Aron, E.N., Tudor, M. and Nelson, G. (1991) 'Close Relationships as Including Other in the Self', *Journal of Personality and Social Psychology*, 60: 241–53.

Atkin, K. and Rolling, J. (1996) 'Looking After Their Own?', in W.I.U. Ahmad and K. Atkin (eds) *'Race' and Community Care*. Buckingham, Open University Press.

Atkinson, M.W., Kessel, N. and Dalgaard, J.B. (1975) 'The comparability of suicide rates', *British Journal of Psychiatry*, 127: 247–56.

Babbie, E. (1998) *The Practice of Social Research*. Belmont, CA, Wadsworth Publishing Co.

Bakermans-Kranenburg, M.J., Van IJzendoorn, M.H. and Juffer, F. (2005) 'Disorganized Infant Attachment and Preventive Interventions: A Review and Meta-Analysis', *Infant Mental Health Journal*, 26(3): 191–216.

Bakermans-Kranenburg, M.J., Van IJzendoorn, M.H. and Juffer, F. (2007) 'Less Is More: Meta-Analytic Arguments for the Use of Sensitivity-Focused Interventions', in *Promoting Positive Parenting: An Attachment-Based Intervention*. Totowa, NJ, Lawrence Erlbaum.

Balen, R., Blyth, E., Calabretto, H., Fraser, C., Horrocks, C. and Manby, M. (2006) 'Involving Children in Health and Social Research: "Human becomings" or "active beings"', *Childhood*, 13(1): 29–48.

Banks, S. (2006) *Ethics and Values in Social Work*. Basingstoke, Palgrave.

Banks, S., Hugman, R., Healy, L., Bozalek, V. and Orme, J. (2008) 'Global Ethics for Social Work: Problems and Possibilities – Papers from *Ethics and Social Welfare Symposium* Durban, July 2008', *Ethics and Social Welfare*, 2(3): 276–90.

Barber, J. (1996) 'Science and Social Work: Are They Compatible?', *Research on Social Work Practice*, 6(3): 379–88.

Bates, S., Clapton, J. and Coren, E. (2007) 'Systematic Maps to Support the Evidence Base in Social Care', *Evidence and Policy*, 3(4): 539–51.

Bauman, Z. (1993) *Postmodern Ethics*. Oxford, Blackwell.

Beauchamp, T.L. and Childress, J.F. (1989) *Principles of Biomedical Ethics*. Oxford, Oxford University Press.

Becker, S. and Bryman, A. (eds) (2004) *Understanding Research for Social Policy and Practice*. Bristol, Policy Press.

Beresford, P. (1999) 'Research Note: Research and Empowerment', *British Journal of Social Work*, 29(5): 671–7.

Beresford, P. (2000) 'Service Users' Knowledge and Social Work Theory: Conflict and Collaboration', *British Journal of Social Work*, 30(4): 489–505.

Beresford, P. and Croft, S. (1986) 'An Empowering Approach to Research', in P. Beresford and S. Croft (eds), *Whose Welfare Private Care and Public Services*. Brighton, Lewis Cohen Urban Studies Centre.

Biestek, B. (1961) *The Casework Relationship*. London, Allen & Unwin.

Booth, C. (1886–1903) *The Survey into Life and Labour in London* (http://booth.lse.ac.uk/static/b/index.html).

Brandon, M., Dodsworth, J. and Rumball, D. (2005) 'Serious Case Reviews: Learning to Use Expertise', *Child Abuse Review*, 14(3): 160–76.

Brannen, J. (2005) 'Mixing Methods: The Entry of Qualitative and Quantitative Approaches into the Research Process', *International Journal of Social Research Methodology*, 8(3): 173–84.

Braye, S. and Preston-Shoot, M. (2007) 'On Systematic Reviews in Social Work: Observations from Teaching, Learning and Assessment of Law in Social Work Education', *British Journal of Social Work*, 37: 313–34.

Briskman, L. (2009) 'Nations', in I. Shaw, K. Briar-Lawson, J. Orme and R. Ruckdeschel (eds) *The Handbook of Social Work Research*. London, Sage.

Broad, B. (1999) *The Politics of Social Work Research*. Birmingham, Venture Press.

Broad, B. and Saunders, L. (1998) 'Involving Young People Leaving Care as Peer Researchers in a Health Research Project: A Learning Experience', *Research Policy and Planning*, 16(1): 1–9.

Bryman, A. (2008) *Social Research Methods*. Oxford, Oxford University Press.

Bulmer, M. (1982) *The Uses of Social Research*. London, Allen & Unwin.

Butler, I. (2000) *A Code of Ethics for Social Work and Social Care Research*. Theorising Social Work Research series. London, Scie.

Butler, I. (2002) 'Critical Commentary (A Code of Ethics for Social Work and Social Care Research)', *British Journal of Social Work*, 32(2): 239–48.

Bywaters, P. (2008) 'Research Strategy for Social Work in the UK', *British Journal of Social Work*, 38(5): 936–52.

CCETSW (1989) 'Requirements and Regulations for the Diploma in Social Work, Paper 30', London, CCETSW.

Challis, D. and Davies, B. (1986) *Case Management and Community Care*. Aldershot, Gower.

Chapman, T. and Hough, M. (1998) *Evidence Based Practice: A Guide to Effective Practice*. London, HMSO.

Clark, C.L. (2000) *Social Work Ethics: Politics, Principles and Practice*. Basingstoke, Palgrave.

Corby, B. (2006) *Applying Research in Social Work Practice*. Maidenhead, Open University Press.

Coren, E. (2009) Presentation to conference on Systematic Reviews held in February 2009 as part of the UK's Researcher Development Initiative (RDI 2).

Coren, E. and Fisher, M. (2006) *The Conduct of Systematic Reviews for Scie Knowledge Reviews*. London, Scie.

Coulshed, V. and Orme, J. (2004) *Social Work Practice: An Introduction*. Basingstoke, Palgrave.

Cresswell, J.W., Fetters, M.D. and Ivankova, N.V. (2004) 'Designing a Mixed Methods Study in Primary Care', *Annals of Family Medicine*, 2: 7–12.

Crittenden, P.M. (1998) 'Dangerous Behavior and Dangerous Contexts: A Thirty-Five Year Perspective on Research on the Developmental Effects of Child Physical Abuse', in P. Trickett (ed.) *Violence to Children*. Washington, DC, American Psychological Association.

Davies, M. (1969) *Probationers and Their Social Environment*. Home Office Research Unit. London, HMSO.

Davies, P. (2004) 'Is Evidence Based Government Possible? Jerry Lee Lecture 2004', *4th Annual Campbell Collaboration Colloquium*, Washington, DC.

D'Cruz, H. and Jones, M. (2004) *Social Work Research Ethical Issues and Political Contexts*. London, Sage.

Delanty, G. (1997) *Social Science Beyond Constructivism and Relativism*. Buckingham, Open University.

Denzin, N.K. and Lincoln, Y.S. (eds) (1998) *The Landscape of Qualitative Research*. London, Sage.

Department of Health (2002) *Requirements for Social Work Training*. London, HMSO.

Department of Health (2005) *Research Governance Framework for Health and Social Care*. London, HMSO.

Department of Health (2008) *Evaluation of the Social Work Degree in England*. London, Department of Health

De Vaus, D. (2001) *Research Design in Social Research*. London, Sage.

Dominelli, L. (2005) 'Social Work Research: Contested Knowledge for Practice', in R. Adams, L. Dominelli and M. Payne (eds) *Social Work Futures: Crossing Boundaries, Transforming Practice*. Basingstoke, Palgrave.

Dominelli, L. and Holloway, M. (2008) 'Ethics and Governance in Social Work Research in the UK', *British Journal of Social Work*, 38: 1009–24.

Douglas, J.D. (1967) *The Social Meaning of Suicide*. Princeton, NJ, Princeton University Press.

Durkheim, E. (1951) *Suicide: A Study in Sociology*. New York, The Free Press.

ESRC (n.d.) (http://www.esrc.ac.uk/ESRCInfoCentre/what_is_soc_sci/index.aspx?ComponentId=1432&SourcePageId=19533).

ESRC (2007) *Research Ethics Framework*. Swindon, ESRC.

Everitt, A., Hardiker, P., Littlewood, J. and Mullender, A. (1992) *Applied Research for Better Practice*. Basingstoke, Macmillan.

Featherstone, B. and Lancaster, E. (1997) 'Contemplating the Unthinkable: Men Who Sexually Abuse Children', *Critical Social Policy*, 17(4): 57–71.

Fernandez, E. and Romeo, R. (2003) 'Implementation of the Framework for the Assessment of Children and Their Families: The Experience of Barnardos Australia', University of New South Wales, report to the UK Department of Health.

Field, A. (2009) *Discovering Statistics: Using SPSS for Windows*. London: Sage.

Fischer, J. (1973) 'Is Casework Effective? A review', *Social Work*, 18: 5–20.

Fisher, M. (1994) 'Man-Made Care: Community Care and Older Male Carers', *British Journal of Social Work*, 24: 659–80.

Fisher, M. (1999) 'Social Work Research, and Social Work Knowledge and the Research Assessment Exercise', in B. Broad (ed.) *The Politics of Social Work Research and Evaluation*. Birmingham, Venture Press.

Fisher, M. (2002) 'The Role of Service Users in Problem Formulation and Technical Aspects of Research', *Social Work Education*, 21(3): 305–12.

Fisher, M., Francis, J. and Fischer, C. (2007) *Social Care Research Capacity Consultation*. SCIE Report 16, London, Scie.

Fisher, M. and Marsh, P. (2001) 'Social Work Research and the 2001 Research Assessment Exercise: An Initial Overview', *Social Work Education*, 22(1): 71–80.

Folkard, S. (1974) *IMPACT*. London, HMSO.

Fonagy, P., Target, M., Steele, H. and Steele, M. (1998). *Reflective-Functioning Manual, Version 5.0, for Application to Adult Attachment Interviews*. London, University College London.

Fortune, R., Briar-Lawson, K. and McCallion, P. (eds) (forthcoming) *Practice Research for the 21st Century*. New York, Columbia University Press.

Fraley, R.C., Waller, N.G. and Brennan, K.A. (2000) 'An Item-Response Theory Analysis of Self-Report Measures of Adult Attachment', *Journal of Personality and Social Psychology*, 78: 350–65.

Frei, J.R. and Shaver, P.R. (2002) 'Respect in Close Relationships: Prototype Definition, Self Report Assessment, and Initial Correlates', *Personal Relationships*, 9: 121–39.

Fuller, R. and Petch, A. (1995) *Practitioner Research: The Reflexive Social Worker*. Buckingham, Open University Press.

Furniss, J. (ed.) (1998) *A Guide to Effective Practice: Evidence Based Practice*. London, HM Inspectorate of Probation.

Gabbay, J., le May, A., Jefferson, H., Webb, D., Lovelock, R., Powell, J. and Lathlean, J. (2003) 'A Case Study of Knowledge Management in Multi-Agency Consumer-Informed "Community of Practice": Implications for Evidence-Based Policy Development in Health and Social Services', *Interdisciplinary Journal for the Social Study of Health, Illness and Medicine*, 7(3): 283–310.

GAfREC (2001) *Governance Arrangements for Research Ethics Committees: A Proposed Harmonised Edition*. London, Department of Health (http://www.

nres.npsa.nhs.uk/news-and-publications/news/harmonised-gafrec-consulta-tion/).

Gambrill, E. (2003) 'Evidence-Based Practice: Sea Change or the Emperor's New Clothes?', *Journal of Social Work Education*, 39(1): 3–23.

Gambrill, E. (2007) 'Views of Evidence-Based Practice: Social Workers' Codes of Ethics and Accreditation Standards as Guides for Choice', *Journal of Social Work Education*, 43(3): 447–62.

Gibbs, D. (1999) 'Disabled People and the Research Community', paper presented to the Theorising Social Work Research ESRC Seminar series (http://www.scie.org.uk/publications/misc/tswr/seminar2.asp).

Gilbert, N. (2008) *Researching Social Life*. London, Sage.

Gilgun, J. (1994) 'Hand in Glove: The Grounded Theory Approach and Social Work Practice Research', in E. Sherman and W.J. Reid (eds) *Qualitative Research in Social Work*. New York, Columbia Press.

Gilgun, J. (2008) 'Lived Experience, Reflexivity, and Research on Perpetrators of Interpersonal Violence', *Qualitative Social Work*, 7(2): 181–98.

Gilgun, J. (2009) 'Methods for Enhancing Theory and Knowledge about Problems, Policies, and Practice', in I. Shaw, K. Briar-Lawson, J. Orme and R. Ruckdeschel (eds) *The Handbook for Social Work Research*. London, Sage.

Glaser, B. and Strauss, A. (1967) *The Discovery of Grounded Theory: Strategies for Qualitative Research*. Chicago: Aldine.

Green, H. (1988) *General Household Survey 1985: Informal Carers*. London, HMSO.

Guba, E. (1990) *The Paradigm Dialogue*. Newbury Park, CA, Sage.

Guba, E.G. and Lincoln, Y.S. (1989) *Fourth Generation Evaluation*. Newbury Park, CA, Sage.

Guba, E.G. and Lincoln, Y.S. (1998) 'Competing Paradigms in Qualitative Research', in N. Denzin and Y. Lincoln (eds) *The Landscape of Qualitative Research*. London, Sage.

Hall, C.J. (1999) *Social Work as Narrative: Storytelling and Persuasion in Professional Texts*. Aldershot, Ashgate.

Hammersley, M. (ed.) (1993) *Social Research: Philosophy, Politics and Practice*. London, Sage.

Hammersley, M. (1995) *The Politics of Social Research*. London, Sage.

Hammersley, M. (2003) 'Social Research Today: Some Dilemmas and Distinctions', *Qualitative Social Work*, 2(1): 25–44.

Harding, S. (1987) *Feminism and Methodology*. Milton Keynes, Open University Press.

Harrington, D. and Dolgoff, R. (2008) 'Hierarchies of Ethical Principles for Ethical Decision-Making in Social Work', *Ethics and Social Welfare*, 2(2): 183–96.

HEFCE (2000) *The Benchmark Statement for Honours Degrees in Social Policy and Administration, and Social Work*.

Henn, M., Weinstein, M. and Foard, N. (2006) *A Short Introduction to Social Research*. London, Sage.

Holosko, M.J. (2001) 'Overview of Qualitative Methods', in B.A. Thyer (ed.) *Handbook of Social Work Research Methods*. London, Sage.

Hood, S., Mayall, B. and Oliver, S. (1999) *Critical Issues in Social Research: Power and Prejudice*. Buckingham, Open University Press.

Horne, M. (1987) *Values in Social Work*. Aldershot, Wildwood House.

Howe, D. (1987) *An Introduction to Social Work Theory*. Aldershot, Arena.

Howe, D., Brandon, M., Hinings, D. and Schofield, G. (1999) *Attachment Theory, Child Maltreatment and Family Support: A Practice and Assessment Model*. London, Macmillan.

Howe, D., Shemmings, D. and Feast, S. (2001) 'Age at Placement and Adopted People's Experience of Being Adopted', *Child and Family Social Work*, 6: 337–50.

Hughes, J. (1990) *The Philosophy of Social Research*. London, Longman.

Hughes, M., McNeish, D., Newman, T., Roberts, H. and Sachdev, D. (2000) *Methods and Tools – Making Connections: Linking Research and Practice*. York, JRF.

Hugman, R. (2009) 'Social Work Research and Ethics', in I. Shaw, K. Briar Lawson, J. Orme and R. Ruckdeschel (eds) *The Handbook of Social Work Research*. London, Sage.

Hugman, R. and Smith, D. (eds) (1995) *Ethical Issues in Social Work*. London, Routledge.

Humm, M. (ed.) (1992) *Feminisms: A Reader*. London, Harvester Wheatsheaf.

Husband, C. (1995) 'The Morally Active Practitioner and the Ethics of Anti Racist Social Work', in R. Hugman and D. Smith (eds) *Ethical Issues in Social Work*. London, Routledge.

IASSW/IFSW (2000) *International Definition of Social Work*. International Association of Schools of Social Work and International Federation of Social Workers (http://www.iassw-aiets.org/index.php?option=com_content&task=view&id=6&Itemid=51).

IFSW/IASSW (2004) *Ethics in Social Work: Statement of Principles*. London: IFSW/IASSW.

Janowitz, M. (1972) *Sociological Models and Social Policy*. Morristown, NJ, General Learning Systems.

Jones, C. (1979) 'Social Work Education 1900–1977', in N. Parry, M. Rustin and C. Satyamurti (eds) *State Social Work, Welfare and the State*. London, Arnold.

Jones, C. (2001) 'Voices from the Front Line: State Social Workers and New Labour', *British Journal of Social Work*, 31: 547–62.

JUC SWEC (2006) *A Social Work Research Strategy in Higher Education 2006–2020*. Joint University Social Work Education Committee (http://www.swap.ac.uk/research/strategy.asp).

Kirk, S.A. and Reid, W.J. (2002) *Science and Social Work: A Critical Appraisal*. New York, Columbia University Press.

Kuhn, T.S. (1970) *The Structure of Scientific Revolutions*. Chicago, University of Chicago Press.

Laming, L. (2003) *The Victoria Climbié Inquiry*. London, HMSO.

Littell, J. H. (2005) 'Lessons from a Systematic Review of Effects of Multisystemic Therapy', *Children and Youth Services Review*, 27(4): 4.

Littell, J. H. (2006) 'The Case for Multisystemic Therapy: Evidence or Orthodoxy?', *Children and Youth Services Review*, 28(4): 458–72.

Lyons, K. (1999) *Social Work in Higher Education: Demise or Development*. Aldershot, Ashgate.

Lyons, K. (2000) 'The Place of Research in Social Work Education', *British Journal of Social Work*, 30(4): 433–48.

Lyons, K. and Orme, J. (1998) 'The 1996 Research Assessment Exercise and the Response of Social Work Academics', *British Journal of Social Work*, 28: 783–792.

McDonald, G. (1994) 'Developing Empirically-Based Practice in Probation', *British Journal of Social Work*, 24: 405–27.

McDonald, G. (1999) 'Social Work and Its Evaluation: A Methodological Dilemma?', in F. Williams, J. Popay and A. Oakley (eds) *Welfare Research: A Critical Review*. London, UCL Press.

McDonald, G., Sheldon, B. and Gillespie, J. (1992) 'Contemporary Studies of Effectiveness in Social Work', *British Journal of Social Work*, 22(6): 615–43.

McLaughlin, H. (2007) *Understanding Social Work Research*. London, Sage.

McLennan, G. (1995) 'Feminism, Epistemology and Postmodernism: Reflections on Current Ambivalence', *Sociology*, 29(2): 391–409.

McNeill, F., Bracken, D. and Clarke, A. (2009) 'Social Work in Criminal Justice', in I. Shaw, K. Briar Lawson, J. Orme and R. Ruckdeschel (eds) *The Handbook of Social Work Research*. London, Sage.

Marsh, P. and Fisher, M. (2005) *Developing the Evidence Base for Social Work and Social Care Practice*. London, Scie.

May, T. (1996) *Situating Social Theory*. Buckingham, Open University Press.

May, T. (1997) *Social Research: Issues, Methods and Process*. Buckngham, Open University Press.

Mayer, J. and Timms, N. (1970) *The Client Speaks*. London, Routledge & Kegan Paul.

Mayhew, H. (1861) *London Labour and the London Poor*. London, Griffin, Bohn, and Company.

Maynard, M. (1985) 'The Response of Social Workers to Domestic Violence', in J. Pahl (ed.) *Private Violence and Public Policy: The Needs of Battered Women and the Response of the Public Services*. London, Routledge & Kegan Paul.

Mertens, D.M. (2008) 'Deep in Ethical Waters', *Qualitative Social Work*, 7(4): 484–503.

Miller, K. (2007) *Preliminary Report on a Survey of Practice-related Research*. Dundee, Institute of Research and Innovation in Social Services (IRISS) (http://www.iriss.org.uk/node/271).

Mills, D., Jepson, A., Coxon, T., Easterby-Smith, M., Hawkins, T. and Spencer, J. (2006) *Demographic Review of the UK Social Sciences*. Swindon, ESRC.

Moriarty, J., Manthorpe, J., Wilcock, J. and Iliffe, S. (2007) 'Consulting with Stakeholders: Using the Expertise of Researchers, Professionals, Carers and Older People in Systematic Reviews', *Dementia: The International Journal of Social Research and Practice*, 6(3): 449–52.

Morris, J. (1993) 'Feminism and Disability', *Feminist Review*, 43: 57–70.

Mullen, E. (2002) 'Problem Formulation in Practitioner and Researcher Partnership: A Decade of Experience at the Centre for the Study of Social Work Practice', *Social Work Education*, 21(3): 323–36.

Mullender, A. (1996) *Rethinking Domestic Violence: The Social Work and Probation Response*. London, Routledge.

Mullender, A., Hague, G., Inam, U., Kelly, L., Malos, E. and Regan, L. (2002) *Children's Perspectives on Domestic Violence*. London, Sage.

Munro, E. (2002) *Effective Child Protection*. London, Sage.

Mutter, R., Shemmings, D., Dugmore, P. and Hyare, M. (2008) 'Restorative Justice and Family Group Conferencing', *Health and Social Care in the Community*, 16(3): 262–70.

National Children's Bureau (2003) *Guidelines for Research* (www.ncb.org.uk/research/research_guidelines.pdf).

Nutley, S.M., Walter, I. and Davies, H.T.O. (2007) *Using Evidence: How Research Can Inform Public Services*. Bristol, Policy Press.

Orme, J. (1995) *Workload: Measurement and Management*. Aldershot, Avebury (now Ashgate) in association with CEDR.

Orme, J. (1997) 'Research into Practice', in G. McKenzie, J. Powell and R. Usher (eds) *Understanding Social Research: Perspectives on Methodology and Practice*. Hove, Falmer Press.

Orme, J. (1998) 'Feminist Social Work Practice', in R. Adam, L. Dominelli and M. Payne (eds) *Social Work: Themes, Issues and Critical Debates*. Basingstoke, Macmillan.

Orme, J. (2000a) 'Interactive Social Sciences: Patronage or Partnership?', *Science and Public Policy*, 27(3): 211–19.

Orme, J. (2000b) 'Social Work: "The Appliance of Social Science" – A Cautionary Tale', *Social Work Education*, 19(4): 323–34.

Orme, J. (2001) '"Bitch or Lover": How Men Construe Women in Violent Relationships', paper presented to British Science Festival, University of Glasgow.

Orme, J. (2003) 'Why Social Work Needs Doctors', *Social Work Education*, 22(6): 541–54.

Orme, J. (2004) '"It's Feminist Because I Say So": Feminism, Social Work and Critical Practice in the UK', *Qualitative Social Work*, 2(2): 131–54.

Orme, J. (2008) 'Feminist Theory', in M. Gray and S.A. Webb (eds) *Social Work Theories and Methods*. London, Sage.

Orme, J. and Briar Lawson, K. (2009) 'Generating or Enhancing Theory and Knowledge about Social Problems and Social Policy and How Best to Enhance Policy Development', in I. Shaw, K. Briar Lawson, J. Orme and R. Ruckdeschel (eds) *The Handbook of Social Work Research*. London, Sage.

Orme, J., Fook, J., MacIntyre, G., Paul, S., Powell, J. and Sharland, E. (2008) *Audit of Research Teaching on the Social Work Degree*. Swindon, ESRC.

Orme, J., MacIntyre, G., Cavanagh, K., Crisp, B., Green-Lister, P., Hussein, S., Manthorp, G., Moriarty, J. and Stevens, M. (2007) 'What (a) Diifference a Degree Makes: An Evaluation of the Social Work Degree in England', *British Journal of Social Work*, 39(1): 161–78.

Orme, J. and Powell, J. (2008) 'Building Research Capacity in Social Work: Process and Issues', *British Journal of Social Work*, 38(5): 988–1008.

Orme, J. and Rennie, G. (2006) 'The Role of Registration in Assuring Ethical Practice', *International Social Work*, 49(3): 333–44.

Pahl, J. (2004) *Ethics Review in Social Care Research: Options, Appraisal and Guidelines*. London, Department of Health.

Pahl, J. (2007) *Ethics Review in Social Care Research: Report from the Planning Group on Ethics Reviews in Social Care Research*. Canterbury, University of Kent.

Paltridge, B. (2007) *Discourse Analysis: An Introduction*. New York, Continuum.

Parton, N. and Kirk, S. (2009) 'The Nature and Purpose of Social Work', in I. Shaw, K. Briar Lawson, J. Orme and R. Ruckdeschel (eds) *The Handbook of Social Work Research*. London, Sage.

Pawson, R., Boaz, A., Grayson, L., Long, A. and Barnes, C. (2003) *Types and Quality of Knowledge in Social Care*. London, Scie.

Payne, M. (1997) *Modern Social Work Theory: A Critical Introduction*. Basingstoke, Macmillan.

Plant, R. (1973) *Social and Moral Theory in Casework*. London, Routledge and Kegan Paul.

Pomerantz, A.M. (1986) 'Extreme Case Formulations: A Way of Legitimizing Claims', *Human Studies* 9: 219–30.

Popay, J. (2006) *Moving beyond Effectiveness: Methodological Issues in the Synthesis of Diverse Sources of Evidence*. London, National Institute for Health and Clinical Excellence.

Popper, K. (1965) *The Logic of Scientific Discovery*. New York, Harper Row.

Potter, J. (1997) 'Discourse Analysis as a Way of Analysing Naturally Occurring Talk', in D. Silverman (ed.) *Qualitative Research: Theory, Method and Practice*. London, Sage Publications.

Powell, J. (2002) 'The Changing Conditions of Social Work Research', *British Journal of Social Work*, 32(1): 17–35.

QAA (2008) *The Benchmark Statement for Honours Degrees in Social Work* (http://www.qaa.ac.uk/academicinfrastructure/benchmark/statements/social-work08.pdf).

Reid, W. and Shyne, A. (1969) *Brief and Extended Casework*. New York, Columbia University Press.

Riessman, C.K. and Quinney, L. (2005) 'Narrative in Social Work: A Critical Review', *Qualitative Social Work*, 4(4): 391–412.

Ritchie, J. and Lewis, J. (eds) (2003) *Qualitative Research Practice*. London, Sage.

Roberts, H. (1981) *Doing Feminist Research*. London, Routledge and Kegan Paul.

Robinson, J. (1970) 'Experimental Research in Social Casework', *British Journal of Social Work*, 1(4): 463–80.

Rossiter, A., Prilleltensky, I. and Walsh-Bowers, R. (2000) 'A Postmodern Perspective on Professional Ethics', in B. Fawcett, B. Featherstone, J. Fook and A. Rossiter (eds) *Practice and Research in Social Work: Postmodern Feminist Perspectives*. London, Routledge.

Rowntree, J. (1901) *Poverty: A Study of Town Life*. London, Macmillan.

Rubin, H. and Rubin, I. (1995) *Qualitative Interviewing*. London, Sage.

Ryle, G. (1990) *The Concept of Mind*. Harmondsworth, Penguin.

Sackett, D.L., Rosenburg, W.M., Gray, J.H.M., Haynes, R.B. and Richardson, W.S. (1996) 'Evidence-Based Practice: What It Is and What It Isn't', *British Medical Journal*, 312(7023): 71–2.

Sainsbury, E. (1975) *Social Work and Families: Perceptions of Social Casework among Clients of a Family Service Unit*. London, Routledge & Kegan Paul.

Sainsbury, E. (1987) 'Client Studies: Their Contribution and Limitations in Influencing Social Work Practice', *British Journal of Social Work*, 17: 635–44.

Sarantakos, S. (1998) *Social Research*. Basingstoke, Palgrave.

Save the Children (2004) *So You Want to Involve Children in Research? A Toolkit Supporting Children's Meaningful and Ethical Participation in Research Relating to Violence against Children*. Stockholm, Save the Children Sweden

Scottish Executive (2006) *Changing Lives: Report of the 21st Century Social Work Review*. Edinburgh, Scottish Executive.

Scourfield, J. (2002) *Gender and Child Protection*. Basingstoke, Palgrave.

Sharland, E. and Taylor, I. (2006) 'Social Care Research: A Suitable Case for Systematic Review?', *Evidence and Policy*, 2(4): 503–23.

Shaw, I. (2005) 'Practitioner Research: Evidence or Critique?', *British Journal of Social Work*, 35: 1231–48.

Shaw, I. (2008) 'Ethics and the Practice of Social Work Research', *Qualitative Social Work*, 7(4): 400–14.

Shaw, I., Arksey, H. and Mullender, A. (2004) *ESRC Research, Social Work and Social Care*. London, Scie.

Shaw, I. and Gould, N. (eds) (2001) *Qualitative Research in Social Work*. London, Sage.

Shaw, I. and Lishman, J. (eds) (1999) *Evaluation and Social Work Practice*. London, Sage.

Shaw, I. and Norton, M. (2007) *The Kinds and Quality of Social Work Research in UK Universities*. London, SCIE.

Shaw, I. and Norton, M. (2008) 'Kinds and Quality of Social Work Research', *British Journal of Social Work*, 38(5): 953–70.

Shaw, I. and Shaw, A. (1997) 'Keeping Social Work Honest: Evaluating as Profession and Practice', *British Journal of Social Work*, 27: 847–69.

Sheldon, B. (2000) 'Cognitive Behavioural Methods in Social Care: A Look at the Evidence', in P. Stepney and D. Ford (eds) *Social Work Models, Methods and Theories*. Lyme Regis, Russel House.

Sheldon, B. (2001) 'The Validity of Evidence-Based Practice in Social Work: A Reply to Stephen Webb', *British Journal of Social Work*, 31: 801–9.

Sheldon, B. and Chilvers, R. (2001) *Evidence-Based Social Care: A Study of Prospects and Problems*. Lyme Regis, Russell House.

Sheldon, B. and Chilvers, R. (2002) 'An Empirical Study of the Obstacles to Evidence-Based Practice', *Social Work and Social Sciences Review*, 10: 6–26.

Sheldon, B. and McDonald, G. (1999) *Mind the Gap*. Exeter, Centre for Evidence Based Social Services, University of Exeter.

Shemmings, D. (1996) *Involving Children in Child Protection Conferences*. Norwich, UEA Monographs.

Shemmings, D. (ed.) (1999) *Involving Children in Family Support and Child Protection*. London: The Stationery Office.

Shemmings, D. (2006) 'Using Adult Attachment Theory to Differentiate Adult Children's Internal Working Models of Later Life Filial Relationships', *Journal of Aging Studies*, 20(2): 177–91.

Shipman, M. (1988) *The Limitations of Social Research*. London, Longman.

SPA (2008) *Social Policy Association Guidelines on Research Ethics* (draft). London, SPA.

SRA (2003) *Ethical Guidelines*. London: SRA (www.thesra.org.uk/documents/pdfs/ethics03.pdf).

Stacey, M. (1969) *Methods of Social Research*. London, Pergamon Press.

Stanley, L. (1990) *Feminist Praxis: Research, Theory and Epistemology*. London, Routledge.

Stanley, L. and Wise, S. (1983) *Breaking Out: Feminist Consciousness and Feminist Research*. London, Routledge and Kegan Paul.

Stepney, P. (2000) 'Implications for Social Work in the New Millennium', in P. Stepney and D. Ford (eds) *Social Work Models, Methods and Theories*. Lyme Regis, Russell House.

Strauss, A. and Corbin, J. (1990) *Basics of Qualitative Research: Grounded Theory Procedures and Techniques*. London, Sage.

Strauss, A. and Corbin, J. (1998) *Basics of Qualitative Research Techniques and Procedures for Developing Grounded Theory*, 2nd edn. London, Sage.

Thomas, J., Sutcliffe, K., Harden, A., Oakley, A., Oliver, S., Rees, R., Brunton, G. and Kavanagh, J. (2003) *Children and Healthy Eating: A Systematic Review of Barriers and Facilitators*. London: EPPI-Centre, Social Science Research Unit, Institute of Education, University of London.

Thyer, B.A. (1989) 'First Principles of Practice Research', *British Journal of Social Work*, 19: 309–23.

Timor, U. and Landau, R. (1998) 'Discourse Characteristics in the Sociolect of Repentant Criminals', *Discourse and Society*, 9(3): 363–86.

TOPSS (2002) *The National Occupational Standards for Social Work*. London: Training Organisation for the Personal Social Services.

Trinder, L. (1996) 'Social Work Research: The State of the Art (or Science)', *Child and Family Social Work*, 1: 233–42.

Trinder, L. and Kellett, J. (2007) 'Fairness, Efficiency and Effectiveness in Court-Based Dispute Resolution Schemes in England', *International Journal of Law Policy and the Family*, 21: 322–40.

Ungar, M. (2005) '"Too Ambitious": What Happens when Funders Misunderstand the Strengths of Qualitative Research', *Qualitative Social Work*, 5(2): 261–78.

Ungerson, C. (1987) *Policy Is Personal: Sex, Gender and Informal Care*. London, Tavistock.

Usher, R. (1997) 'Introduction', in G. McKenzie, J. Powell and R. Usher (eds) *Understanding Social Research: Perspectives on Methodology and Practice.* London, Falmer Press.

Walker, S. (1999) 'Children's Perspectives on Attending Statutory Reviews', in D. Shemmings (ed.) *Involving Children in Family Support and Child Protection.* London, The Stationery Office.

Walliman, N. (2006) *Social Research Methods: A Course Companion.* London, Sage.

Walter, I., Nutley, S., Percy-Smith, J., McNeish, D. and Frost, S. (2004) *Improving the Use of Research in Social Care Practice.* London, SCIE.

Ward, H. (2000) *The Development Needs of Children: Implications for Assessment.* London, Department of Health.

Watson, D.A., Abbott, D. and Townsley, R. (2006) 'Listen to Me, Too! Lessons from Involving Children with Complex Healthcare Needs in Research about Multi-Agency Services', *Child: Care Health and Development*, 33(1): 90–5.

Webb, S. (2001) 'Some Considerations on the Validity of Evidence-Based Practice in Social Work', *British Journal of Social Work*, 31: 57–79.

Webb, S. and Webb, B. (1968) *Methods of Social Study.* New York, A.M. Kelley.

Wiener, C. and Strauss, A. (eds) (1997) *Where Medicine Fails*, 5th edn. New Brunswick, NJ, Transaction.

Wenger, E. (1998) *Communities of Practice: Learning, Meaning and Identity.* Cambridge: Cambridge University Press.

Wetherell, M. (1998) 'Positioning and Interpretative Repertoires: Conversation Analysis and Post-Structuralism in Dialogue', *Discourse and Society*, 9: 387–412.

White, S. (1997) 'Beyond Retroduction? Hermeneutics, Reflexivity abd Social Work Practice', *British Journal of Social Work*, 27: 739–53.

White, S. and Featherstone, B. (2005) 'Communicating Misunderstandings: Multi-Agency Work as Social Practice', *Child and Family Social Work*, 10: 207–16.

White, S. and Hall, C. (2005) 'Editorial', Special Issue on Discourse Narrative and Ethnographic Approaches in Social Work, *Qualitative Social Work*, 4(4): 379–90.

Williams, F., Popay, J. and Oakley, A. (eds) (1999) *Welfare Research: A Critical Review.* London, UCL.

WMA (1964) *Declaration of Helsinki* (as amended 2004). Ferney-Voltaire, World Medical Association.

Wooff, D.A. and Schneider, J. (2006) 'A Bayesian Belief Network for Quality Assessment: Application to Employment Officer Support', *Journal of Intellectual Disability Research*, 50: 109–26.

Wooffitt, R. (1993) 'Analysing Accounts', in N. Gilbert (ed.) *Researching Social Life.* London and Beverly Hills, CA, Sage.

Index